Fundamentals of Software Testing

I would like to dedicate this book to a number of persons:

– to those who came before me and opened the way in the field of testing, many of them are listed in the bibliography;

– to those who will follow me, hoping that this book will provide you with a good start in this wonderful career;

– to my colleagues and dear friends who read the draft and proposed suggestions;

– to my spouse and children who have to suffer a husband and father who is too frequently away and quite demanding.

Fundamentals
of
Software Testing

Bernard Homès

First published 2012 in Great Britain and the United States by ISTE Ltd and John Wiley & Sons, Inc.

ISTE Ltd
27-37 St George's Road
London SW19 4EU
UK

www.iste.co.uk

John Wiley & Sons, Inc.
111 River Street
Hoboken, NJ 07030
USA

www.wiley.com

© ISTE Ltd 2012

Library of Congress Cataloging-in-Publication Data

Homès, Bernard.
Fundamentals of software testing / Bernard Homès.
p. cm.
Includes bibliographical references and index.
  ISBN 978-1-84821-324-1
  1. Computer software--Testing. I. Title.
  QA76.76.T48H674 2012
  005.1--dc23
                                                                    2011040335

British Library Cataloguing-in-Publication Data
A CIP record for this book is available from the British Library
ISBN: 978-1-84821-324-1

Printed and bound in Great Britain by CPI Group (UK) Ltd., Croydon, Surrey CR0 4YY

Table of Contents

Preface

Why this book

Software testing is becoming more and more important in the industry, reflecting the increasing importance of software quality in today's world.

Due to the lack of formal and recognized training in software testing, a group of specialist consultants gathered together in 2002 and founded the International Software Testing Qualifications Board (ISTQB). They defined the minimal set of methodological and technical knowledge that testers should know depending on their experience. This was gathered into what is called a syllabus. The foundation level syllabus was reviewed in 2011 and is the basis of an international certification scheme, already obtained by more than 200,000 testers worldwide. For testers who wish to prepare for the ISTQB foundation level exam, this book can serve as reference material and a study guide. It references the 2011 version of the ISTQB Certified Tester Foundation Level syllabus.

This book follows the order and chapters of the syllabus, helping you to successfully complete the certification exam. It is a one-stop reference book offering you:

– more detailed explanations than those found in the ISTQB syllabus;

– definitions of the terms (i.e. the Glossary) used in the certification exams;

– practice questions similar to those encountered during the certification exam;

– a sample exam.

For testers who want to acquire a good understanding of software and system tests, this book provides the fundamental principles as described by the ISTQB and recognized experts.

This book provides answers and areas of discussion allowing test leaders and managers to:

– improve their understanding of testing;

– have an overview of process improvement linked to software testing;

– increase the efficiency of their software development and tests.

Throughout this book, you will find learning objectives (noted FLO-…) that represent the ISTQB foundation level syllabus learning objectives. These are the topics that certification candidates should know and that are examined in the ISTQB certification exams.

Prerequisite

Software testing does not require specific prerequisites. Although it is not mandatory, a common understanding of data processing and software allows you to have a better understanding of software testing.

The reader with software development knowledge, whatever the programming language, will understand certain aspects faster, but a simple practice as a user should be enough to understand this book.

ISTQB, CFTL (Comité Français des Tests Logiciels) and national boards

The ISTQB is a not-for-profit international association grouping national software testing boards covering approximately 50 countries. These national boards are made up of software testing specialists, consultants, and experts, and together they define the syllabi and examination directives for system and software testers. The CFTL represents France on the ISTQB and offers the ISTQB certification in France.

To define the syllabus content for all three software tester certification levels (i.e. foundation, advanced, expert), and the applicable exam directives, the ISTQB has created a number of working groups, each in charge of a specific subject (i.e. foundation level syllabus, advanced level syllabus, expert level syllabi, training provider accreditation, examination specification, etc.). These work groups are, as the national boards, made up of software testing experts and specialists, consultants, presenters at conferences, professors and national or international specialists in software testing and systems quality. Their combined expertise enables them to synthesize knowledge from numerous fields (aeronautics, space, medical, commercial, rail, telecoms, etc.) and various levels (technicians, analysts, project leaders, specialists, experts, researcher, managers, etc.).

A number of prominent authors of software testing books participate in the creation of the syllabi, ensuring that these reflect what a tester should know depending on his/her level of experience (foundation, advanced, expert) and on his/her objectives (test management, functional testing, and test techniques, specialization in software security or performance testing, etc.).

Glossary and syllabus

The ISTQB is aware of the broad diversity of terms used and the associated diversity of interpretation of these terms depending upon the customers, countries, and organizations. A common glossary of software testing terms has been set up and national boards provide translation of these terms in national languages to promote better understanding of the terms and the associated concepts. This becomes more and more important in a context of international cooperation and offshore sub-contracting.

The syllabi define the basis of the certification exams; they also help to define the scope of training and are applicable at three levels of experience: foundation level, advanced level and expert level. This book focuses on the foundation level.

The foundation level, made up of a single module, is detailed in the following chapters.

The advanced level is made up of three modules:

– test manager, which focuses on the test management and test process improvements aspects;

– test analyst, which focuses on the testing of characteristics of the software and systems, mostly without the use of tools; and

– technical test analyst, which focuses on the testing of non-functional characteristics of software and systems, mostly with the use of tools.

The expert level focuses on specific aspects, such as test management, test process improvement, or performances.

ISTQB certification

The ISTQB proposes software tester certifications, which are recognized as equivalent by all ISTQB member boards throughout the world. The level of difficulty of the questions and the exams are based on the same criteria (defined in the syllabi) and the same terms (defined in the Glossary).

The certification exams proposed by the CFTL and the national boards of the ISTQB enable the candidates to validate their knowledge, and assure employers or potential customers of a minimum level of knowledge from their testers, whatever their origin.

These certifications are recognized as equivalent throughout the whole world, enabling international cross-recognition. In France, more than 1,500 people have successfully passed the certification, and more than 200,000 have acquired such a certification worldwide. This shows the need from the industry to have an independent certification of the software testing activities.

Key for understanding the content

To be used efficiently, this book has the following characteristics:

FLO-xxx: text that starts with FLO-xxx is a reminder of the learning objectives present in the ISTQB foundation level syllabus for certified testers. Those objectives are expanded in the paragraphs following this tag.

The titles of the chapters correspond to those of the ISTQB foundation level syllabus, version 2011. This is often the case too for the section heads; the syllabus reference is provided in the form (FLx.y) where x.y stands for the chapter and section head of the ISTQB foundation level syllabus. The example below shows that the section of the book refers to the 2.4 section of the foundation syllabus:

2.4. Tests and maintenance (FL2.4)

A synopsis closes each of the chapters, summarizing the aspects covered and identifying the terms of the glossary to know for the certification exam. Sample exam questions are also provided at the end of each chapter. These questions were developed by applying the same criteria as for the creation of real exam questions.

The sample questions provided in Chapters 1, 2, 3, 4, 5 and 6 are reproduced with kind permission of © Bernard Homès 2011.

Glossary

The definitions hereafter are extracted from the International Software Testing Qualifications Board (ISTQB) *Standard Glossary of Terms used in Software Testing*. Only the terms used for the Foundation Level certification exams are mentioned, so as not to drown the reader in terms that are used at other levels or in other syllabi.

ACM: (Association for Computer Machinery) professional and scientific association for the development of information technology as science and profession.

Acceptance testing: Formal testing with respect to user needs, requirements, and business processes conducted to determine whether or not a system satisfies the acceptance criteria and to enable the user, customers, or other authorized entity to determine whether or not to accept the system.

Alpha testing: Simulated or actual operational testing by potential users/customers or an independent test team at the developers' site, but outside the development organization. Alpha testing is often employed as a form of internal acceptance testing.

Attack: Directed and focused attempt to evaluate the quality, especially reliability, of a test object by attempting to force specific failures to occur.

Beta testing: Operational testing by potential and/or existing users/customers at an external site not otherwise involved with the developers, to determine whether or not a component or system satisfies the user/customer needs and fits within the business processes. Beta testing is often employed as a form of external acceptance testing in order to acquire feedback from the market.

Black-box technique: See *black-box testing*.

Black-box testing: Testing, either functional or non-functional, without reference to the internal structure of the component or system.

Boundary value analysis: A black-box test design technique in which test cases are designed based on boundary values.

Branch coverage: The percentage of branches that have been exercised by a test suite. One hundred percent branch coverage implies both 100% decision coverage and 100% statement coverage

Bug: see *defect*.

CFTL: Comité Français des Tests Logiciels, French association [LOI 01] for the development of testing in France and French-speaking countries.

Code coverage: An analysis method that determines which parts of the software have been executed (covered) by the test suite and which parts have not been executed, e.g. statement coverage, decision coverage, or condition coverage.

Commercial off-the-shelf software (COTS): See *off-the-shelf software*.

Compiler: A software tool that translates programs expressed in a high-order language into their machine language equivalents.

Complexity: The degree to which a component or system has a design and/or internal structure that is difficult to understand, maintain, and verify. See also *cyclomatic complexity*.

Component integration testing: Tests executed to identify defects in the interfaces and interactions between integrated components.

Component testing: The testing of individual software components.

Configuration control: An element of configuration management, consisting of the evaluation, co-ordination, approval or disapproval, and implementation of changes to configuration items after formal establishment of their configuration identification.

Configuration item: An aggregation of hardware, software or both, that is designated for configuration management and treated as a single entity in the configuration management process.

Configuration management: A discipline applying technical and administrative direction and surveillance to: identify and document the functional and physical characteristics of a configuration item, control changes to those characteristics, record and report change processing and implementation status, and verify compliance with specified requirements.

Confirmation testing: See *re-testing*.

Control flow: An abstract representation of all possible sequences of events (paths) in the execution through a component or system.

Coverage: The degree, expressed as a percentage, to which a specified coverage item has been exercised by a test suite.

Coverage measurement tool: See *coverage tool*.

Coverage tool: A tool that provides objective measures of what structural elements, e.g. statements, branches, have been exercised by the test suite.

Cyclomatic complexity: The number of independent paths through a program. Cyclomatic complexity is defined as: $L - N + 2P$, where:

– L = the number of edges/links in a graph;

– N = the number of nodes in a graph;

– P = the number of disconnected parts of the graph (e.g. a calling graph and a subroutine).

Data-driven testing: A scripting technique that stores test input and expected results in a table or spreadsheet, so that a single control script can execute all of the tests in the table. Data driven testing is often used to support the application of test execution tools such as capture/playback tools. See also *keyword-driven testing*.

Data flow: An abstract representation of the sequence and possible changes of the state of data objects, where the state of an object is any of creation, usage, or destruction.

Debugging: The process of finding, analyzing, and removing the causes of failures in software.

Debugging tool: A tool used by programmers to reproduce failures, investigate the state of programs, and find the corresponding defect. Debuggers enable programmers to execute programs step-by-step, to halt a program at any program statement, and to set and examine program variables.

Decision coverage: The percentage of decision outcomes that have been exercised by a test suite. One hundred percent decision coverage implies both 100% branch coverage and 100% statement coverage.

Decision table testing: A black-box test design technique in which test cases are designed to execute the combinations of inputs and/or stimuli (causes) shown in a decision table.

Defect: A flaw in a component or system that can cause the component or system to fail to perform its required function, e.g. an incorrect statement or data definition. A defect, if encountered during execution, may cause a failure of the component or system.

Defect density: The number of defects identified in a component or system divided by the size of the component or system (expressed in standard measurement terms, e.g. lines-of-code, number of classes, or function points).

Defect management: The process of recognizing, investigating, taking action, and disposing of defects. It involves recording defects, classifying them, and identifying the impact.

Defect management tool: See *incident management tool.*

Driver: A software component or test tool that replaces a component that takes care of the control and/or the calling of a component or system.

Dynamic analysis tool: A tool that provides run-time information on the state of the software code. These tools are most commonly used to identify unassigned pointers, check pointer arithmetic, and to monitor the allocation, use, and de-allocation of memory and to highlight memory leaks.

Dynamic testing: Testing that involves the execution of the software of a component or system.

Entry criteria: The set of generic and specific conditions for permitting a process to proceed with a defined task, e.g. test phase. The purpose of entry criteria is to prevent a task starting that would entail more (wasted) effort compared to the effort needed to remove the failed entry criteria.

Equivalence partition: A portion of an input or output domain for which the behavior of a component or system is assumed to be the same, based on the specification.

Error: A human action that produces an incorrect result [IEEE 610]

Error guessing: A test design technique where the experience of the tester is used to anticipate what defects might be present in the component or system under test as a result of errors made, and to design tests specifically to expose them.

Exit criteria: The set of generic and specific conditions, agreed upon with the stakeholders, for permitting a process to be officially completed. The purpose of exit criteria is to prevent a task from being considered completed when there are still outstanding parts of the task which have not been finished. Exit criteria are used by testing to report against and to plan when to stop testing.

Exhaustive testing: A test approach in which the test suite comprises all combinations of input values and preconditions.

Exploratory testing: Testing where the tester actively controls the design of the tests as those tests are performed and uses information gained while testing to design new and better tests.

Failure: Actual deviation of the component or system from its expected delivery, service, or result (according to Fenton). The inability of a system or system component to perform a required function within specified limits. A failure may be produced when a fault is encountered [EUR 00].

Failure rate: The ratio of the number of failures of a given category to a given unit of measure, e.g. failures per unit of time, failures per number of transactions, failures per number of computer runs.

Fault attack: See *attack*.

Field testing: See *beta testing*.

Finite state testing: See *state transition testing*.

Formal review: A review characterized by documented procedures and requirements, e.g. inspection.

Functional requirement: A requirement that specifies a function that a component or system must perform.

Functional testing: Testing based on an analysis of the specification of the functionality of a component or system. See also *black-box testing*.

Horizontal traceability: The tracing of requirements for a test level through the layers of test documentation (e.g. test plan, test design specification, test case specification, and test procedure specification).

IEEE: Institute for Electrical and Electronic Engineers, a professional, not for profit association for the advancement of technology, based on the electrical and electronic technologies. This association is active in the design of standards. There is a French chapter of this association providing publications useful for software testers.

Impact analysis: The assessment of change to the layers of development documentation, test documentation, and components, in order to implement a given change to specified requirements.

Incident: Any event occurring during testing which requires investigation.

Incident report: A document reporting on any event that occurs during the testing which requires investigation.

Incident management tool: A tool that facilitates the recording and status tracking of incidents found during testing. They often have workflow-oriented facilities to track and control the allocation, correction, and re-testing of incidents and provide reporting facilities. See also *defect management tool.*

Incremental development model: A development life cycle where a project is broken into a series of increments, each of which delivers a portion of the functionality in the overall project requirements. The requirements are prioritized and delivered in priority order in the appropriate increment. In some (but not all) versions of this life cycle model, each sub-project follows a "mini V-model" with its own design, coding and testing phases.

Independence of testing: Separation of responsibilities, which encourages the accomplishment of objective testing.

Informal review: A review not based on a formal (documented) procedure.

Inspection: A type of review that relies on visual examination of documents to detect defects, e.g. violations of development standards and non-conformance to higher-level documentation. The most formal review technique and, therefore, always based on a documented procedure. See also *peer review.*

Intake test: A special instance of a smoke test to decide whether the component or system is ready for detailed and further testing. An intake test is typically carried out at the start of the test execution phase. See also *smoke test.*

Integration: The process of combining components or systems into larger assemblies.

Integration testing: Testing performed to expose defects in the interfaces and in the interactions between integrated components or systems. See also *component integration testing, system integration testing.*

Interoperability testing: The process of testing to determine the interoperability of a software product. See also *functionality testing.*

ISTQB: International Software Testing Qualifications Board, a nonprofit association developing international certification for software testers.

Keyword driven testing: A scripting technique that uses data files to contain not only test data and expected results, but also keywords related to the application being tested. The keywords are interpreted by special supporting scripts that are called by the control script for the test. See also *data-driven testing.*

Master test plan: See *project test plan.*

Maintainability testing: The process of testing to determine the maintainability of a software product.

Metric: A measurement scale and the method used for measurement.

Mistake: See *error.*

Moderator: The leader and main person responsible for an inspection or other review process.

Modeling tool: A tool that supports the validation of models of the software or system.

N-switch coverage: The percentage of sequences of N+1 transitions that have been exercised by a test suite.

N-switch testing: A form of state transition testing in which test cases are designed to execute all valid sequences of N+1 transitions (Chow). See also *state transition testing.*

Non-functional requirement: A requirement that does not relate to functionality, but to attributes of it such as reliability, efficiency, usability, maintainability, and portability.

Off-the-shelf software: A software product that is developed for the general market, i.e. for a large number of customers, and that is delivered to many customers in identical format.

Oracle: See *test oracle*

Peer review: See *technical review*.

Performance testing: The process of testing to determine the performance of a software product.

Performance testing tool: A tool to support performance testing and that usually has two main facilities: load generation and test transaction measurement. Load generation can simulate either multiple users or high volumes of input data. During execution, response time measurements are taken from selected transactions and these are logged. Performance testing tools normally provide reports based on test logs and graphs of load against response times.

Portability testing: The process of testing to determine the portability of a software product.

Probe effect: The effect on the component or system when it is being measured, e.g. by a performance testing tool or monitor. For example performance may be slightly worse when performance testing tools are being used.

Product risk: A risk directly related to the test object. See also *risk*.

Project risk: A risk related to management and control of the (test) project, e.g. lack of staffing, strict deadlines, changing requirements, etc. See also *risk*.

Project test plan: A test plan that typically addresses multiple test levels. See *master test plan*.

Quality: The degree to which a component, system or process meets specified requirements and/or user/customer needs and expectations.

RAD: Rapid Application Development, a software development model.

Regression testing: Testing of a previously tested program following modification to ensure that defects have not been introduced or uncovered in unchanged areas of the software, as a result of the changes made. It is performed when the software or its environment is changed.

Reliability testing: The process of testing to determine the reliability of a software product.

Requirement: A condition or capability needed by a user to solve a problem or achieve an objective that must be met or possessed by a system or system component to satisfy a contract, standard, specification, or other formally imposed document.

Requirement management tool: A tool that supports the recording of requirements, attributes of requirements (e.g. priority, knowledge responsible), and annotation, and facilitates traceability through layers of requirements and requirement change management. Some requirement management tools also provide facilities for static analysis, such as consistency checking and violations to pre-defined requirement rules.

Re-testing: Testing that runs test cases that failed the last time they were run, in order to verify the success of corrective actions.

Review: An evaluation of a product or project status to ascertain discrepancies from planned results and to recommend improvements. Examples include management review, informal review, technical review, inspection, and walk-through.

Review tool: A tool that provides support to the review process. Typical features include review planning and tracking support, communication support, collaborative reviews, and a repository for collecting and reporting of metrics.

Reviewer: The person involved in the review who identifies and describes anomalies in the product or project under review. Reviewers can be chosen to represent different viewpoints and roles in the review process.

Risk: A factor that could result in future negative consequences; usually expressed as impact and likelihood.

Risk-based testing: An approach to testing to reduce the level of product risks and inform stakeholders on their status, starting in the initial stages of a project. It involves the identification of product risks and their use in guiding the test process.

Robustness testing: Testing to determine the robustness of the software product.

SBTM: Session-based test management, an ad hoc and exploratory test management technique, based on fixed length sessions (from 30 to 120 minutes) during which testers explore a part of the software application.

Scribe: The person who has to record each defect mentioned and any suggestions for improvement during a review meeting, on a logging form. The scribe has to ensure that the logging form is readable and understandable.

Scripting language: A programming language in which executable test scripts are written, used by a test execution tool (e.g. a capture/replay tool).

Security testing: Testing to determine the security of the software product.

Site acceptance testing: Acceptance testing by users/customers at their site, to determine whether or not a component or system satisfies the user/customer needs and fits within the business processes, normally including hardware as well as software.

SLA: Service level agreement, service agreement between a supplier and its client, defining the level of service a customer can expect from the provider.

Smoke test: A subset of all defined/planned test cases that cover the main functionality of a component or system, to ascertain that the most crucial functions of a program work, but not bothering with finer details. A daily build and smoke test is among industry best practices.

State transition: A transition between two states of a component or system.

State transition testing: A black-box test design technique in which test cases are designed to execute valid and invalid state transitions. See also *N-switch testing*.

Statement coverage: The percentage of executable statements that have been exercised by a test suite.

Static analysis: Analysis of software artifacts, e.g. requirements or code, carried out without execution of these software artifacts.

Static code analyzer: A tool that carries out static code analysis. The tool checks source code, for certain properties such as conformance to coding standards, quality metrics, or data flow anomalies.

Static testing: Testing of a component or system at specification or implementation level without execution of that software, e.g. reviews or static code analysis.

Stress testing: A type of performance testing conducted to evaluate a system or component at or beyond the limits of its anticipated or specified workloads, or with reduced availability of resources such as access to memory or servers. See also *performance testing, load testing*.

Stress testing tool: A tool that supports stress testing.

Structural testing: See *white-box testing.*

Stub: A skeletal or special-purpose implementation of a software component, used to develop or test a component that calls or is otherwise dependent on it. It replaces a called component.

System integration testing: Testing the integration of systems and packages; testing interfaces to external organizations (e.g. electronic data interchange, the internet).

System testing: The process of testing an integrated system to verify that it meets specified requirements.

Technical review: A peer group discussion activity that focuses on achieving consensus on the technical approach to be taken. A technical review is also known as a peer review.

Test: A set of one or more test cases.

Test approach: The implementation of the test strategy for a specific project. It typically includes the decisions made that follow based on the (test) project's goal and the risk assessment carried out, starting points regarding the test process, the test design techniques to be applied, exit criteria, and test types to be performed.

Test basis: All documents from which the requirements of a component or system can be inferred. The documentation on which the test cases are based. If a document can be amended only by way of formal amendment procedure, then the test basis is called a frozen test basis.

Test case: A set of input values, execution preconditions, expected results, and execution post conditions, developed for a particular objective or test condition, such as to exercise a particular program path or to verify compliance with a specific requirement.

Test case specification: A document specifying a set of test cases (objective, inputs, test actions, expected results, and execution preconditions) for a test item.

Test comparator: A test tool to perform automated test comparison.

Test condition: An item or event of a component or system that could be verified by one or more test cases, e.g. a function, transaction, quality attribute, or structural element.

Test control: A test management task that deals with developing and applying a set of corrective actions to get a test project on track when monitoring shows a deviation from what was planned. See also *test management*.

Test coverage: See *coverage*.

Test data: Data that exists (for example, in a database) before a test is executed, and that affects or is affected by the component or system under test.

Test data preparation tool: A type of test tool that enables data to be selected from existing databases or created, generated, manipulated and edited for use in testing.

Test design: The process of transforming general testing objectives into tangible test conditions and test cases. See *test design specification*.

Test design specification: A document specifying the test conditions (coverage items) for a test item, the detailed test approach, and identifying the associated high level test cases.

Test design technique: A method used to derive or select test cases.

Test design tool: A tool that supports the test design activity by generating test inputs from a specification that may be held in a CASE tool repository, e.g. requirements management tool, or from specified test conditions held in the tool itself.

Test-driven development: Agile development method, where the tests are designed and automated before the code (from the requirements or specifications), then the minimal amount of code is written to successfully pass the test. This iterative method ensures that the code continues to fulfill requirements via test execution.

Test environment: An environment containing hardware, instrumentation, simulators, software tools, and other support elements needed to conduct a test.

Test execution: The process of running a test by the component or system under test, producing actual results.

Test execution schedule: A scheme for the execution of test procedures. The test procedures are included in the test execution schedule in their context and in the order in which they are to be executed.

Test execution tool: A type of test tool that is able to execute other software using an automated test script, e.g. capture/playback.

Test harness: A test environment comprised of stubs and drivers needed to conduct a test.

Test leader: See *test manager.*

Test level: A group of test activities that are organized and managed together. A test level is linked to the responsibilities in a project. Examples of test levels are component test, integration test, system test, and acceptance test.

Test log: A chronological record of relevant details about the execution of tests.

Test management: The planning, estimating, monitoring, and control of test activities, typically carried out by a test manager.

Test manager: The person responsible for testing and evaluating a test object. The individual, who directs, controls, administers, plans, and regulates the evaluation of a test object.

Test monitoring: A test management task that deals with the activities related to periodically checking the status of a test project. Reports are prepared that compare the results with what was expected. See also *test management.*

Test objective: A reason or purpose for designing and executing a test.

Test oracle: A source to determine expected results to compare with the actual result of the software under test. An oracle may be the existing system (for a benchmark), a user manual, or an individual's specialized knowledge, but should not be the code.

Test plan: A document describing the scope, approach, resources, and schedule of intended test activities. Amongst others, it identifies test items, the features to be tested, the testing tasks, who will do each task, the degree of tester independence, the test environment, the test design techniques, and test measurement techniques to be used, and the rationale for their choice, and any risks requiring contingency planning. It is a record of the test planning process.

Test policy: A high-level document describing the principles, approach, and major objectives of the organization regarding testing.

Test procedure: See *test procedure specification.*

Test procedure specification: A document specifying a sequence of actions for the execution of a test; also known as the test script or manual test script.

Test report: See *test summary report*.

Test script: Commonly used to refer to a test procedure specification, especially an automated one.

Test strategy: A high-level document defining the test levels to be performed and the testing within those levels for a program (one or more projects).

Test suite: A set of several test cases for a component or system under test, where the post-condition of one test is often used as the precondition for the next one.

Test summary report: A document summarizing testing activities and results. It also contains an evaluation of the corresponding test items against exit criteria.

Tester: A technically skilled professional who is involved in the testing of a component or system.

Testware: Artifacts produced during the test process required to plan, design, and execute tests, such as documentation, scripts, inputs, expected results, setup and clear-up procedures, files, databases, environment, and any additional software or utilities used in testing.

Thread testing: A version of component integration testing where the progressive integration of components follows the implementation of subsets of the requirements, as opposed to the integration of components by levels of a hierarchy.

Traceability: The ability to identify related items in documentation and software, such as requirements with associated tests. See also *horizontal traceability*, *vertical traceability*.

Usability testing: Testing to determine the extent to which the software product is understood, easy to learn, easy to operate, and attractive to the users under specified conditions.

Use case testing: A black-box test design technique in which test cases are designed to execute user scenarios.

User acceptance testing: See *acceptance testing*.

V-model: A framework to describe the software development life cycle activities from requirement specification to maintenance. The V-model illustrates how testing activities can be integrated into each phase of the software development life cycle.

Validation: Confirmation by examination and through provision of objective evidence that the requirements for a specific intended use or application have been fulfilled.

Verification: Confirmation by examination and through the provision of objective evidence that specified requirements have been fulfilled.

Version control: See *configuration control.*

Vertical traceability: The tracing of requirements through the layers of development documentation to components.

Walk-through: A step-by-step presentation by the author of a document in order to gather information and to establish a common understanding of its content.

White-box testing: Testing based on an analysis of the internal structure of the component or system.

Chapter 1

Fundamentals of Testing

1.1. Why is testing necessary? (FL1.1)

FLO-1.1.1. Describe, with examples, the way in which a defect in software can cause harm to a person, to the environment, or to a company (K2)

In our everyday life, we are more and more dependent on the correct execution of software, whether it is in our equipment (cell phones, engine injection, etc.), in the transactions we undertake each day (credit or debit card purchases, fund transfers, Internet usage, electronic mail, etc.), or even those that are hidden from view (back office software for transaction processing), software simplifies our daily lives. When it goes awry, the impact can be devastating.

1.1.1. *Software systems context*

Testing software and systems is necessary to avoid *failures* visible to customers and avoid bad publicity for the organizations involved. This is the case for service companies responsible for the development or testing of third-party software, because the customer might not renew the contract, or might sue for damages.

We can imagine how millions of Germans felt on January 1st, 2010, when their credit cards failed to work properly. No early warning sign informed them, and they found themselves, the day after New Year celebrations, with an empty fridge, totally destitute, without the possibility of withdrawing cash from ATMs or purchasing anything from retail outlets. Those most pitied were probably those who took advantage of the holiday period to go abroad; they did not even have the possibility to go to their bank to withdraw cash.

On November 20th, 2009, during its first week of commercial operation on the Paris to New York route, the autopilot function of the Airbus A380, the pride of the Air France fleet, suffered a software failure such that it was forced to return to New York. The passengers were dispatched to other flights. Such a software problem could have been a lot more serious.

Software problems can also have an impact on an individual's rights and freedom, be it in the USA, where voting machines failed during the presidential elections, preventing a large number of votes from being included [KER 04], or in France where, during local elections in 2008, a candidate from the Green party obtained 1,765 votes from 17,656 registered voters, and the software from the Ministry of Interior allowed the person to sit in the next stage of the election as the 10% threshold was reached. However, the software did not compute three digits after the decimal point and an "unfortunate rounding error to 10% was computed while the candidate only had 9.998% of the registered voters". The end result was that the candidate was not allowed to participate in the next stage of the election. [ELE].

Software problems are not limited to small inconveniences, such as those listed above. They can be the root cause of accidents and even fatalities. This happened with the radiotherapy system Therac-25 [LEV 93, pp. 18-41], which led to six accidental releases of massive overdoses of radiation between 1985 and 1987, leading to the death of three patients. In the case of Therac-25, the root cause of the software failures – and of the death of the patients – were determined as being:

– a lack of code reviews by independent personnel;

– software design methods that were not adapted and thus incorrectly implemented for safety critical systems;

– lack of awareness regarding system reliability for evaluation of software *defects*;

– unclear error messages and usability problems in the software;

– a lack of full acceptance tests for the complete system (hardware and software).

Other examples of software failures that have caused major incidents have occurred in the space industry, such as:

– the first flight of the Ariane 5 launcher, where a component that was developed and used reliably on the Ariane 4 launchers was used outside its normal operational context and led to the loss of the launcher and all the satellites it carried;

– NASA's (National Aeronautics and Space Administration) Mars Climate Orbiter mission, where a unit conversion problem, between the units used by the European Space Agency (ESA; using metric-based units) and the units used by NASA (nautical mile) led to the loss of the spaceship and the full mission;

– NASA's Mars Polar Lander, where a speck of dust led to an incorrect response from one of the three landing gear, and a lack of software testing led to the shutdown of the probe's engine some 40 meters above the surface, leading to the loss of the probe and the mission.

These three examples each cost hundreds of millions of Euros and US dollars, even with the high level of quality and tests done on such systems. Every year software failures generate financial losses evaluated to be hundreds of millions of Euros. Correct testing of software is necessary to avoid frustration, lost financial expenditure, damages to property, or even death; all this due to failures in software.

1.1.2. Causes of software defects

FLO-1.1.2 Distinguish between the root cause of a defect and its effects (K2)

There is a causality link between errors and defects, and between defects and failures generated. The initial cause – the root cause – of defects is often found to be caused by the actions (or lack of action) of humans:

– misunderstanding of the specifications by functional analysts, resulting in a software design or architecture that prevents the expected goals from being reached or objectives stated by the customers;

– mistakes, such as replacing a greater than sign by a greater than or equal to sign, resulting in abnormal behavior when both variables are equal.

Some failures are not directly caused by human action, but are caused by the interactions between the *test object* and its environment:

– software malfunctions when electronic components overheat abnormally due to dust;

– electrical or electronic interferences produced by power cables near unshielded data cables;

– solar storms or other activities generating ionizing radiation that impacts on electronic components (this is important for satellite and airborne equipment);

– impact of magnets or electromagnetic fields on data storage devices (magnetic disks or tapes, etc.).

FLO-1.1.5 Explain and compare the terms error, defect, fault, failure, and the corresponding terms mistake and bug, using examples (K2)

Many terms describe the incorrect behavior of software: bug, error, failure, defect, fault, mistake, etc. These terms are sometimes considered as equivalent, which may generate misunderstandings. In this book, just as for the International Software Testing Qualifications Board (ISTQB), we will use the following terms and definitions:

– error: human action at the root of a defect;

– defect: result, present in the test object, of a human action (i.e. error);

– failure: result from the execution of a defect by a process (whether the process is automated or not).

These terminological differences are important and will result in different activities to limit their occurrence and/or impact.

In order to reduce human errors – and thus the number of defects introduced in the software – training activities can be implemented, or more strict processes can be set in place. Tests are executed to identify the failures, by displaying abnormal behavior. Using the information provided by testers, designers can identify and remove defects that cause incorrect behavior. The software defects can be identified by submitting the software to reviews (code or architecture reviews, etc.), or by executing the software and identifying failures that result from the presence of defects.

NOTE: Defects may be located in software, but can also be present in documents. A large number of software problems are caused by requirements or specifications that may be ambiguous, or even incoherent or incompatible. The error is thus made by those who write these requirements, the defect in the specification, and in the code, before the failure is identified during test execution.

FLO-1.1.3 Give reasons why testing is necessary by giving examples (K2)

Our software and systems become more and more complex, and we rely more and more on their faultless operation. Our cell phones and personal digital assistants (PDAs) are more powerful than the mainframes of 30 years ago, simultaneously integrating agenda, notepad, and calendar functions, plus global positioning systems (GPSs), cameras, emails, instant messaging, games, voice recorders, music and video players, etc., not forgetting the telephone functionalities of course. Vehicles are equipped with more and more electronic circuits and data processing systems

(ESP (trajectory control for vehicles, anti-skid), GPS, fuel injection, airbags, course control, cruise control, etc.), our cell phones connect automatically (via Bluetooth) to our vehicles and its audio system. We only need a small software problem and our vehicle or our cell phone becomes unusable.

We also rely on other software, such as those in our credit or debit cards, where a defect can directly impact millions of users [LEM 10], such as occurred in early 2010 where German users were victims of a major failure for over a week. We have also seen exploding virtual high-speed trains [LEP 10] (without actual victims) or the availability of customer data for rail companies available on the Internet [LET 10], as well as problems with bank software, administrations, etc.

Our lives rely on software, and it is necessary to test this software. Software testing is undertaken to make sure that it works correctly, to protect against defects and potentially fatal failures.

1.1.3. *Role of testing in software development, maintenance and operations*

Testing is – and should be – present throughout the software life cycle, from the beginning of its design to the end of its maintenance, and during the whole operation of the software. Rigorous testing of software and systems, including their documentation, allows a reduction in the probability of failure during execution of the software, and contributes to improving the quality of these software and systems.

Tests also provide information that allows managers to make informed decisions, with a better understanding of the level of quality and the impacts of their decisions.

1.1.4. *Tests and quality*

FLO-1.1.4 Describe why testing is part of quality assurance and give examples of how testing contributes to higher quality (K2)

Tests are sometimes mistaken with quality assurance. These two notions are not identical:

– quality assurance ensures that the organization's processes (its best or recommended practices) are implemented and applied correctly. Continuous process improvements to increase their efficiency and their effectiveness – and thus the organizations' efficiency and effectiveness – and attain a higher maturity level are additional goals for quality assurance;

– testing identifies defects and failures, and provides information on the software and the risks associated with their release to the market.

We can clearly see the complementarities of these two aspects.

The software testing community is not uniform. Two main approaches are visible:

– the "traditional" approach, where tests are based on requirements and specifications, and the software is analyzed systematically, sometimes leading to a large volume of documentation. This approach is based on a definition and organization of the activities (test design, test case design, creation of the test data associated with the test cases, execution of the test cases on the software). This approach generates a testing workload (and a cost) before the discovery of the first defect or the first failure;

– the "agile" approach, where tests are executed based on the Agile Manifesto [AGI] recommendations, highlighting the search for defects associated with risks and context. This approach is based on a pragmatic evaluation of the test activities that require execution prior to software delivery.

Proponents of each approach have arguments in favor of their approach and against the other. It is a pity to see high-level professionals unable to recognize the complementarities of both approaches. One approach is more adapted to one type of project, while the other is more suited to other projects.

The "traditional" or "systematic" approach is more applicable to large projects or those of a long duration, where the test team are associated relatively early with the project, even from the beginning of the design phase. This allows a more detailed analysis of the software and a test case design phase for a longer period. This approach requires sequential development cycles.

The "agile" approach is more suited for qualification of smaller-sized software, and for shorter time periods. It is applicable, among others, to "agile" development cycles.

1.1.5. *Terminology*

A number of terms and concepts are used in testing, sometimes correctly sometimes incorrectly. To aid understanding, the ISTQB proposed a unique set of definitions for the terms used in software testing. Some terms, for which the definition is noted here, are noted in italic (i.e. *test*), and their definition, extracted from the ISTQB Glossary, is provided in the glossary of this book. In the index of this publication, the location where these terms are used is provided. The latest version of the glossary is available from the ISTQB web site (www.istqb.org).

In general, the definitions included in this book come from norms and international standards, or from the ISTQB Glossary of terms used in software testing. The following definitions come from the ISO 9000 [ISO 05] standard.

Verification: confirmation, through the provision of objective evidence, that specified requirements have been fulfilled.

"Objective evidence" is the set of data supporting the evidence or verity of something, which can be obtained through observation, measurement, testing, or other means.

Verification ensures that the requirements have been fulfilled, whether these requirements are applicable to the product or process. The qualifier "verified" designates the corresponding status.

Thus, verification provides a response to the question: "have we produced what is specified?"

Validation: confirmation, through the provision of objective evidence, that the requirements for a specific intended use or application have been fulfilled

Just as for verification, "objective evidences" is a set of data supporting the evidence or reality of something, which can be obtained through observation, measurement, testing, or other means.

The purpose of validation is to verify that the requirements have been fulfilled for a specific intended usage. Contrary to verification, which focuses only on specified requirements, validation focuses on the usage of the validated component. Usage conditions may be real or simulated, where "validated" is the corresponding status.

Thus, "validation" provides a response to the question: "have we built the correct product?"

Verification and validation are complementary but not identical. These differences will have an impact on the burden of proof to be provided by the testers.

1.2. What is testing? (FL 1.2)

Testing is a set of activities with the objective of identifying *failures* in a software or system and to evaluate its level of quality, to obtain user satisfaction. It is a set of tasks with clearly defined goals.

Detection of failures by a user, in the normal usage of the software or system, does not make a tester of that user. If a hacker studies a software to find failures and use them to gain access to the system, that does not make that hacker a tester either.

1.2.1. *Origin of defects*

Defects are not the product of a "gremlin" sprinkling defects in the software when the developers have their back turned away. Defects are introduced at the same time the code is written, by the same persons.

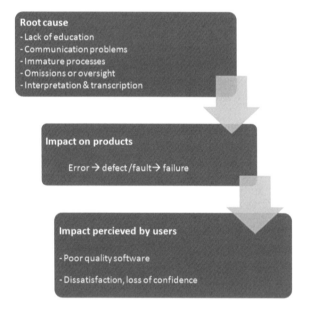

Figure 1.1. *Origin and impacts of defects*

Defects and failures can arise from different root causes, such as gaps in the developer's training, communication problems between the customer and the designers, immature design processes – from requirements gathering, to detailed design and architecture – or even oversights or misunderstanding or incorrect transcriptions of the requirements. Among other things, these causes may result from stress or fatigue of the design teams.

The impact of human error on a product is called a "defect", which will produce a "failure" (a mode of operation that does not fulfill user's expectations) if it is executed when the software or system is used.

1.2.2. *Common goals of testing*

FLO-1.2.1 Recall the common objectives of testing (K1)

Contrary to what some might think, testing is not something that is done if there is time between the end of the design activities and the delivery of the product.

Over the years, testing has seen its goals change and evolve. From verification that the software works correctly, the software underwent verification that it did not have defects, through to a phase where it delivers information that allows decisions to be made, and has now become a set of techniques and methods that enables decisions for delivery to users, taking into account the objectives of cost reduction, time to market, and risks.

Software testing focuses on two complementary but distinct aspects:

– defect and failure detection, so that these can be fixed and thus the quality of the product delivered to customers and users is improved;

– allows decisions to be made on the basis of the information provided regarding the level of risks associated with the delivery of the software to the market, and on the efficiency of the organization's processes which are the root cause of the identified defects and/or failures.

1.2.3. *Examples of objectives for testing*

FLO-1.2.2 Provide examples for the objectives of testing in different phases of the software life cycle (K2)

Test objectives vary depending on the phase of the life cycle of the software. The objectives are not identical during the initial design, the maintenance, or at the end of the software usage. Similarly, they differ also according to the test level.

During the general design or detailed design phase, testing will focus on finding the highest number of defects (or failures), in the shortest possible timescale, in order to deliver high-quality software.

During the customer acceptance phase, testing will show that the software works properly to obtain customer approval for usage of that software.

During the operational phases, where the software is being used, testing will focus on ensuring that the requirement levels (SLA: service level agreement, explicit or implicit) are reached.

During evolutive or corrective maintenance of the software, testing aims to ensure the absence of defects via corrections or evolutions, and also that no side effects (regression) occur on the unchanged functionalities of the system or software.

When the software is discarded and replaced by another, testing takes a snapshot of the software, to ensure which functionalities are present and guarantee the quality of data, so that migration goes smoothly to another platform, whether this is new hardware or new software. Data transfer from the old to the new environment is also important and must be tested.

Thus, we can see that the testing objectives vary depending on the phase of the software's life cycle.

1.2.4. *Test and debugging*

FLO-1.2.3 Differentiate testing from debugging (K2)

Testing is the identification of one or more characteristics according to a defined procedure [ISO 05]. The characteristics can be inherent or implied, qualitative or quantitative, and grouped according to different criteria (physical, sensory, behavioral, temporal, ergonomic, functional, etc.). A procedure is defined here as a specified way to carry out an activity or process. The result from test execution is that the characteristic is present or is not.

There are many aspects that are associated with what is usually called a test:

– an objective (the characteristic that we want to ascertain),

– a way to determine the characteristic (the defined procedure and its execution),

– an activity (the execution of the procedure to obtain a result),

– a result (the presence or absence of the characteristic to the expected level).

More precise definitions and terms will be provided later in this book. Generally, when we determine that an expected characteristic is not present, we will talk of a "failure". Failures are the result of the execution of a defective piece of code, of a defect in the software. To remove the failure, it is necessary to fix the defect.

Developers fix software defects, which is called "debugging" and consists of finding and removing the exact cause of the failure. This is not a task involved in the testing process.

1.3. Paradoxes and main principles (FL1.3)

FLO-1.3.1 Explain the seven principles in testing (K2)

During the last 50 years, a number of major principles have been identified, that apply to any test project, whatever their environment.

1.3.1. *Testing identifies the presence of defects*

Testing enables the identification of defects present in a piece of code, but does not show that such defects are not present. In order to demonstrate absence of defects, all combinations of all possible actions on all reachable objects of the software, for all combinations of input data, in all possible contexts have to be tested, i.e. hardware: mother board, central processing unit (CPU) and number of CPUs, bus, network, random-access memory (RAM), I/O speed, hard disk drive speed and capacity, and software (operating system and its parameter settings, other software that could interact with the software, either at a software or hardware level, etc.) which is, to all intent and purpose, impossible.

It is not possible to demonstrate the real absence of a defect in software, but only the presence of such defects.

Test execution of software enables the reduction of risks of residual – unidentified – defects, but cannot guarantee that all defects have been identified.

1.3.2. *Exhaustive testing is impossible*

Second principle: it is impossible to undertake exhaustive testing, to test "everything".

When testing a small calculator, "testing everything" would mean trying all combinations of input values, actions, configurations (hardware and software), resulting in an almost infinite number of test cases, which is not realistic to design or to execute. Exhaustive testing is not possible, except in some rare trivial cases.

We must reduce the number of tests that are designed and/or executed, so as to obtain a number of tasks that it is economically possible to execute. Therefore this involves choosing which tests to design and execute. This is risk management. The test team activities are software risk limitation (mitigation) activities.

1.3.3. *Early testing*

Third principle: test early in the development cycle, or "early testing"

This principle is based on the fact that costs, whether development costs, testing costs, defect correction costs, etc. increase throughout the project. It is economically more sensible to detect defects as early as possible; thus avoiding the design of incorrect code, the creation of test cases, which require design and maintenance of the created test cases, the identification of defects that have to be logged, fixed, and retested.

A ratio usually applied in industry (validated numerous times in Europe, USA and Asia) is as follows: for a specific unit of cost, the cost of finding (and fixing) a defect in the design phase is "1". If the defect is identified in the coding phase, it is multiplied by "10". If the defect is found during the test phase (system test or acceptance test) then the cost is multiplied by "100". Finally, if the defect is found in production (by the customer or by a user) then the cost is multiplied by "1,000".

Thus, it is economically more efficient to find defects as early as possible.

NOTE: calculation of the return on investment of testing is either empirical or based on statistics of the cost of fixing defects. Empirically, it is clear that fixing a requirement (i.e. changing a minus sign to a plus sign in a requirement specification) is easier and cheaper during the requirements review than after the code or the tests have been designed and created. For defects found in the field, it is necessary to take into account the cost of restoring the software and the data on the customer site (including installation, cost of travel for the technician, etc.) and also any loss of business or of prospective customers, because of bad publicity, etc.

1.3.4. *Defect clustering*

Fourth principle: defects aggregation.

Even if bugs do not have a real life, it is frequent that a number of defects are concentrated according to identical criteria. These can be a piece of code (such as a complex section of an algorithm), a sub-assembly of components designed by the same person (where a similar error is repeated), or a group of components designed in the same period of time, or even a defective off-the-shelf component (COTS). This principle means also that if you find a defect, it might be efficient to look for other defects in the same piece of code.

1.3.5. *Pesticide paradox*

Fifth principle: the pesticide paradox, or lack of efficiency of tests when they are used over a period of time.

This loss of efficiency is due to the re-execution of identical tests (same data, same actions) on software paths that have already been tested. If a failure has been identified and corrected during a previous execution of that test, it will not be detected anymore during the re-execution of that test at a later time. Other defects could be evidenced, aside from those already identified. In the end, the re-execution of that test will work without problem and will not identify any additional defect. Test efficiency will decrease, just as pesticide efficiency decreases over time and usage.

It is strongly suggested that tests are changed over time, so as to modify them and so that the impact of this principle will be negligible. Uses of other test techniques, variation in test data, or in the order of execution of the tests are ways to counter this principle.

Reuse, without modification, of tests can be necessary to ensure that no side effects (i.e. regression) have been introduced in the software as result of changes in that software or in its execution context. Such activities are called regression tests.

1.3.6. *Testing is context dependent*

Sixth principle: testing is dependent on the context.

Safety-critical systems will be tested differently and with a more intense effort, than most e-commerce systems. However, this principle goes much further, because it also applies to the evolution of the context of your own software application. During the first tests of your software, you will design tests based on your knowledge of the software at that moment in time. During subsequent tests, or tests of the next version of the software, your knowledge of the software will have evolved, and you will design other tests, focusing, for example, on identified risks, on components where defect clustering occurred, or taking into account the pesticide paradox. Your test effort will be influenced by the available time and resources, by previous defects, code quality, and the objectives you have been assigned.

Reuse of test plans, test design, test conditions, or test cases from other software or projects is thus counterproductive, even though it might seem intuitively valid. This does not mean that you should not take heed of the experience acquired by others, but that you should – at all times – be aware of your own environment, of its evolution, and any mandatory adaptation to your context.

1.3.7. *Absence of errors fallacy*

Seventh principle: absence of errors fallacy.

Very frequently, the reduction of number of defects is considered to be the ultimate goal of testing. However, it is not possible to assure that a software application, even if it has no defect, suits the needs of the public. If the software does not correspond to what the users need or to their expectations, identification and correction of defects will not help the architecture or the usability of the software, nor the financial success of the software.

1.4. Fundamental test process (FL1.4)

FLO-1.4.1 Recall the five fundamental test activities and respective tasks from planning to closure (K1)

Testing is not limited to the execution of software with the aim of finding failures: it is also necessary to plan, define goals, identify test conditions, create test data, start and exit criteria, test environments, and of course, control all these activities

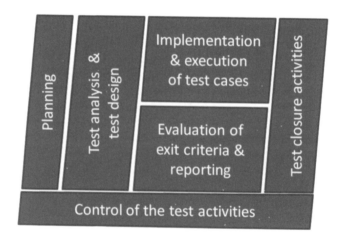

Figure 1.2. *Fundamental test processes*

These activities are grouped in a number of major fundamental processes:

– test planning and control;

– analysis and design of tests;

– implementation and execution of tests;

– evaluation of the exit criteria and production of test reports;

– test closure activities.

These activities are repeated at each test level and for each test campaign, whatever the software or system to be tested.

1.4.1. *Planning*

Before any human activity, it is necessary to organize and plan the activities to be executed. This is also applicable for software and system testing.

Test planning is detailed in Chapter 5, and consists of the definition of test goals, and the definition of the activities to reach these goals.

Test planning activities include organization of the tasks, and coordination with the other stakeholders, such as development teams, support teams, user representatives, management, customers, etc.

The level of detail will depend on the context: a complex safety-critical software will not be tested with the same goals or the same focus as a video game or e-commerce software.

1.4.2. *Control*

Control activities are executed throughout the test campaign. They are often grouped with planning activities because they ensure that what has been planned is correctly implemented.

Control identifies deviations from planned operations, or variations with regards to planned objectives, and proposes actions to reach these objectives. This implies the ability to measure the progress of activities in terms of the resources used (including time) as well as in terms of objectives reached.

Similar to test planning activities, test control activities are described in Chapter 5 in more detail.

1.4.3. *Test analysis and design*

The analysis and design phase is where global test objectives, as defined by the organization at the test plan level, are used to create the test conditions for the software. The high-level test objectives, identified during the planning phase, are used to create the test design documents, test conditions, and test procedures. These activities are described in Chapter 5 and include analysis of the basis of the test as well as the creation of test conditions.

1.4.3.1. *Analysis of the basis of the test*

Analysis of the basis of the test is the study of the reference documents used to design the software and the test objectives. This includes, but is not limited to:

– contractual documents, such as the contract, statement of work, and any amendments or technical attachments, etc.;

– software specifications, high-level design, detailed architecture of the components, database organization or file system organization;

– user documentation, maintenance or installation manuals, etc.;

– the risks identified or associated with the use or the development of the software;

– applicable standards, whether they be company specific, profession specific, or mentioned in the contractual documents.

A test basis that requires a specific or formal process, such as negotiations, contract change notice, or other similar documentation, before it can be changed is called a frozen test basis.

The analysis of the test basis allows the definition of the objectives of the test, their prioritization, and the evaluation of the testability of the test basis and test objectives. During this phase, we will identify the risks and test priorities (*integrity level*), as well as test environments (including test data) to be acquired. We will also select the measurements and *metrics* that will allow us to measure test progress.

The integrity level indicates the criticality of the software for the stakeholders, and is based on attributes of the software, such as risks, safety, and security level, etc. The integrity level will impact the depth and breadth of tests to be executed, type and the level of detail of test documentation and the minimal set of testing tasks to be executed.

Integrity levels as defined by the IEEE 829-2008 [IEE 08a, pp. 13-14] standards are:

– level 4: catastrophic: software must execute correctly or grave consequences (loss of life, loss of system, environmental damage, economic or social loss) will occur. No mitigation is possible;

– level 3: critical: software must execute correctly or the intended use (mission) of system/software will not be realized causing serious consequences (permanent injury, major system degradation, environmental damage, economic or social impact). Partial-to-complete mitigation is possible;

– level 2: marginal: software must execute correctly or the intended function will not be realized causing minor consequences. Complete mitigation possible;

– level 1: negligible: software must execute correctly or the intended function will not be realized causing negligible consequences. Mitigation not required.

IEEE 829-2008 integrity levels can be linked to the failure conditions categorizations described in D0178B /ED12B [EUR 00, pp. 7-8]:

– catastrophic (category A): failure conditions that would prevent continued safe flight and landing;

– hazardous/severe-major (category B): failure conditions that would reduce the capability of the aircraft or the ability of the crew to cope with adverse operating conditions to the extent that there would be:

- a large reduction in safety margins or functional capabilities,

- physical distress or higher workload such that the flight crew could not be relied on to perform their tasks accurately or completely, or

- adverse effects on occupants including serious or potentially fatal injuries to a small number of those occupants;

– major (category C): failure conditions that would reduce the capability of the aircraft or the ability of the crew to cope with adverse operating conditions to the extent that there would be; for example, a significant reduction in safety margins or functional capabilities; a significant increase in crew workload or in conditions impairing crew efficiency; or discomfort to occupants, possibly including injuries;

– minor (category D): failure conditions that would not significantly reduce aircraft safety, and that would involve crew actions that are well within their capabilities. Minor failure conditions may include, for example, a slight reduction in safety margins or functional capabilities, a slight increase in crew workload, such as, routine flight plan changes, or some inconvenience to occupants;

– without effect (category E): failure conditions that do not affect the operational capability of the aircraft or increase crew workload.

Analysis of the test basis allows you to identify the aspects to test (test objectives) and to determine how they will be tested. Traceability from the test basis to the test objectives and test conditions, to allow quick impact analysis of change requests to the test basis should be ensured.

1.4.3.2. *Test design*

Test objectives correspond to the reasons or goals that we have, during test design and execution. These will guide our actions and will lead to the detailed design of the test cases.

Test design consists of applying the test objectives under obvious test conditions, and then applying them to test cases. Test conditions are usually abstract while test cases are usually precise and include both test data and expected results. For more details on the difference between the design of test conditions and test cases, see Chapter 4.

The test design phase comprises:

– identification and prioritization of the test conditions based on an analysis of the test objects, of the structure of the software and system;

– design and prioritization of high-level test cases;

– identification of the test environment and test data required for test execution;

– provision for control and tracking information that will enable evaluation of test progress.

Bi-directional traceability between the test basis, the requirements, and risks on one hand and the test conditions on the other hand, enables all the requirements and all the risks to be covered by the tests, and that all test conditions are attached to a higher-level test objective.

The integrity level enables the approximation of the depth and breadth of the test to execute, and thus helps to devise the test conditions.

1.4.4. *Test implementation*

Test implementation is the conversion of test conditions towards test cases and test procedures, with specific test data and precise expected results. Detailed information on test environment and test data, as well as on the sequence of the test cases are necessary to anticipate test execution.

Test implementation tasks are (non-exhaustive list):

– finalize, implement, and order test cases based on the priorities defined. This can come from the integrity levels or other considerations such as risk analysis or the relative criticality of the components;

– develop and sequence the test procedures, by organizing test cases and test data. This can require the creation of drivers or stubs, or even automated test cases;

– create test suites (scenarios) from test procedures and test cases, to facilitate test execution;

– define the test environment and design test data;

– ensure that bi-directional traceability, started during the analysis and test design phases is continued until the test case levels;

– provide information on the evolution of the process (metrics and measurement), so that project control and management can be efficient.

A test case is defined by a starting environment, input data, actions, and expected results, which included the expected data and resulting environment.

Last minute changes, from changes to the test environment or a reorganization of priorities will modify the test cases, test procedures, or test suites, or even of the test data. Full and detailed traceability will save time – via an impact analysis – and ensure tracking and control of the tests in such difficult conditions.

1.4.5. *Test execution*

Test execution in the test environment enables the identification of differences between the expected and the actual results and includes tasks linked to the execution of test cases, test procedures, or test suites. This includes:

– ensuring that the test environment is ready for use, including the availability of test data;

– executing test cases, test procedures, and test suites, either manually or automatically, according to the planned sequence and priority;

– recording test execution results and identifying the version of the component tested, of the test tools, and test environment;

– comparing expected results with actual results;

– identifying and analyzing any discrepancy between expected and actual results, and clearly defining the cause of the discrepancy. Recording these differences as *incidents* or defects, by providing the highest level of detail possible to facilitate defect correction in the future;

– providing tracking and control information to allow efficient management of test activities.

Test execution activities include activities re-executed for each fix of identified defects. It is necessary to ensure that the fixes have corrected the defect (confirmation testing or retest) and that the modifications introduced have not generated side effects or regressions (regression test).

Traceability initiated in earlier phases must continue, so that these can be associated with the test objectives, test conditions and test cases, information on test execution, and obtained test results. In the case of the presence of defects, this will allow determination of the integrity level associated with the test condition, and thus the importance and impact of the defect as seen by the user, and the need for urgent correction of this defect.

1.4.6. *Analysis of exit criteria*

Analysis of the exit criteria evaluates the test object with regards to the test objectives and criteria defined during the planning phase. This evaluation takes place during test execution and depending on the results enables other test activities to be envisaged.

Test completion evaluation includes:

– analysis of the test execution logs and reports (notes taken during test execution);

– comparison of the objectives reached versus objectives identified during the planning phase, and evaluation of the need to test more thoroughly or to modify the exit criteria.

If one or more of the exit criteria have not been reached after execution of the planned tests, additional tests must be designed and executed to ensure that these new tests enable the intended *exit criteria* to be reached.

A detailed analysis can identify areas where there is no justification to undertake further tests in order to reach the expected exit criteria, such as exceptional or unreachable situations, or in case of *dead code*.

1.4.7. *Reporting*

Test activity results interest a large number of stakeholders:

– testers, to evaluate their own progress and efficiency;

– developers, to evaluate the quality of their code, and the remaining workload, whether it is on the basis of remaining defects to be fixed, or components to deliver;

– quality assurance managers, to determine the required process improvement activities, whether in the requirement elicitation phase or reviews, or during design or test phases;

– customers and end users, or marketing, to advise them when the software or system will be ready and released to the market;

– upper management, to evaluate the anticipated remaining expenses and evaluate the efficiency and effectiveness of the activities to date.

These stakeholders must be informed, via progress reports, statistics, and graphs, of the answer to their queries, and enable them to take appropriate decisions with adequate information.

Reporting activities are based on the tracking and control data provided by each test activity.

1.4.8. *Test closure activities*

Once the software or system is considered ready to be delivered (to the next test phase, or to the market), or the test project is considered complete (either successfully or because it was cancelled), it is necessary to close the test activities. This consists of:

– ensuring that the planned components have been delivered;

– determining the actions that must be taken to rectify unfixed incidents or remaining defects. This can be closure without any action, raising change requests on a future version, delivery of data to the support team to enable them to anticipate user questions;

– document the acceptance of the software or system;

– archive test components and test data, drivers and stubs, test environment parameters and infrastructure for future usage (i.e. for the next version of the software or system);

– if necessary, delivery of the archived components to the team in charge of software maintenance;

– identify possible lessons learned or return on experience, so as to document them and improve future projects and deliveries, and raise the organization's maturity level.

Amongst the archived components, we have the test tools, test scripts, test data, test execution results, but also everything related to the test environment (parameters, operating systems, etc.). These archived data can be used years later, in case of litigation, or to compare against a future version of the software.

1.5. Psychology of testing (FL 1.5)

FLO-1.5.1 Recall the psychological factors that influence the success of testing (K1)

Testers and developers have different ways of thinking, linked to their specific objectives:

– a developer will try to find *one* solution – the best – to a particular problem, and will design the program based on the solution envisaged;

– a tester will try to identify *all* possible failures that might have been forgotten.

A developer usually has two hats: the developer's and the tester's [BEI 95, pp. 6]. The developer is the first person to see and test the software. We are all more or less blind to our own failings and our own errors: when we read what we have written, we may identify a number of spelling mistakes, but our intended reader identifies a number of other defects. What is more, our brain has a tendency to hide defects because it is looking for usual patterns. It is thus important to have different points of view on the same software from different people. When evaluating a piece of software, the ideal is to have input from people with different levels of independence, so that the views will not be biased. Nowadays, software is designed by teams, where each member is specialized in one area (architecture, databases, networks, security, etc.), and has only a limited understanding of the activities of the other members of the team.

FLO-1.5.2 Contrast the mindset of a tester and of a developer (K2)

For a tester, it is necessary to, simultaneously or alternately, consider the requirements of:

– the manager, who wishes to deliver the software on time and within budget;

– the architect, who designed and organized the software;

– the developer, who programmed the code;

– the database specialist, who designed the requests and organized the data;

– the customer and users, who will use the software or system;

– the hacker who will attempt to circumvent the existing security protections;

– etc.

Searching for defects in a software or system requires a level of curiosity, critical thinking, attention to details, knowledge of the business, and end-user processes, understanding of the system and of programming, an extensive experience and good human and communication relationships, to understand and be understood. It is obvious why testing can be defined as "an extremely creative activity and an intellectual challenge" [MYE 79, pp. 16].

1.5.1. *Levels of independence*

As we are all relatively blind to our own defects, it is important to have other people look at the software being designed. A level of independence of the test from the development allows an independent evaluation, and thus limited interference between the contradicting objectives of test and design. The ISTQB syllabus defines different independence levels:

– the lowest level of independence is where the test design and execution is done by the same person who designed and coded the software;

– slightly more independent, tests are designed and executed by another person from the development team who is not a specialized tester. This includes pair programming;

– sometimes a tester is assigned to a development team to identify defects. Often these testers are supposed to also correct the identified defects, and are incorporated in the development team when there is a shortage of developers (who will do the testing then?);

– an increased independence level is reached when a specific team focuses on testing, in the same company where development takes place. This team can either be hierarchically independent from the development team (stronger independence), or be under the same management (weaker independence);

– the highest level of independence is reached when testers from a totally separate organization are responsible for testing the software. This can be the case for independent consultants (freelance), specialists of one domain, or external subcontractors.

Use of external resources that are co-located and depend on their customers for their day-to-day tasks (also called staff augmentation) is not considered as an adequate level of independence.

Independence can be attained with teams geographically co-located or distant. If the teams belong to the same economic entity or are from distinct entities, an increased level of independence is often reached.

Independence has advantages (such as reduction of team size, better understanding of the product, etc.) and drawbacks (such as longer processes, weaker knowledge of the product or its environment, etc.). When selecting a level of independence these advantages and drawbacks must be measured and evaluated. The level of independence can also be linked to the level of integrity of the software [IEE 08a; pp. 91-99]. Chapter 5 describes the impact of independence in test management.

1.5.2. *Adaptation to goals*

Usually we all try to reach the goals that have been assigned to us. This is also applicable in projects, where each participant tries to reach a common goal. It is thus important to define clear and pragmatic objectives, both for the development teams and for the test teams. If the goals are clearly unattainable, those to whom they are assigned will start with a psychological handicap (they will consider the goal as unreachable) and will not attempt to reach that goal, making it a self-fulfilling prediction.

Different objectives are or can be assigned to test teams:

– ensure that the software works correctly. This goal was assigned to test teams 40 years ago. The major drawback of this goal is that it focuses on the correct operation of the software, not on finding potential defects or on finding rare combinations of values and actions that can generate failures of the software;

– find defects present in the software, or even, find "all" defects in the code. Finding all defects is an unrealistic objective and adjusting the incomes from the testers depending on the number of defects found is very risky: we could be swamped by a large number of insignificant defects (easy to find) and artificially increase the number of defects (and thus the income of the testers). Note that the opposite is also true: it is dangerous to associate the income of the development team to the number of defects corrected, as those defects that are easily found will be corrected first, leaving the difficult to fix defects (those that will have a large impact and require a long time to implement) until the end of the project. Similarly, with an objective defined in terms of number of defects found, we may have defects that are found but insufficiently detailed or documented, and thus generate a larger workload to fix, or a higher rate of "non-reproducible defects" rejected by developers;

– find information that will allow quick and easy correction of the defects identified. Such an objective may have the impact of reducing the number of identified defects and may require development expertise on the part of the testers. However, it is important that defects are described as exhaustively as possible by testers, so that – with a better understanding – bug triage can be faster (bug triage is the process of deciding whether the defect is fixed now or deferred), correction can be quicker and more effective, and retesting (aka confirmation testing) can be more efficient;

– provide information on the quality of the software or system. This objective allows simultaneous coverage of multiple aspects: make sure of what is working properly or not, evaluate risks associated with identified failures and defects. Continuous improvements of development and test processes also belong to the level of information that can be supplied by testers, as is the estimation of financial profits or losses associated with defects, and potential gains that can be obtained by improving test and development processes.

The definition of test objectives is important at the project level, but also at the company level. They demonstrate the worth of the upper management team associated with improving quality, and thus, impacts the status of the testers in the company.

1.5.3. *Destructive or constructive?*

Testers find failures in software designed by development teams, or defects in documents. Testers are seen as people with a knack for destroying software, while developers strive to design and create software. Although this is an understandable viewpoint, it is nevertheless incorrect: test teams do not introduce defects in software, they only try to identify such defects. Defects are introduced in the software by the developers during the design and coding processes.

Identification of defects in a product can be perceived as a slight on the product, or even of its authors. This may be felt as a destructive activity, while it is in fact a constructive identification – and afterwards limitation – of software risks.

1.5.4. *Relational skills*

All the members of the development and testing teams do their best to develop software without defects. Identification of failures and their transmission to the developers for correction can be seen by the developers as bad news: on the one hand it shows they are fallible (a first blow to morale) and on the other hand this forces corrections of components that they thought were complete (a second blow to morale).

It is important that testers take into account these psychological aspects and consider measures to minimize them.

If identified errors, defects, and failures are transmitted in a constructive manner, antagonism of analysts, architects, designers, and developers can be avoided. This applies to defects identified during reviews as well as to those identified during testing.

Testers and testing project leaders need good relational skills because they often provide unpleasant information: higher workload, delays to the time to market, risks, etc. It is thus important that they provide their information in a constructive and positive manner. It must be for the author of the document or software information to help them improve their skills and provide cheaper better quality software. Indeed, early correction of defects avoids higher subsequent correction costs.

Communication problems can happen, especially if the testers are seen as messengers of bad news, providing unwanted information on defects. There are several ways to improve relations between testers and developers:

– start by collaborating and by reminding each other of the common objectives for improving the quality of the delivered software;

– communicate in a neutral manner, based on facts, and not on the individual who created them, via, for example, writing factual and objective reports on identified incidents;

– try to understand the feelings of your correspondents and their reactions;

– make sure your interlocutor understood what you meant and vice versa.

1.5.5. *Change of perspective*

As mentioned by Boris Beizer [BEI 84, pp. 308-309], the usual attitude of developers is to glorify development and denigrate testing. The first question that a developer often considers is "how can I implement this?"; whereas a project manager wonders "how can I do this within budget and on schedule?" Neither party is concerned with testing. Testing is often considered a necessary activity that uses between half and two-thirds of the time. Therefore, it frequently occurs that developers take shortcuts and tend not to focus on the readability or maintainability of the software they design. This mode of operation can no longer apply in complex systems, which forces us to apply simpler and clearer programming. Therefore, the perspective changes and the question asked is "how can I test my code implementation?" and "how can I produce a properly tested program on time and within budget?"

This will have an impact:

– anticipation of testing activities by the development teams;

– a better understanding and recognition of the role of testers, and an appreciation of the specificities of testing;

– better quality software design that is cheaper and easier to maintain.

It is evident that clear, unambiguous, and testable requirements are mandatory, and this can be obtained by different techniques such as those associated with requirements engineering (such as REQB).

1.6. Testers and code of ethics (FL 1.6)

The aspects of ethics and good conduct are becoming increasingly important in today's industries. ACM (Association for Computing Machinery) and IEEE (Institute for Electrical and Electronic Engineers) have defined a code of ethics for software engineers. The ISTQB has adapted this code of ethics for systems and software testers.

This code of ethics was deemed necessary to prevent the use of information in inappropriate situations. Testers undergoing certification exams should accept and implement this code of ethics in their everyday life. The following sections have been taken and adapted from the code of ethics for the ACM/IEEE as available on their respective web sites.

The recommendations described below will increase the awareness of professionals to ethical issues and to the customer, changing their feelings toward software and systems testing.

1.6.1. *Public*

Certified software testers shall act consistently with the public interest.

This implies:

– acceptance of full responsibility for their work;

– to moderate the interests of testers, developers, employers, customers, and users with the interest of the public;

– to approve software only if there is good reason to believe that it is safe, meets the requirements, has passed the appropriate tests, and does not reduce the quality of life, private life, and does not damage the environment. The ultimate goal should be public good;

– to disclose to the appropriate authorities or persons, any risk real or potential towards the user, the public, or the environment, they think are linked to the software or its associated documentation;

– to cooperate in efforts to address public concerns caused by the installation, maintenance, support, or documentation of the software;

– to be fair and avoid deception in all claims, in particular public claims, regarding the software, its associated documentation, methods and tools;

– to take into account the physical infirmities, the allocation of resources, the economic disadvantages and any other factors that can reduce access to the benefits of the software;

– to encourage the provision of professional skills to good causes and to contribute to public education concerning the testing discipline.

1.6.2. *Customer and employer*

Certified software testers shall act in a manner that is in the best interests of their client and employer, consistent with the public interest.

Testers as software engineers must act simultaneously for the interests of their customers, employers, and the public good. This implies, where applicable that:

– the service should be provided in the field of competence of the tester, with honesty and candidness about any limit on the tester's experience and education;

– the software used is not knowingly obtained or kept via illegal sources or by unethical behavior;

– the property of a customer or an employer is used only in an authorized manner, with the knowledge and approval of the client or employer;

– any document on which design or tests are based has been approved, where applicable, by a person with the authority for the approval;

– all confidential information obtained in the tester's professional work is kept private, where this confidentiality is consistent with the public interest and the law;

– in cases where, in the tester's opinion, a project may fail, be too expensive or problematic in one way or another, or violate intellectual property rights; this should be identified, documented, evidence collected, and the client or employer should be informed;

– the tester identify, document, and inform their employer or client on all important social issues or aspects, of which they are aware, with regards to the software or associated documents;

– the tester accept annex work that can be detrimental to the work carried out for its main employer;

– the tester must not promote interests opposite to their client or employer, unless a higher ethical aspect is compromised, and in this case to inform their employer or the appropriate authority of this ethical aspect.

1.6.3. *Product*

Certified software testers shall ensure that the deliverables they provide (on the products and systems they test) meet the highest professional standards possible.

Software testers must ensure that their deliverables and the changes they apply to it, meet the highest possible professional standards. In particular, testers shall ensure, where appropriate, that they:

– achieve the highest possible quality, within an acceptable budget and reasonable schedule, ensuring clear identification of compromises and their acceptance by their employer and customer, and their availability for evaluation by users and the public;

– ensure that correct and achievable targets are present for any project on which the tester works or which it offers;

– identify, define, and address ethical, economic, cultural, legal, and environmental issues related to projects;

– ensure proper qualification of any project that the tester is working on, or proposes to work on, achievable by a suitable combination of education, training and experience;

– ensure that adequate methods are implemented on any project on which the tester works or proposes to work;

– work according to professional standards, when they are available, standards appropriate to the tasks to achieve, and to stray away from these standards only when it is justified from an ethical or technical point of view;

– endeavor to fully understand the specifications for the software or system on which it works;

– ensure that specifications for the software or system on which the tester works are properly documented, meet the requirements of users and have the required approvals;

– ensure that realistic costs, schedules, personal, quality and results' estimates are provided for each project on which the tester works, and that an assessment of the level of uncertainty associated with these estimates is provided;

– make sure that tests, reviews, and appropriate fixes are performed for software, systems, and documentation on which the tester works;

– provide appropriate documentation, including significant problems discovered and solutions implemented, for each project on which the tester works;

– strive to develop software, systems and associated documentation, in line with privacy of those who will be affected by this software or system;

– are careful to use only correct data obtained ethically and legally, and that such data are used only in a properly authorized manner;

– maintain data integrity, while being aware of that data can be incomplete or outdated;

– treat all forms of software maintenance with the same professionalism as for a new development.

1.6.4. *Judgment*

Certified software testers shall maintain integrity and independence in their professional judgment.

Testers shall maintain their integrity and independence when providing professional judgment. Specifically and depending on the case, testers:

– will adapt technical judgments to support and uphold human values;

– will support only documents if they have been prepared under its supervision or in its field of competence and with which they have agreed;

– will keep their professional objectivity with regards to any software or associated documents with which it is asked to evaluate;

– will not participate in illegal financial activities, such as corruption, double billing, or other unauthorized practices;

– will divulge to all stakeholders conflicts of interest that cannot reasonably be avoided;

– will refuse to participate as a member or adviser, in private, governmental or professional organizations, involved in software or systems where he/she, their employer or its customers may have a potential undeclared conflict of interest.

1.6.5. *Management*

Certified software test managers and leaders shall subscribe to and promote an ethical approach to the management of software testing.

Test managers and leaders will share and promote an ethical approach to management, development, and maintenance of software and systems. Specifically, where appropriate, those managing or directing testers:

– shall ensure proper management of the projects on which they work, including processes to improve quality and reduce risks;

– shall ensure that testers are aware of the standards before enforcing these standards;

– shall ensure that testers know their employers or clients policies concerning the protection of passwords, files, and confidential information, whether they be owned by the employer or by third-parties;

– shall assign work only after taking into account the contribution of education and experience, modulated by the desire to promote such education and experience;

– shall make sure of the realism of quantitative estimates of cost, load, schedule, personnel, quality and results on any project where they work or are considering working for, and provide an evaluation of an uncertainty factor for these estimates;

– shall attract potential testers only with a complete and accurate description of the conditions of employment;

– shall provide a correct and fair compensation;

– shall not unfairly hinder employment of a person in a position for which she is properly qualified;

– shall ensure that there is a correct agreement concerning ownership of any software, process, research, written document or other intellectual property on which the tester has contributed;

– shall provide evidence of violation of policies of the employer or the code of ethics;

– shall not request that a tester does anything inconsistent with the code of ethics;

– shall not punish anyone questioning the ethical aspects of a project.

1.6.6. *Profession*

Certified software testers shall advance the integrity and reputation of the profession consistent with the public interest.

Software testers shall develop the integrity and reputation of the profession consistently with the general interest. In particular, testers:

– shall help foster business development compatible with ethical activities;

– shall promote knowledge by making public software and systems testing;

– shall develop knowledge of testing by participating in professional organizations, meetings, and publications;

– shall support, as members of the profession, other testers wishing to follow this code of ethics;

– shall not develop their own interests to the detriment of the profession, their clients or their employer;

– shall comply with the laws governing their work unless, in exceptional circumstances, such compliance is inconsistent with the interests of the public;

– shall be accurate in the affirmation of characteristics of software or systems on which they work, avoiding not only false assertions, but also assertions that can reasonably be considered speculative, hollow, misleading, false, or suspicious;

– shall be responsible to identify, detect, and notify errors in software, systems and associated documents, on which they work;

– shall ensure that supervisors, employers, and clients know the implications of this code of ethics for the tester and the ramifications of such code of ethics;

– shall avoid association with companies or organizations that are in conflict with this code of ethics;

– shall recognize that violation of this code of ethics is incompatible with the profession of software or systems tester;

– shall voice their concerns to the appropriate persons when significant violations of the code of ethics are identified, unless this is impossible, counterproductive, or dangerous;

– shall inform authorities of violations to this code of ethics when it is impossible, counterproductive, or dangerous to speak with the people concerned.

1.6.7. *Colleagues*

Certified software testers shall be fair to and supportive of their colleagues, and promote cooperation with software developers.

Software or systems testers will be fair and supportive of their colleagues, in particular and where appropriate, testers:

– shall encourage their colleagues to adhere to this code of ethics;

– will attend to their colleagues in their professional development;

– will attribute merit to those who carried out the work and will not take the credit for work done by others;

– shall revise the work of others objectively, candidly, and with proper documentation;

– shall honestly hear opinions, concerns, and complaints from their colleagues;

– shall help their colleagues be aware of current practices, including policies and procedures for protection of passwords, files, and other confidential information, and other general safety measures;

– shall not unfairly intervene in the career of colleagues; however, concerns about the employer, client, or public interest may require testers, in good faith, to question the competence of a colleague;

– in situations outside of their areas of competence, will ask the opinion of other professionals with expertise in this area.

1.6.8. *Self*

Certified software testers shall participate in lifelong learning regarding the practice of their profession and shall promote an ethical approach to the practice of the profession.

Systems and software testers shall participate in a process of continuous improvement of their knowledge and of their profession, and promote an ethical approach to the practice of the profession. In particular the testers will seek to:

– improve their knowledge in aspects of testing and review of analysis, requirements, specifications, design, and maintenance of software and systems, and associated documentation, and their management process for software design, development, and testing;

– improve their ability to create quality software and test components, reliable, safe, and useful, at a reasonable cost and delay;

– improve their ability to produce accurate, informative, and well-written documentation;

– improve their understanding of testing, software, and systems, as well as the associated documentation and the environment in which they will be used;

– develop their knowledge of applicable standards and laws governing software and systems, as well as the documentation on which they work;

– improve their knowledge of this code of ethics, of its interpretation, and its application in their work;

– not treat persons unfairly for reasons without relation to the subject at hand;

– not influence others to perform actions that would violate this code of ethics;

– remind and remember that personal violations of this code of ethics are incompatible with being a professional tester.

1.7. Synopsis of this chapter

The following is a short synopsis of what was described in this chapter.

In section 1.1 we describe why tests are necessary, their context, and the reasons why it is important to test software throughout their existence and not only when they are created. You should know the following terms from the glossary: bug, defect, error, failure, fault, mistake, quality, risk, software and test.

From section 1.2 the causes of software defects and the objectives of testing of software should be noted. Section 1.3 identified the paradoxes and principles applicable to all tests, whatever their context. You should know the following terms from the glossary: debug, requirement, review, test case, test objective and exhaustive test.

Section 1.4 allowed us to identify the fundamental test principles and other important aspects such as traceability from requirements until test execution and the need for metrics to measure the progress of testing activities. You should know the following terms from the glossary: confirmation test, incident, regression test, test basis, test condition, test coverage, test data, test execution, exit criteria, test log, test plan, test strategy, test procedure, test policy, test suite, test summary report and testware.

In section 1.5 a number of important psychological aspects for testers and developers were identified, as well as the different levels of independence available for test teams, including their advantages and drawbacks. You should know the following glossary terms: error guessing and test independence.

The last section, 1.6, allowed us to understand the code of ethics applicable to software testers, its impacts and its utility.

1.8. Sample exam questions

Section 1.1. Why is Testing Necessary? (K2)

FLO-1.1.1   Describe, with examples, the way in which a defect in software can cause harm to a person, to the environment or to a company (K2)

FLO-1.1.2   Distinguish between the root cause of a defect and its effects (K2)

FLO-1.1.3   Give reasons why testing is necessary by giving examples (K2)

FLO-1.1.4   Describe why testing is part of quality assurance and give examples of how testing contributes to higher quality (K2)

FLO-1.1.5   Explain and compare the terms error, defect, fault, failure, and the corresponding terms mistake and bug, using examples (K2)

Ref	Question
1.	FLO-1.1.1 (K2) Which of the following scenarios describes a way in which a software defect may cause damage primarily and to a company directly? A. A bank that does 10% of its business online suffers a network outage due to a software defect. B. A drawing tool generates the same graphics for toll roads and highways. C. A software that controls liquid effluent from a plant underestimates the percentage of toxic products released by the plant. D. An employee mistakenly types the letter O instead of the number 0 in a post code, and a quotation is not sent correctly, leading to the loss of an important project.

Ref	Question
2.	FLO-1.1.2 (K2) Take the following sequence of events: I. A manager decides to remove code reviews from the process in order to enable a faster development time. II. An operation, required for another part of the system, is removed by a developer maintaining another part of the code that he/she is not familiar with. III. A front office bank clerk is unable to modify a customer address after installation of the new software version. IV. The customer, upset by the use of bad quality software in an establishment that manages its money, decides to change bank. Which of the following is true? A.I is the defect, II is the root cause, III and IV are the effects. B.I is the failure, II is the root cause, III and IV are the defects. C.I is the root cause, II and III are the defects, IV is the effect. D.I is the root cause, II is the defect, III and IV are the effects.
3.	FLO-1.1.3 (K2) An organization recently purchased billing software. Acceptance testing is envisaged before introducing this software into production. Which is the potential reason for such tests? A. To find defects in the software. B. To acquire a level of confidence in the software. C. To obtain evidences in case of litigation. D. To train the users.
4.	FLO-1.1.4 (K2) Which example best describes the value added by testers to quality? A. A project leader asks the test leader to evaluate the test workload. B. A tester installs a test component in the test environment to ensure that the installation package works properly. C. A tester identifies a defect that is corrected before delivery. D. A tester identifies a defect that could be fixed in a future version.

Ref	Question
5.	FLO-1.1.5 (K2) The relation between the terms "error" and "mistake" is the same as the one between which pairs of words? A. "failure" and "bug". B. "error" and "defect". C. "failure" and "defect". D. "fault" and "bug".
6.	Terms (K1) A quality software component is one that: A. Fits the user's needs. B. Corresponds to the functional specifications. C. Is finished within the allocated time. D. Is finished within budget.

Section 1.2. What is testing? (K2)

FLO-1.2.1   Recall the common objectives of testing (K1)

FLO-1.2.2   Provide examples for the objectives of testing in different phases of the software life cycle (K2)

FLO-1.2.3   Differentiate testing from debugging (K2)

Ref	Questions
7.	FLO-1.2.1 (K1) Consider the following objectives: I. Find defects. II. Acquire confidence in the level of quality. III. Provide useful information to help the decision process. IV. Fix defects. V. Prevent defects. Which of the following lists usual test objectives? A. I, II, III, IV B. I, II, IV, V C. I, II, IV, V D. I, II, III, V

Ref	Questions
8.	FLO-1.2.2.(K2) Consider the following objectives: I. Acquire confidence on the level of quality. II. Find defects. III. Provide useful information to help the decision process. IV. Check the absence of side effects. V. Prevent defects. A tester executes tests after evolutive maintenance of software. Which are the objectives aimed at? A. I, II, III, V B. I, III, IV, V C. I, II, IV, V D. I, II, III, IV
9.	FLO-1.2.3(K2) Consider the following activities: I. Analyze specifications in order to detect defects. II. Analyze code in order to detect defects. III. Analyze code execution in order to identify failures. IV. Analyze code in order to identify root cause. Which are debugging activities and which are testing activities? A. I and II are test activities, III and IV are debugging activities B. I and IV are test activities, II and III are debugging activities C. I and III are test activities, II and IV are debugging activities D. II and IV are test activities, I and III are debugging activities

Section 1.3. Seven testing principles (K2)

FLO-1.3.1   Explain the seven principles in testing (K2)

Ref	Questions
10.	FLO-1.3.1. (K2) Consider the following scenario: you tested some software and detected 100 defects, spread over six modules of equivalent size and complexity. Fifty percent of these defects are in the user interface, the rest are spread equally over the five other modules. Which principle is identifiable here? A. Test shows the presence of defects. B. Defects are frequently grouped. C. Testing is context dependent. D. It is necessary to test early.
11.	FLO-1.3.1. (K2) Consider the following scenario: you test a new version of software that has been maintained for a couple of years. Your regression tests do not show any side effects and your manual tests have not identified any defects. What principle is identifiable here? A. Defect clustering. B. Pesticide paradox. C. The absence of errors fallacy. D. Testing shows the presence of defects.
12.	Terms (K1) Exhaustive testing means: A. All pairs of input values and pre-conditions. B. At least one value from each equivalence partition. C. That testers are exhausted by the test effort. D. All combination of input values and preconditions.

Section 1.4. Fundamental test process (K1)

FLO-1.4.1   Recall the five fundamental test activities and respective tasks from planning to closure (K1)

Ref	Questions
13.	FLO-1.4.1. (K1) Which of the following is an activity included in the planning phase? A. Evaluate testability of requirements. B. Specification of exit criteria. C. Conversion of test conditions to test cases. D. Definition of the list of test cases to run.
14.	Terms (K1) What is confirmation testing? A. Confirmation that defects are present to convince developers. B. Confirmation that the software runs properly after a defect is corrected. C. Confirmation that a defect has been fixed correctly. D. Confirmation that an error has been fixed correctly.

Section 1.5. The psychology of testing (K2)

FLO-1.5.1   Recall the psychological factors that influence the success of testing (K1)

FLO-1.5.2   Contrast the mindset of a tester and of a developer (K2)

Ref	Questions
15.	FLO-1.5.1. (K1) Why is it important to clearly define test objectives? A. Because individuals have a tendency to try and reach the goals assigned by management. B. Because coverage objectives help insure quality software. C. Because risks must be covered by tests. D. Because tester independence is a major objective.
16.	FLO-1.5.2. (K2) Which of the following is the most important to promote and maintain good relations between testers and developers? A. Understand what management wants from testing. B. Explain defects in a neutral fashion. C. Identify possible workaround for identified defects. D. Promote software quality whenever possible.

17.	Terms (K1)
	What is the aim of tester's independence?
	A. Better recognition of the importance of testers in delivering quality software.
	B. The ability for testers to use their own budget instead of depending on development budgets.
	C. A more efficient defects and failures detection through a vision that is independent from development.
	D. A better specialization of testers by training and coaching, that cannot be reached if testers are too close to developers.

Section 1.6. Code of ethics (K2)

This section does not have specific learning objectives, the learning objectives are left at the discretion of the ISTQB national boards.

Ref	Questions	Level
18.	FLO-1.6.1 (K2)	K2
	Why is a code of ethics important for testers?	
	A. Because testers must have an independent vision and evaluate the quality of software developments.	
	B. Because the quality of the delivered software is important for the public, and testers identify failures that can impact the public.	
	C. Because quality of delivered software is important for the organization, otherwise it might have to pay penalties and damages.	
	D. Because it allows testers and developers to maintain a good reputation.	

Chapter 2

Testing Throughout the Software Life Cycle

Software and systems tests are mostly executed during the creation phase of such software or system. Tests are also performed during operation of the software or system, during corrective or adaptive maintenance phases, or to take into account evolution of their environment.

2.1. Software development models (FL 2.1)

FLO-2.1.1 Explain the relationship between development, test activities, and work products in the development life cycle, by giving examples using project and product types (K2)

There are many development cycles, and testing can be applied to all of these development models. Testing is based on the same input information as software development and delivers data used to improve the quality of the product (software or system) or the efficiency of the development project. In general, any design activity can introduce defects, and should be associated with one or more activity tasked to identify and extract these defects. These will be described in more detail in Chapter 5.

Software development models can be grouped in three main categories:

– *sequential models*, where the activities are executed in sequence, one after the other, with milestones that allow the accomplishment of the objectives to be identified;

– *iterative development models* where the activities are executed iteratively until the required level of quality is reached. These models use regression testing extensively;

– a third model, titled *incremental model*, can combine the two previous models.

Testing is always present in the software development cycle, sometimes it is implemented differently depending on the model, but the main principles are always applicable.

2.1.1. *Sequential models*

The sequential development model has been used since the dawn of time in many areas, first planning and creating the foundations, then building the different layers. The principle is to first define the objectives, then design the different components, in a specific sequence, and finish with the delivery of the finished product, after we have ensured that the product fits the requirements.

2.1.1.1. *Waterfall model*

The waterfall model is a simple representation of the basic sequential model.

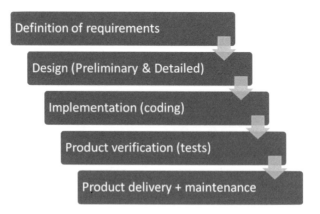

Figure 2.1. *Waterfall model*

It adapts very well to an explosion of generic activities into more detailed activity. It can be easily imported into project management tools.

It is possible to add verification tasks after each design activity, but the principle is that it is not possible to revisit an activity that is considered finished. Each activity ends with a milestone clearly identifying whether the objectives of the activity have been reached, and deciding on the start of the next activity. Any going back would imply a re-execution of the completion milestone for this activity.

The major drawback of a strict application of the waterfall cycle is that a defect generated in one phase, and detected in a latter phase, should not imply correction of that defective initial phase. Another drawback is that testing starts very late in the project, with the associated risk of being skipped altogether due to timing constraints.

2.1.1.2. *The V-model (FL 2.1.1)*

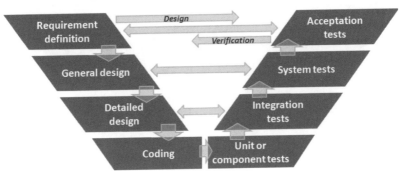

Figure 2.2. *V model*

The V model for development was proposed by Barry Boehm in 1979 and links each design activity to a test activity of the same level, thus of the same importance.

The duration between the design activity (the left descending side of the V) and the testing activity (right ascending side of the V), is the period when the tests of that level can be developed. The tests are designed to verify what has been defined during the design phase of that level.

Additional levels, beyond those identified in Figure 2.2, can be envisaged to take into account aspects such as equipment, sub-systems, and systems, when speaking of systems-of-systems or complex systems.

The main advantage of this model is that it associates a test activity to each design activity. It is to be noted that the activities are not specifically sequential, but can overlap with higher and lower level activities.

The major drawback of this model is that is shows the test activities as occurring after development, while test design activities should occur at the same time as development.

2.1.1.3. *W and VVV models*

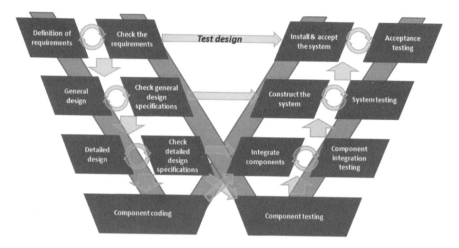

Figure 2.3. *W model*

Other development models, derived from the V-model are available: the W model and the VVV model.

The W model adds a parallel V model to the V design model, with specific testing activities: the left hand (downwards) side of this additional V is there to review the design phases, and the right-hand side of the V is there to process any change to the test execution (such as correction of test, re-execution, etc.).

The VVV cycle is a sequence of V models, where each subsequent V can be of a less important level than the previous one. This allows a visualization of the sequences of corrections or enhancements for a single software. The number of Vs is not limited.

The W model – and the VVV model – correct a number of problems identified in the V model, but are much more difficult to explain and understand.

2.1.2. *Iterative models (FL 2.1.2)*

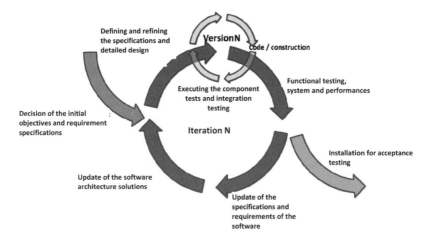

Figure 2.4. *Iterative model*

Problems linked to sequential models have led to the development of models where requirements for information completeness beforehand (in the requirements and specification phases) are not so stringent. Such a model would offer greater flexibility by splitting one single activity in a number of smaller ones. This would enable the design team to show results and obtain customer feedback earlier, so that eventual defects could be corrected earlier.

Such models can be the merging or blending of different sequential models (such as VVV), each focusing on a larger perimeter, or other models such as those described hereafter.

2.1.2.1. *Spiral model*

Proposed by Barry Boehm in 1986 [BOE 86; BOE 88], the spiral model is an evolution of the waterfall model on large governmental systems in the USA. The radial aspect represents the increased cost of design as more and more prototypes are delivered, and iterations increase in the spiral.

Each cycle in the spiral starts with the identification of objectives, evaluation of possible alternatives and definitions of applicable constraints.

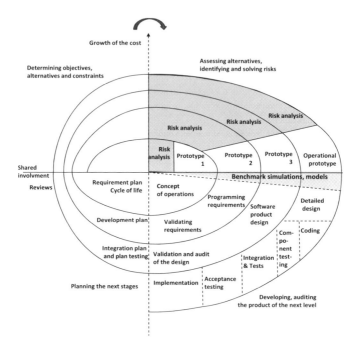

Figure 2.5. *Spiral model*

Subsequent phases are the analysis of risks, design of a more detailed prototype, and, according to the phases, validation of the different levels of requirements, and, at the end of the detailed design stage, coding, test of the components, their integration and verification, followed by their acceptance.

When comparing this model to the waterfall model, it can be observed that this later model is very complete for all the aspects of requirements, specifications, and risk analysis, i.e. for all activities before coding. Component testing, integration testing, system and acceptance testing can be identified for all aspects regarding verification and validation. The moment when specifications are sufficiently stable to enable test design only occurs relatively late in the last iteration, sometimes after the risk analysis, but always after validation of the operational prototype.

This model presupposes that there will be no requirement changes during this last iteration.

2.1.3. *Incremental model*

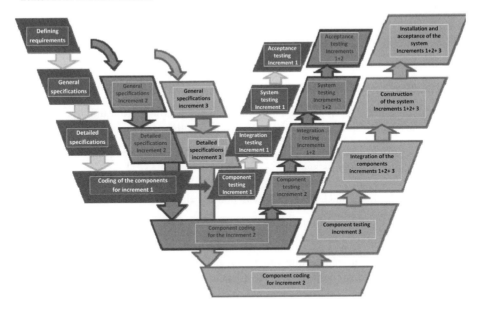

Figure 2.6. *Incremental model*

The principle of incremental development is the design of an initial sub-assembly of components – or functionalities – to which the development team adds additional components or functionalities (the increments) until development is complete.

The incremental model can be considered in two ways:

– where the increments are anticipated before design, such as during requirements definition. This is called "batch" (or "parts") and each development can be considered as an evolution of sequential models;

– where the increments are defined during design, in order to facilitate development. It is then possible, after the product has been broken down in its constituting elements, to separately design – and test – each of these components, then to integrate them before delivering the product. This split of the project can be done using an iterative or sequential design model.

Incremental development often includes a sequential development mode for the main product, and sequential or iterative development models for the sub-elements of this main product. Delivery of a main product with an incremental increase of functionalities is another implementation of the incremental model.

At the whole-system level, the incremental model can be implemented as a spiral model, with the replacement of each prototype stage by a number of functional increments (first the first increment, then the second increment, etc., until the final increment). Incremental development models are frequently used in the aerospace and defence industries.

The advantages of the incremental model are:

– the possibility to split a very large development effort into a number of more reasonable sized projects that can be executed in parallel or in sequence;

– the ability to identify the important or critical functionalities and those that can be implemented at a later stage.

The principal drawbacks of the incremental development model are:

– the tendency to use too much time to develop an increment, which delays the start (and delivery) of subsequent increments;

– the tendency to reduce the functional perimeter of an increment, hoping to deliver the other functionalities in a subsequent increment, or by creating additional increments, with the end result that the later increments are either larger or the finished product is delayed (due to the supplementary increments).

2.1.4. *RAD*

The RAD (acronym of rapid application development) model is a parallel development of diverse functions and constituting parts of the software, followed by their integration. The components are developed in parallel as mini-projects (usually from a sub-set of templates) then assembled as prototypes, enabling the customer to have a first overview of the software and provide feedback. Rapid modifications of the components are possible, but at a certain time it will become necessary to freeze the requirements and the specifications to ensure that the components are correctly managed before delivery to the market.

RAD can be considered a precursor of agile models, but is not really agile, as all the requirements are supposed to be available from the start.

RAD is often supported by tools, and encourages reuse of components and customer interaction. Configuration management aspects are very important due to the number and frequency of component changes.

Validation of components by the users, which occurs relatively early and iteratively in the development cycle, is one of the main points of this development model.

According to Wikipedia[2], RAD is organized in five phases (of which three are systematic):

– initialization, which prepares the organization and determines the software perimeter and communication plan;

– scoping, which defines the objectives, solutions and means;

– design, which models the solution and verifies system coherence;

– construction, which creates active prototypes with permanent validation;

– finalization, which is reduced to a final control of the quality level at a pilot site.

The advantages of the RAD method are:

– promotion of a collaborative organization with a dynamic requirements gathering;

– user involvement in the validation of the prototype, from test case design to unit test execution;

– adaptability to large projects through the sequential and parallel development of the different components.

The drawbacks of the RAD model are:

– dependency on strongly coherent teams, and required individual involvement in the project;

– decision mode based on the functional characteristics with a shared decision process, with lower centralization by engineering or project management.

RAD was at the origin of a large number of other agile methods such as eXtreme programming (XP) and Scrum.

---

1 http://fr.wikipedia.org/wiki/D%C3%A9veloppement_rapide_d'applications and http://en.wikipedia.org/wiki/Rapid_application_development

2.1.5. *Agile models*

The "agile development models" are based on the principles exposed in the "Agile Manifesto" [AGI] and are based on human and project realities, on learning aspects, innovation, and continuous changes for better results. These methods are based on:

– cross-functional teams (developers, testers, and customers) empowered to take design or implementation decisions, in opposition to long decision cycles and functional compartmentalization;

– numerous and rapid iterations, with user feedback, instead of larger and less frequent deliveries.

Two agile methods have attained a level of acceptance: XP and Scrum.

XP is a known development model, promoting:

– the generation of user stories or business stories that define the functionalities that will be designed;

– constant feedback from the customers (or users), who must be close to the development team to define and explain the "stories" and execute acceptance testing of the delivered code;

– pair programming and design of a test system before the code is designed, so as to design only the amount of code that is necessary;

– frequent integration of the components, up to a number of times per day, and

– implementation of the simplest solution to solve the problem at hand.

XP requires a large number of iterations, and can only be planned if supported by strong configuration of management policies, and automated test tools, so that all tests can be re-executed after each integration and iteration.

Evaluation of the development workload is done for each "story". As the stories are provided one after the other, it is difficult to predict in advance the overall development costs for a project. Moreover, previous experience will influence future estimations: if previous stories were easy to implement, estimation of the development time for a complex "story" may be underestimated, and vice-versa for a simple "story" if the previous ones were complex.

The main problems with this model are:

– the use of testing as a tool to specify a "story" provided by the customer, instead of using testing as an independent method to independently verify or validate a system under development;

– the inability to anticipate the overall cost, duration, and effort, of the development activities, before the start of the project, and for each iteration or "user story", and the impact in terms of code rewrite;

– the code is less maintainable, due to the lack of refactoring and the tendency by a number of developers to only write the minimum amount of code. Over the lifetime of the software, this lack of documentation – in the code or separate from the code – will negatively impact the maintenance costs.

Advantages of this method are:

– frequent interaction with the customer, testers, and developers;

– quick delivery of working software, even if with a restricted sub-set of functionalities.

Agile development principles are sometimes integrated in sequential development models, where – after an initial preliminary design phase – a number of "stories" are provided to the development teams, and an acceptance phase of the finished product is proposed at the end of the development phase. Agile development is then only used for components of the software, not for the overall system.

2.1.5.1. *EVO*

One of the derivations of the incremental model is EVO (proposed by Tom Gilb [GIL 05, pp. 293-319]), where complex tasks are split into many simpler, smaller tasks. EVO is characterized by:

– frequent delivery of system level increments;

– increments useful to the stakeholders (users and customers);

– feedback from the stakeholders to define the following stages/increments;

– use of the present system as initial reference;

– very small increments, ideally between 2% and 5% of the cost and workload of the overall project;

– prioritization of the increments based on the added value for each delivery;

– feedback from stakeholders is used to immediately adapt long-term planning and requirements, and to decide at which stage to implement a global approach;

– focus on deliverable results.

Review activities, component tests, integration tests, system tests, and acceptance tests can also be split into very small increments.

NOTE: EVO and Scrum are not required by the International Software Testing Qualifications Board (ISTQB) syllabus.

2.1.5.2. *Scrum*

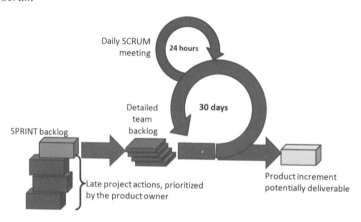

Figure 2.7. *Scrum development model*

Scrum is based on development iterations (called sprints) to execute the project's actions. These actions are planned and kept in a "backlog" that comprises all the planned actions for the project. Actions are prioritized according to owner-defined priorities (one of the stakeholders). The development team selects the actions to execute in a sprint, according to the established priorities, and these actions will not evolve during that iteration. In each sprint, shorter duration cycles (from a few hours to a couple of days, but less than a week) will occur. A daily meeting allows the definition of the day's priorities, and re-prioritization of efforts based on project events. At the end of each cycle, the project team meets with the stakeholders to demonstrate (validate and accept) developments executed in this iteration. Feedback from the stakeholders enables adaptation of the product in the next iteration (the next sprint cycle).

One of the major principles of Scrum is the ability given to the development team to learn and to adapt to the project events, through the use of small increments.

A typical Scrum team is from five to nine people, with multiple skills such as analysis and design, coding, test, interface and database design, architecture, and documentation, etc. One person can be in charge of project management. The Scrum model also puts forward the ScrumMaster as coach and consultant of the Scrum team. This person is there in a purely consultative role, not in the role of project leader or of product owner.

The advantages of the Scrum model are:

– an increase in productivity for teams previously hindered by a complicated process;

– the possibility to prioritize the work and to change its organization depending on current project risks;

– use of a Backlog in order to complete development in a series of small iterations;

– daily project measurement and daily communication in the team.

The drawbacks of the Scrum model are:

– dependency upon a ScrumMaster, who might not have the required skills or authority to help the development team;

– dependency on self-managed teams and rejection of centralized control, which can lead to a power struggle that can paralyze the team;

– major difficulties in integrating this type of development in the context of very large projects;

– requirement of specialist teams that adapt to less experienced teams;

– difficulty to determine the time or cost of the project – or even a cost bracket – for the whole project before project commencement.

2.1.5.3. *Test driven development*

Test driven development (TDD) is a variation of the agile model that builds on automated test tools.

The principle is as follows: the customer defines the way the software is supposed to work (a.k.a. the user story), the tester defines a test case that represents the expected operation, the developer then designs the minimum amount of code to ensure successful operation of the test. Next a new iteration occurs with a new test case or a new functionality. It may be necessary to reorganize (refactor) the code, but regression is automated, as all tests must be able to run and execute all the user stories.

Test cases are usually supported by tools that allow backup and re-execution of tests as often as needed.

The advantages of this method are:

– frequent interaction between tester, developer and customer;

– the possibility to use tests as development comments;

– the availability of working code, even if it is only a sub-set of the expected functionalities.

The major drawbacks of this development method are:

– use of tests as specifications, and not as a method to ensure verification and validation of specifications written previously,

– inability to determine the overall cost beforehand and thus the project duration.

2.1.6. *Selection of a development model*

FLO-2.1.2 Recognize the fact that software development models must be adapted to the context of project and product characteristics (K1)

Selection of the development model will depend on the development context. A development model is frequently associated with a formalization level for documentation, and thus with the data used by testers to design and develop tests. Similarly the industrial development context for the software or the system will also impact the design and documentation requirements:

– in a formal environment a sequential model (either incremental or not) will often be selected, with service level agreements (SLAs) defined between the different stakeholders, whether within a single organization or between different organizations, in the same geographical location or thousands of kilometers away;

– in an informal environment, incremental iterative models will frequently be used, with developers, testers, and customers grouped in a single geographic location;

– regulated or governmentally overseen projects, such as medical, aerospace, military, and nuclear applications, sequential development models will be privileged, as they allow verification milestones, which allow early regulatory organization verification such as PDR (Preliminary Design Review) or CDR (Critical Design Review).

The required availability of customers, users, and other stakeholders is one of the characteristics of the agile methods. Unfortunately, such people are frequently unavailable for development teams, which render these methods less efficient.

Important aspects of the mode	Waterfall	V-Model	Increm.	Spiral	Agile
Clear implementation for management	Y	Y	Y	Y	N
Easy reporting	Y	Y	Y	Y	N
All requirements necessary before start	Y	Y	N[*]	N	N
Ease of resources allocation	Y	Y	Y	Y	N
Quick availability of running software	N	N	Y	Y	Y
Risk and cost control via prototyping	N	N	Y	Y	Y
Lack of clear objectives problematic for management	N	N	Y	Y	Y
Requires clear interfaces between modules	N	N	Y	Y	Y
Not very compatible with formal reviews	N	N	Y	Y	Y
Tendency to push problems to a future delivery	N	N	Y	Y	Y
[*]The incremental model can start with fully defined requirements or with less-defined objectives.					

Table 2.1. *Development cycle comparison*

The selection of a development model often depends on the designer's habits and the selection of the design organization.

2.1.7. *Positioning tests*

FLO-2.1.3 Recall characteristics of good testing that are applicable to any life cycle model (K1)

To ensure a reduction of the number of defects introduced in the software designed, and whatever the development model selected, it is necessary to begin testing as early as possible. This is not always possible, due to time, budget, or resources constraints.

However, regardless of the development model selected, it is possible to set up test activities that increase the quality of the software. Principles to implement are as follows:

– each design activity, and each deliverable, must have a corresponding test activity that will search for defects introduced by this activity or in this deliverable;

– each test level has its own specific objectives, associated with that test level, so as to avoid testing the same characteristic twice;

– analysis and design of tests for a given level start at the same time as the design activity for that level, thus saving as much time as possible;

– testers are involved in document review as soon as drafts are available, whichever the development model selected.

Test levels and associated deliverables may be combined, split, or reorganized depending on the software or system being designed, on the specific context and on the required *integrity level*.

NOTE: It is important that the term "test" is used correctly and to note that test objectives (variable depending on the organizations) include verification and validation of requirements and specifications, and delivery of evidence and useful management information.

Generic reference development models are available in CMMI (Capability Maturity Model Integration) and in ISO/IEC 12207 (software life cycle processes). The standard that defines the test deliverables based on product integrity level is IEEE 829-2008. These reference models and templates can be adapted to the specific context of the product or project.

2.2. Test levels (FL 2.2)

FLO-2.2.1 Compare the different levels of testing: major objectives, typical objects of testing, typical targets of testing (e.g. functional or structural) and related work products, people who test, types of defects, and failures to be identified (K2)

Whichever development model is selected, a number of design activities are executed: creation of components, integration of these components together, then – when all components have been integrated – it is necessary to ensure that the system works properly in end-to-end operation, and that the system is accepted by the users, so that it can be delivered to the market. Whether these tasks are executed once only or multiple times, it is not important with regards to the generic objectives of each task.

To facilitate understanding, we will use a sequential model (V-model) to group the testing tasks in four levels:

– component tests;

– component integration tests;

– system tests, on the completely integrated system;

– acceptance tests, a prerequisite for delivery to the market or production.

Some aspects are generic and applicable regardless of the test activity, such as:

– *test object*, i.e. the target of the tests, be it a function, a sub-program, or a program, a software application, or a system made up of different sub-systems;

– *specific objectives*, associated with that activity, which are the reasons why the tests will be executed. These can be to discover certain types of defects, to ensure correct operation, or provide any other type of information (such as coverage);

– *test basis*, a referential or set of information that can be used to define what the test object is supposed to do;

– *entry and exit criteria*, which will define when a task can start (the pre-requisites) and when it can be considered as finished.

2.2.1. *Component level testing or component tests*

Test object: components, program modules, functions, programs, database modules, SQL requests, depending on the granularity of the software or system to test.

Objective: detect failures in the components, verifies whether the mode of operation of the component, module, program, object, class, etc., is functional or non-functional.

Reference material: requirements applicable to the component, detailed specifications, source code, algorithms.

Entry criteria: the component is available, compiled, and executable in the test environment; the specifications are available and stable.

Exit criteria: the required coverage level, functional and technical (or non-functional), has been reached; defects found have been corrected; and the corrections have been verified; regression tests on the rest of the component have been executed on the last version and do not identify any regression; traceability from requirements to test execution is maintained and statistical data are available.

Component tests, also called "unit tests", are applicable on the components and verify the operation in reference to a set of requirements and specifications (e.g. detailed design specification documents). Usually, component tests are executed on components that can be tested separately. This frequently occurs in isolation from the rest of the system, and requires the use of drivers and stubs, and sometimes of simulators and emulators.

The characteristics investigated at this level can be functional or non-functional, such as those associated with resource usage (central processing unit (CPU), memory usage, etc.) robustness or performance.

The types of tests that can be executed at the component test level can be based on the structure (*white-box tests*) or on the requirements or the interfaces (*black-box tests*).

Generally, these tests are executed with access to the source code, often with the help – or by – the developers. Frequently, the defects identified are directly fixed without being reported in the defect-tracking process or tool. This can lead to invalid statistics with regards to the number of defects per component.

2.2.2. *Integration level testing or Integration tests*

Test object: components, infrastructure, interfaces, database systems, and file systems.

Objective: detect failures in the interfaces and exchanges between components.

Reference material: preliminary and detailed design documentation for the software or system, software or system architecture, *use cases*, workflow, etc.

Entry criteria: at least two components that must exchange data are available, and have passed component test successfully.

Exit criteria: all components have been integrated and all message types (sent or received) have been exchanged without any defect for each existing interface; statistics (such as *defect density*) are available; the *defects* requiring correction have been corrected and checked as correctly fixed; the impact of not-to-fix defects have been evaluated as not important.

Component integration testing focuses on the interfaces between components and between the different parts of the software and the system (including the hardware). This includes the interface with the operating system, file systems, database systems, hardware (plugs, voltage, etc.), and software (protocol, messages, etc.); interfaces inside the system or between systems.

Based on the granularity of the components, there can be many levels of integration:

– integration of software components, typically executed during component integration tests;

– integration of software components with hardware components, and integration of these components (hardware + software) together in order to create equipment or sub-systems;

– integration of equipment or sub-systems within a higher-order system (such as a system of systems), typically executed after the system tests for each of these equipments or sub-systems and before the systems tests of the higher-level system.

Characteristics tested at this level can be functional or non-functional, such as those linked to resource usage (CPU, memory usage, etc.), to robustness, or to performance, and can also include physical characteristics (such as heat generated or radiation).

The type of tests executed at this component integration test level can be based on the architecture of the code (white-box tests) or on the specifications (black-box tests). Component integration tests are frequently executed with the help of development teams and their support.

The way in which the components will be integrated depends on how they will be delivered by the development team. Depending on component granularity, drivers and stubs will be used.

There are many ways to integrate components, each with advantages and drawbacks. It is important for testers to understand the architecture of the software, the influence of the different components, and to coordinate with the development and design teams, before deciding on one integration method. The identification of the root cause of failure becomes increasingly difficult as the number of simultaneously integrated components increases (due to the large number of added interfaces). If we integrate a few components at a time, the integration process is longer.

2.2.2.1. *Big bang integration*

Big bang integration occurs when all (or most of) the components are integrated simultaneously. The advantage of such integration is that drivers and stubs are not necessary to test the interfaces between the components. Conversely, this type of integration often ends up with a large number of defects that are difficult to isolate quickly, and these are passed on to the system test phase without being identified.

2.2.2.2. *Bottom-up integration*

Bottom-up integration starts with the integration of the lower-level components, followed by integration of higher-level components, to finish with the highest level components. This will necessitate the design of a number of drivers to pilot each of these integration levels.

2.2.2.3. *Top-down integration*

This type of integration starts with the design of highest level component and replacing all next (lower) level components by stubs. As the design of the components progresses, stubs will be replaced by real components. This type of integration requires the design of a large number of stubs to replace components that have not yet been developed.

2.2.2.4. *Other types of integration*

A number of other integration [JOR 08s, pp. 201-227] types exist and can be implemented. We can note:

– sandwich integration, which combines top-down and bottom-up integration;

– integration by functionalities, which focuses on functionalities delivered and the delivery of the components required to implement that functionality. It ensures that the required functionalities are delivered, and required drivers and stubs;

– neighborhood integration, which is based on the technical proximity of components, their links being technical instead of functional. This allows a reduction in the number of drivers and stubs from bottom-up and top-down integration. Such integration requires analysis of the software – or system – architecture and the cooperation of the development team. Backbone integration is a kind of neighborhood integration where the technical backbone is used as point of origin for the integration.

2.2.3. *System tests*

Test object: the complete software or system, its documentation (user manual, maintenance and installation documentation, etc.), the software configuration and all the components that are linked to it (installation and de-installation scripts, etc.).

Objective: detect failures in the software, to ensure that it corresponds to the requirements and specifications, and that it can be accepted by the users.

Reference material: requirements and specifications of the software or system, use cases, risk analysis, applicable norms, and standards.

Entry criteria: all components have been correctly integrated, all components are available.

Exit criteria: the functional and technical (i.e. non-functional) level of coverage has been reached; must-fix defects have been corrected and their fixes have been verified; regression tests have been executed on the last version of the software and do not show any regression; bi-directional traceability from requirements to test execution is maintained; statistical data are available, the number of defects that do not require correction is not too important; the summary test report has been written and approved.

Sample exit criteria for system tests:

1. No changes – design, code, or characteristics – except to fix defects identified by system tests;

2. No unexpected stops, failures, or termination of process has occurred on any server software or hardware during the last 3 weeks;

3. No client system became inoperative due to a failing update during system tests;

4. The test team successfully executed all planned tests on the software version that is candidate for release;

5. The development team corrected all the defects categorized as "must fix" by the sales, marketing and customer support teams;

6. Test team checked that all items identified in the defect tracking management system have either been closed or postponed to a future version, and where appropriate have been verified by regression tests and confirmation tests;

7. Test metrics indicate product stability and reliability, completion of all planned test and adequate coverage of all "critical" risks;

8. The project management team accepts that the product, as defined during the last round of system level tests, will satisfy the reasonable expectations of a client;

9. The project management team implements an end-of-system-test phase meeting, and accepts that the systems test be terminated.

Tests at system level focus on how the overall system works. It will thus process end-to-end transactions, from installation to operation of the system, user management, and interactions with other systems or software.

The system test will focus on functional and non-functional aspects of the software. It will also ensure that the software operates in an environment similar to the expected (production) environment, so that user acceptance is facilitated.

Usually, the types of tests executed at system test level are based on specifications (black-box tests). However, it is possible to base some tests on the architecture of the system – call graph for example – and to execute some white-box tests. Analysis of the coverage reached will help focus remaining activities on components that are not yet sufficiently covered.

System tests are usually executed by test teams, sometimes with a high degree of independence.

2.2.4. *Acceptance tests*

Test object: the complete software or system, its documentation (user manuals, installation and maintenance documentation, etc.), all necessary configuration items, forms, reports and statistics from previous test levels, user processes.

Objective: obtain customer or user acceptance of the software.

Reference material: contract, specifications, and requirements for the system or software, use cases, risk analysis, applicable standards, and norms.

Entry criteria: all components have been correctly tested at system test level and are available, the software installs correctly, the last fixes have been implemented and tested (confirmation tests and regression tests) without identification of failures, the software is considered sufficiently mature for delivery.

Exit criteria: the expected coverage level has been reached; must-fix defects have been corrected and the fixes have been verified; regression tests have been executed on the latest version of the software and do not show regression; traceability from requirements to test execution has been maintained (including for contractual requirements, whether functional or not); user and customer representatives who participated in the acceptance test accept that the software or system can be delivered in production.

Acceptance tests are aimed at reaching a level of confidence in the system, whether for functional or non-functional aspects. The search for defects and failures is only a byproduct, not the main goal. If too many failures are observed the confidence in the software or system will not be reached, and the customer will be more skeptical about future deliveries of the software.

Acceptance tests are executed by user or customer representatives, augmented by testers, generally independent from the development team. Other types of stakeholders can also participate at this test level. Acceptance test are mostly black-box tests (based on requirements and specifications), though some structure based tests can be executed.

Acceptance tests can occur at different levels in the life of software:

– during design of the software;

– when the software is integrated with other software;

– when the software is being acquired by a new customer;

– for acceptance of new functionalities or features.

There are many types of acceptance tests:

– user acceptance, verifying whether the software fulfills the user requirements;

– operational acceptance, when system administrators will check that normal operation can be executed without failures: data backup, retrieval and restoration, user and priority management, security vulnerability verifications, data migration and upload, backup and restoration of the software and its data in case of major disaster, maintenance tasks, installation, and de-installation;

– contractual acceptance, verifying that all the contractual requirements have been fulfilled. Usually the contractual requirements and acceptance criteria are defined between the parties in advance;

– regulatory acceptance, where an authorized regulatory organism (i.e. Food and Drug Administration (FDA), FAA, DoD, etc.) ensures that applicable rules and standards have been applied and complied with during design and testing of the software or system. Such acceptance tests are mostly undertaken for software in regulated industries (aerospace, medical, or rail systems). This type of acceptance mostly focuses on the evidences provided by the design and test teams that regulatory requirements have been complied with;

– alpha tests, executed by potential users belonging to the design organization, using the software as a customer would, in order to have an independent vision from the design team;

– beta tests, where potential customers use the software for a limited period, free of charge, in their own environment, in order to identify potential problems with some particular environments. Beta tests are sometimes used for marketing purposes (to create "buzz" around the product), instead of a real, efficient, test phase. This is because there is no mandatory usage of the product, nor information of the development team in case of dissatisfaction.

– pilot phase, where the software – frequently after acceptance tests – is rolled out on a limited geographical or logical scale. This phase allows the use of the different functionalities by real users and can help adapt the user processes;

– plant acceptance – and FAI (First Article Inspection) – is often used for systems and equipment, and checks that the system designed corresponds to the contractual, technical, and functional requirements. This verification includes a review of all test deliverables and all test documentation for the project. It is thus important to have complete traceability from contract and requirements until delivery of the final completed system.

2.2.5. *Other levels*

In complex systems and systems-of-systems, other test levels can occur: sub-system acceptance tests, equipment integration tests, pre-operational and operational test phases, etc.

Safety critical systems, or critical components in complex systems, can also have some of their test levels executed by regulatory organizations that are accepted by the governmental or regulatory authority (e.g. FDA for medical software).

2.3. Types of tests (FL 2.3)

FLO-2.3.2 Recognize that functional and structural tests occur at any test level (K1)

We have identified different levels of tests. We also have tests applicable to different software or systems quality characteristics.

You probably have a car, and selected it based on criteria that were specific to you, such as price, color, brand, horsepower, reliability, comfort, miles to the gallon, speed, price of spare parts or of maintenance, etc. For you the functional characteristic – ability to go from point A to point B – was probably not the determining factor (all vehicles have that functionality), your selection was thus aimed mostly towards non-functional characteristics.

In terms of selection of software and systems, functional and non-functional characteristics are also important, and their evaluation – through testing – allows their measurement. International standard ISO 9126 [ISO 01, p. 7] proposes a quality model for software and systems. This model is organized around six major characteristics (functionality, reliability usability, efficiency, maintainability, and portability). These characteristics possess sub-characteristics.

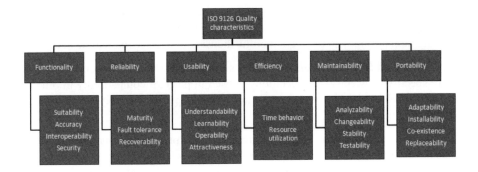

Figure 2.8. *ISO 9126 quality characteristics*

Each of these characteristics and sub-characteristics can be subject to testing. Usually these characteristics are divided as follows:

– functional characteristics, which includes the functions and functionalities provided by the system;

– non-functional characteristics, which comprise other (non-functional) characteristics such as reliability, usability, efficiency, maintainability and portability.

These characteristics, whether functional or not, can be tested at each test level, with different test techniques.

Test design based on the structure of the software can be executed at any test level: the only change will be the granularity of the component being studied. For a test level, we can have a focus on instructions and branches, (component test), in another we will have pieces of the software (integration test), sub-systems or other software (system test and acceptance test).

2.3.1. *Functional tests*

Functional tests focus on the functions of the software, what they do, the services provided, and the requirements covered.

Functional tests include, for ISO 9126, the following aspects:

Suitability: the capability of the software to provide an appropriate set of functions for specified tasks and user objectives. This also covers the suitability of the tasks and the operability of the software. Example: the process will allow opening, modification and closing of files.

Accuracy: the capability of the software to provide the correct or agreed results or effects with the required degree of precision. Example: depending on the usage of the software, accuracy to the second or the thousandth of a second will be necessary.

Interoperability: the capability of the software product to interact with one or more specified systems. Interoperability is used in place of compatibility in order to avoid possible ambiguity with replaceability. Example: interaction with a specific emailing or operating system.

Security: the capability of the software product to protect information and data so that unauthorized persons or systems cannot read or modify them and authorized persons or systems are not be denied access to them. This is also applicable to data in transmission. Safety is defined as a characteristic of quality in use, as it does not relate to software alone, but to a whole system. Generally, it is important to make sure that operating systems, file systems, database management systems, and network management systems are secure.

Functional compliance: the capability of the software to adhere to standards, conventions, or regulations in laws and similar prescriptions relating to functionality. Example: accounting software should not allow physical removal of an entry, but only its logical removal by the creation of another entry between the same accounts, for the same amount, but with an inverse direction.

These aspects are usually defined in requirements and specifications documents and are well understood by customers and users. They represent the way the system is supposed to function in the commercial or management context of its users.

Functional tests are executed at all test levels (component – or unit – test level, component integration level, system test level, or acceptance test level).

2.3.2. *Non-functional tests*

FLO-2.3.3 Identify and describe non-functional test types based on non-functional requirements (K2)

Contrary to functional tests, which focus on the services provided by the software, non-functional tests focus on the way the services are provided.

Similar to functional tests, non-functional tests can be executed at all test levels (component – or unit – test level, component integration level, system test level, or acceptance test level).

Non-functional aspects of the ISO 9126 standard contain the following characteristics and sub-characteristics:

– reliability, which is the capability of the software product to maintain a specified level of performance when used under specified conditions, and comprises:

- maturity,

- fault tolerance,

- recoverability,

- reliability compliance;

– usability, which is capability of the software product to be understood, learned, used and attractive to the user, when used under specified conditions and comprises:

- understandability,

- learnability,

- operability,

- attractiveness,

- usability compliance;

– efficiency, which is the capability of the software product to provide appropriate performance, relative to the amount of resources used, under stated conditions and includes:

- time behavior,

- resource utilization,

- efficiency compliance;

– maintainability or the capability of the software product to be modified. Modifications may include corrections, improvements, or adaptation of the software to changes in environment, and in requirements and functional specifications, which includes:

- analyzability,

- changeability,

- stability,

- testability,

- maintainability compliance;

– portability, which is the capability of the software product to be transferred from one environment to another and includes:

- adaptability,

- installability,

- co-existence,

- replaceability,

- portability compliance.

Frequently, non-functional tests are delayed after functional tests. It is recommended that non-functional tests are executed at the same time, or even before, functional tests, because non-functional defects are very important – regarding long-term issues – and take a long time to correct.

Example: transactions response time per number of users, also called performance tests are often left until the end of system tests. However, the root causes of performance issues are frequently to be found in the organizational design and architecture of the software. In order to fix them, it will be necessary to return to an early phase of the design. Early detection (see section 1.3.3) is possible, if the precaution to allocate performance objectives to each of the sections of the transactions has been undertaken. This is called "budgetization" of transactions sections and is illustrated in Figure 2.9.

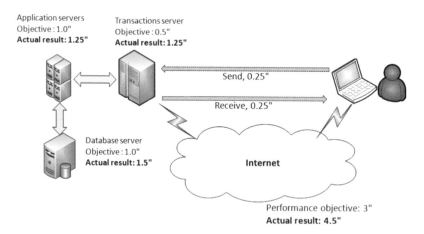

Figure 2.9. *Example of transaction budget*

If we have a 3" second maximum requirement for a transaction, we could budget 0.5" for sending the transaction request and 0.5" to receive the transaction response (network section), 1" for the processing by the transaction server, and 1" for data retrieval in the database. A performance test to evaluate the response time for each separate component will allow the tester to ascertain that a section of the transaction does not take more that the allocated (budgeted) time, and thus does not impact the overall transaction. If the performances from one section or one component are inadequate, it is possible to think of corrective actions without waiting for the results of performance tests done at the end of systems tests, or to mitigate these bad performances with increased performances of the other sections.

2.3.3. *Tests based on the structure or architecture of the software*

FLO-2.3.4 Identify and describe test types based on the analysis of a software system's structure or architecture (K2)

White-box tests, based on the structure of the software (structural tests) can be executed at any test level.

If these tests are executed at component test level, they will focus on instructions, branches, and conditions in the code.

If they are executed at component integration test level, they will be able to focus on components call graphs, and on the interactions of the different modules for the processing of messages and transactions.

If they are executed at system test level, structural tests of the software can focus on how the different components interact with each other, including the frequency with which they are called (call graphs) or on the analysis of the modules used to process transactions or messages.

Usually, the level of completion of structural tests for a test level is defined as "coverage level" (e.g. code coverage) based on the objective of the coverage level. Identification of the coverage percentage is obtained after dynamic tests – manual or automated – on a version that is said to be "instrumented". The dynamic tests will have been chosen to test the highest number of aspects of the code, and the evaluation of coverage level (if it is below 100%) will allow you to identify which portions of the code have not been covered, and thus design other tests or test conditions.

Code instrumentation usually has a negative impact on the performances and forces testers to re-execute tests with and without this instrumentation. Such negative impact is called "probe effect" (or side effect).

2.3.4. *Tests associated with changes*

FLO-2.3.5 Describe the purpose of confirmation testing and regression testing (K2)

When a defect has been corrected, two types of tests should be executed:

– confirmation tests or retests, which focus on verifying that the defect has been corrected and the software operates as expected; and

– regression tests that will make sure that the correction did not introduce any side effects (regression) on the rest of the software (see Regression test policies, page 78).

Confirmation test – or retest – is the re-execution of the tests that identified the failure resulting from the defect that was corrected. The purpose here is to make sure that the software works correctly and that the defect is not present anymore. An additional objective is to make sure that the corrected defect did not mask another defect (defect masking).

Regression testing consists in the re-execution of tests that were already executed, on the whole software, to ensure that modifications implemented elsewhere in the software did not have side effects (regressions) in the software. Modifications to take into account include:

– defect fixes;

– introduction of additional functionalities or removal of obsolete functionalities;

– integration of new components;

– modification of any component with which the software interfaces, whether it be other software, the operating system, file systems, network, or database management systems (non-exhaustive list).

Component fixes occurring at all test levels, confirmation test and regression tests also occur at all levels. Thorough impact analysis can help to focus and limit regression tests. The underlying assumption is that the impact analysis is complete.

Regression tests and impact analysis of modifications are very important during maintenance and correction of software. In Figure 2.10, we see the structure of calls between components of a software. If component 22 must be updated, then components 1, 23, 24, 25, 26, and 27 will have to be verified to make sure that they are not impacted by the changes to component 22. Components 14, 15, 6, 8, 2, 3, 4, and 13 could also be indirectly impacted by a change in component 22 and should also be tested. A similar impact analysis (via data flow and control flow) should be executed for all variables used or referenced in component 22 to make sure that all potential impacts are identified.

Tests on these components (updated or not) should be documented and associated with the software version of these components and on the version of the overall software.

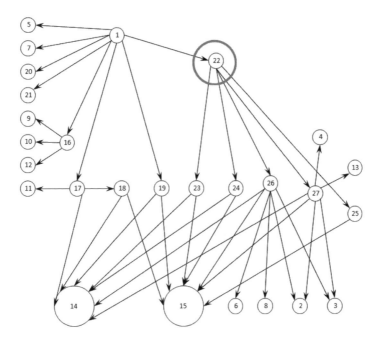

Figure 2.10. *Impact analysis*

2.3.5. Comparisons and examples

FLO-2.3.1 Compare four software test types (functional, non-functional, structural and change related) by examplef (K2)

Functional tests are those associated with the functions offered by the software, such as the ability to create bank accounts, deposit or withdraw cash, send or receive money orders and view transactions on accounts. In general the functional aspects – what the software must execute – are defined in software requirements document specified by the customer, and detailed in specifications documents.

Non-functional tests focus on aspects such as response time, maintainability, or usability of the software, usage of hardware, network, or other system resources (a list of non-functional characteristics is available in Figure 2.8). We could test the response time, network bandwidth usage, or readability or understandability of the code. Non-functional aspects are frequently forgotten by customers, but are linked to numerous litigations or non-acceptance of software products.

Structural tests are those linked to the structure and architecture of the software and include analysis of the internal workings of the software, whether inside the software (e.g. source code analysis, control graph, etc.) or during software execution (e.g. call graph and frequency of calls to specific modules). These tests enable evaluation of the software quality both for maintenance purposes and for its operational usage.

Tests associated with changes are those applicable when evolutive or corrective updates are implemented, allowing the software to adapt to changes in its context.

2.4. Test and maintenance (FL 2.4)

Software maintenance applies to modifications of software already used or delivered to the market. Constraints associated with this type of test are more important than those associated with the development of similar new software.

FLO-2.4.1 Compare maintenance testing (testing an existing system) to testing a new application with respect to test types, triggers for testing, and amount of testing (K2)

During maintenance, evolutions or fixes are usually caused by external events such as changes in regulations that translate in a corresponding change in the software. Development and testing time become a major constraint. Of course it is also paramount to ensure that there is no impact on other functionalities provided by the software.

Maintenance testing has different constraints from the testing of new software:

– timing constraints, for development and testing;

– impact constraints, to ensure that other functionalities are not impacted.

Many aspects impact the development effort when maintaining software:

– quick identification of required modifications, via an easier analyzability of the software, to quickly diagnose causes of failures and areas to update;

– readability of the software, to have an understandable software, where the variables, functions, and sections are easily recognizable, identifiable, and adequately documented;

– software stability, so as to prevent the impact of changes outside the area modified;

– adherence of the software to applicable maintainability standards or conventions.

Identification of regressions – the ability to ensure that the rest of the software is not impacted by changes – is another major aspect of software maintenance.

FLO-2.4.2 Recognize indicators for maintenance testing (modification, migration and retirement) (K1)

There are three main reasons to initiate maintenance tests:

– when the software is modified, updated, when defects are corrected, and when the operating environment is modified or patched;

– when the software is migrated to a new software or hardware environment;

– when the software or sub-system is retired, which will require its replacement.

The principles associated with maintenance testing is to make sure that all areas that are changed are correctly changed, and that all areas that are not changed are not changed, either in form (content), or in terms of supported functionalities.

2.4.1. *Maintenance context*

Software is developed during a relatively short period of time, but is used for many years. COBOL programs, developed in the 1980s and 1990s are still used at this time (20 to 30 years later) in some organizations. Maintainability (ability of the software product to be modified, corrected, improved, or adapted to changes in its environment, in its requirements or its functional specifications) includes aspects of developers reading and understanding the code, naming rules for variables and functions, and can include rules on the amount and type of comments to make the code more readable, and ease its comprehension.

These aspects, which continue long after the software is delivered to its market, have an impact on the costs – and duration – of fixes before software delivery (ease of defect identification and correction during the tests phases), and an impact throughout the life of the software and its maintenance. Taking care of these aspects as early as possible in the development cycle is thus important and will provide an increased return on investment.

Many important aspects are associated with maintenance of software:

– all quality characteristics defined by the ISO 9126 standard are important and should be considered;

– maintenance is not limited to modification of the software, but includes changes to the design and test documentation;

– components should be managed in configuration exactly as in the case of new developments;

– traceability to documentation should be maintained, whether design documentation or test documentation (test conditions, test cases and test execution).

2.4.2. *Evolutive maintenance*

Evolutive maintenance focuses on the development of new functions in existing software. In this case it is important to ensure that the new developments do not have any side effects on the existing functions. Generally, evolutive maintenance does not have the same time constraints as corrective maintenance.

Example: corrective maintenance includes evolution of the software and the evolution of the context in which the software operates (interfaces, operating system, etc.).

We may remember the portability issues associated with migration from Windows XP to Windows Vista, or from a 32 bit system to a 64 bit system, or from a single processor computer to a multicore machine.

When the environment is modified all the functionalities of the software must remain available. This is done through the execution of regression tests, which are frequently functional, on the software and all software with which it exchanges data. End-to-end functional tests at the acceptance level are another solution.

2.4.3. *Corrective maintenance*

Corrective maintenance takes into account the correction of defects found by customers or users. In such cases there are more important time constraints than during evolutive maintenance.

The first stage is to identify the extent of the modification required, and the tests that are impacted by the corrections. This will enable evaluation of the effort and duration of changes.

In a second stage, the testing activities must focus on two aspects:

– ensuring that the software fits the user's needs, through:

- confirmation tests or retesting, to verify that the fixes correct the identified defects,

- regression tests to ensure no side-effects occur in the rest of the software;

– analyzing the reasons why the defect was allowed to reach the market, in order to improve existing processes and thus avoid these in the future. Possible causes can include:

- incorrect risk evaluation and thus incorrect tests of the software,

- incorrect understanding of the requirements or specifications,

- test cases or test data that do not fit the test objectives,

- test techniques that were misunderstood or incorrectly implemented,

- misunderstandings between the stakeholders,

- etc.

Identification of the root causes of defects that are to be fixed during maintenance enables process improvement, increases in productivity, efficiency, and effectiveness of the testing activities.

2.4.4. *Retirement and replacement*

When software or systems are retired and replaced, it is also necessary to execute tests. These can include:

– verification of the data conversion and data transfer software, to ensure that the data from the old system or software will be correctly migrated to the new system or software. It is also necessary to ensure that conversion from the new system to the old works correctly so that if the new system does not work correctly, a rollback of the data is available;

– verification of the backup, archival, and restoration of data, to ensure that the software in charge of conversion of backups and archives are able to process the data from the old software version, and archive the data from the new software in compatible form. This is important with regards to mandatory access to archived electronic data;

– optionally, the design of end-to-end functional tests (business tests) on the old version of the software could be necessary to generate acceptance tests on the new version of the software.

2.4.5. Regression test policies

FLO-2.4.3 Describe the role of regression testing and impact analysis in maintenance (K2)

We have seen previously that maintenance requires us to ensure that no regression occur on areas that are not modified. There are different types of regression:

– modification introduces a new defect;

– modification exposes a defect that is already present in the software or in the functionality that was modified;

– correction or change exposes a defect already present in an unrelated area of the software.

The two first cases can usually be identified through tests in the software area that underwent the change, while the last case will require exhaustive regression tests throughout the software.

Regression tests are:

– either re-execution of all tests designed during the creation of the software, possibly with an emphasis on system and acceptance tests levels. This re-execution, if manual, can result in a large (and costly) workload;

– or re-execution of a sub-set of the above-mentioned tests. It is clear that the selection of tests that will be included in this sub-set is of paramount importance, so as to avoid holes (areas that would not be covered correctly and fail to detect regressions) or redundancies (areas that are tested multiple times without adding any value).

Automated tests can be a solution to execute a large number of tests in a short time frame. However, the fact that automated tests must be maintained and kept in synch with the software and its interfaces must be taken into account.

The selection of a sub-set of tests for regression depends on multiple aspects such as:

– impact analysis (see Figure 2.10);

– traceability to specifications, software components, existing test cases, and procedures, available test data, etc.;

– risk evaluation, both for the project and the product;

– the time frame available and effort required.

2.4.5.1. *Efficiency of regression tests*

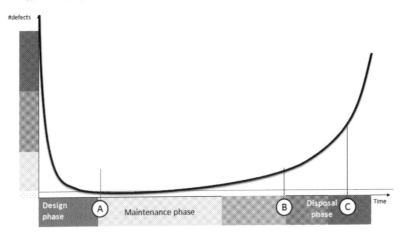

Figure 2.11. *Bathtub curve*

Regression tests cannot be evaluated with the same metrics as other types of tests: the aim is to check that no regression or side effects have been induced by the development of the software.

If we assume that the software was correctly tested when it was designed, the number of possible defects exposed will be small, with a much lower failure rate than that for the software component undergoing modification.

However, as time goes on, changes and fixes are added, evolution occurs and, new functionalities are introduced, etc., which are designed by different developers; this increases complexity, hinders readability, and generates more defects, as well as making software updates more difficult. Some complex components of the software will no longer be updated for fear of introducing complex defects and side effects. The curve in Figure 2.11 illustrates this evolution associated with the software life cycle. This curve, called bathtub curve, shows that during the design phase the number of defects decreases until the software is provided to the market (A). During maintenance, the number of defects continues to decrease then increases until (B) this number becomes too large and justifies the retirement of the software and it is replaced by different software. Development and test costs for new software are often lower than the maintenance costs for the existing software, and will enable the organization to reach – again – a period of diminishing defects and costs. There are many examples of such changes in versions of operating software at Microsoft or Apple to illustrate this type of replacement. However, it should be noted that the two systems may co-exist for some time and the design costs – for the new version of the software – will have to be added to the maintenance cost of the old version.

Throughout maintenance phases, it is thus important to continue to measure the number of defects and the workload for fixing (including testing and regression testing) software, so as to anticipate the time when retirement and replacement of the software is economically justifiable.

2.4.5.2. *Regression strategy and policy*

Different policies can direct the selection of regression tests:

– repeat all functional tests that were designed, at system test and acceptance test level, plus any non-functional tests (performance and security for example) that might be necessary; or

– repeat a sub-set of representative functional user actions and major risks associated with the software, so as to cover all major functionalities and all those with the highest risks; or

– repeat a sub-set of tests for components, based on their usage or their complexity or on their – previously computed – defect density, so as to cover the most important technical risks.

It is clear that technical and functional risks, such as coverage of the specifications or of the code, testing techniques and methods, as well as economic imperatives must be taken into account when deciding on a regression strategy or policy.

In terms of possible solutions for delivery of changes, we have:

– delivery of (urgent) fixes at the same time as new features, to include regression tests and defect fixes with the tests of new features;

– delivery at set dates, such as every year or every 6 months, instead of every month or every week, so as to ensure that regression tests have been executed exhaustively, for all changes and fixes, instead of being forgotten or skimped.

Delivery of patches and quick fixes without an exhaustive verification of regression aspects through adequate tests has demonstrated its inefficiency time and again, as well as its dangerous impact for customers and users.

2.4.6. *SLA validation and acceptance*

The use of sub-contractors and service providers to resolve maintenance or operation of software, whether they are called third-party maintenance or another service offering, is a reality. In order to ensure the quality of the services provided to the users, an SLA (service level agreement) can be established. These SLAs define the quality level, which is often identified as the level of availability of the software, or maximum downtime duration, or longest time to correct identified defects.

Such statistics correspond to data provided by the test teams to evaluate the maturity of the software. Periodic delivery of these data is one implication of tests of the delivery of operational data. Analysis of the data will enable test teams to anticipate the different aspects of the bathtub curves, and will allow delivery of quality software to the user.

2.5. Oracles

Once we have defined the test conditions and test cases, it is necessary to identify quickly whether defects are present or not during test execution. This requires the availability of a validated reference state.

Comparison of the actual result with the expected result will indicate whether the software has successfully passed the test (or not) and should have three main attributes:

– a source, which will predict the expected result for each test;

– a comparator, which will compare the expected results with the actual results;

– an evaluator, which will determine whether the two results are close enough for the test to be considered successful.

The source of expected data for comparison is called an "oracle", which is based on the Oracle of Delphi in ancient Greece.

2.5.1. *Problems with oracles*

One of the main problems with oracles is their "pertinence":

– the number of input and output values associated with a test are limited;

– formulas used, whether mathematical or not, only use a limited number of values, thus their precision is limited;

– the methods used to define expected results are usually approximations and their values can differ from those obtained with the software.

This means that the evaluation of test results can be based on incomplete or even incorrect results.

Even though it is better to compare the software to a limited series of results rather than no results at all, it should be noted that oracles may fail and provide erroneous data in some cases.

2.5.2. *Sources of oracles*

Oracles are frequently automated and data can be generated from:

– software specifications, commercial assertions, requirements whether they are regulatory or contractual;

– results of previous tests on this version of the software;

– operation of previous versions of the software or from competing software;

– standard functions,

– a specific model.

Test oracles can be created manually or using tools. It is also possible to capture the results from a reference, and use that as oracle. Predictions can also be generated using the software or system specifications, requirements (either contractual or based on standards and norms), or from other sources. Oracle information should have been validated to ensure that the prediction is valid.

2.5.3. *Oracle usage*

Using oracles in order to predict how the software should function assumes that the prevision model of the oracle has been validated with regards to the software operating environment. It is unrealistic to consider that a prediction model (an oracle) can provide results on the whole range of data that might be needed to validate a software or system. Usually an oracle can only validate a sub-set of the data, and more than one oracle may be required to cover the whole system.

It is thus necessary to make sure that the input and exit conditions of the software correspond to those of the prediction model, and to remember that an oracle can also fail and deliver incorrect data.

2.5.3.1. *Pre-conditions*

Before usage of an oracle it is necessary to determine:

– the need to use an oracle, the validity of the oracle based on the range of data provided by the oracle;

– the level of detail and precision of the oracle with regards to the required level of detail of the software or system responses;

– the range of input values where the oracle is valid and coherent with the software;

– how the data coming from the oracle and from the software or system are gathered before being compared;

– how the data coming from the oracle and from the software or system are compared, and what percentage of difference can be accepted and the result still be considered valid.

2.5.3.2. *Post-conditions*

Post-conditions to the use of an oracle are to:

– verify whether the conditions for use correspond to the valid ranges of operation for this oracle, as usage of an oracle outside of its validated range of operation could provide incorrect data and we would compare against an incorrect reference;

– determine the level of validity, which is to identify whether the data produced by the software is in a valid range of data, or outside that range, and – if outside that range – whether the data are close or far from the limits of correct values.

2.6. Specific cases

2.6.1. *Performance tests*

Performance testing is often executed when the system is complete and works correctly, which is very close to the planned delivery date. Usually performance defects are linked to the software architecture and require a thorough rework of most of the components, which should trigger new integration system and acceptance tests. It is thus recommended that performance problems are resolved early in development, such as from the time of system architecture and throughout the development of the software. One way to do this can be to define, for each part of a user transaction, the allotted duration of that part, and to ensure that none of the parts (or sections) of the transaction take more time than that allocated. This enables performance objectives to be defined for each component, sequence of integrated components, and functionalities, and these objectives to be tested at the earliest possible time, such as at the component test level or at the component integration test level.

When a performance problem is identified on a component, the issue will be identified at the earliest possible time instead of at acceptance test time, and corrective or mitigating actions will be easier to implement. This will have a positive impact on the duration and costs of development and design.

2.6.2. *Maintainability tests*

As mentioned in section 2.4.1, software is frequently developed over a relatively short period of time, but is used over a period of many years. There are still many COBOL legacy software versions running even though that language had its heyday in the 1980s and 1990s. Maintainability testing is important for longevity and ease of use in the long term, as well as reduced maintenance costs.

2.7. Synopsis of this chapter

Let us recap what was covered in this chapter.

Section 2.1 described development cycles; we saw that there were two main types: sequential or iterative. We also noted the following terms present in the glossary: commercial off-the-shelf (COTS), iterative-incremental development model, validation, verification, V-model.

In section 2.2 we covered the four test levels, their objectives, the objects on which they focus, their input data, and deliverables. We also noted the definitions of the following terms, present in the glossary: alpha testing, beta testing, component testing, driver, field testing, functional requirement, integration, integration testing, non-functional requirement, robustness testing, stub, system testing, test environment, test level, test-driven development, user acceptance testing.

Section 2.3 familiarized us with the types of tests and when they are used. We noted the definitions of the following terms, present in the glossary: black-box testing, code coverage, functional testing, interoperability testing, load testing, maintainability testing, performance testing, portability testing, reliability testing, security testing, stress testing, structural testing, usability testing, white-box testing.

Section 2.4 focused on tests associated with maintenance of software and allowed us to identify the following terms: impact analysis, maintenance testing.

In section 2.5 we developed the aspects associated with oracles, their use to check the actual results obtained during test execution and determine the presence or absence of defects. We also identified the term oracle.

Section 2.6, highlighted two special cases explaining when some performance tests were useful and the requirement for maintainability testing as previously mentioned in section 2.4.

2.8. Sample exam questions

Section 2.1. Software development models (K2)

FLO-2.1.1   Explain the relationship between development, test activities and work products in the development life cycle, by giving examples using project and product types (K2).

FLO-2.1.2   Recognize the fact that software development models must be adapted to the context of project and product characteristics (K1).

FLO-2.1.3   Recall characteristics of good testing that are applicable to any life cycle model (K1)

Ref	Questions
19.	FLO-2.1.1. (K2) Assume you work as sole tester on a small project that just published a first draft of requirements specifications. Consider the following possibilities: I. You should participate in a review of this document, even if it is just a draft. II. You should use this document as the basis for test planning and design activities, as well as for acceptance testing. III. These requirement specifications can act as a frozen test basis. IV. These requirement specifications can act as a test basis. Which of the following is true? A. I, II and III are true. B. II, III and IV are true. C. I, III and IV are true. D. I, II and IV are true.

20.	FLO-2.1.2. (K1)
	Which of the following sentences is true regarding the possibility to adapt software development life cycle models?
	A. It is better not to modify them as they are standards and created by experts.
	B. Development models have no impact on testing.
	C. You should avoid modification of these models as they can impact the quality of the products.
	D. Development models can be adapted to the characteristics and context of project and products.
21.	FLO-2.1.3. (K1)
	Which of the following sentences is true, whichever development life cycle is used?
	A. Testers should be involved after each design activity.
	B. Testers should be involved only after each design activity that created a deliverable for the customer.
	C. Testers should be involved as soon as the code is delivered by the development team.
	D. Testers only add value at the end of the development project.
22.	Terms (K1)
	What is validation?
	A. Confirmation that the product conforms to the customer's specifications.
	B. Confirmation that the product conforms to the customer's requirements.
	C. Confirmation that the product conforms to the customer's needs.
	D. A group of activities implemented to ensure a level of quality for software.

Section 2.2. Test levels (K2)

FLO-2.2.1   Compare the different levels of testing: major objectives, typical objects of testing, typical targets of testing (e.g. functional or structural) and related work products, people who test, types of defects, and failures to be identified (K2)

Ref	Questions
23.	FLO-2.2.1. (K2)
	Testing a sub-program, whether for functional or non-functional aspects, is the main goal of which test level?
	A. Component testing.
	B. Component integration testing.
	C. System testing.
	D. Acceptance testing.

Ref	Questions
24.	Terms (K1) What is the purpose of acceptance testing? A. To ensure that software have good operational performances. B. To determine the ability for these software to withstand incorrect data in operation. C. To verify the software in an operational environment. D. To ensure that medical software can be used in operating theaters.

Section 2.3. Types of tests (K2)

FLO-2.3.1   Compare four software test types (functional, non-functional, structural, and change related) by example (K2)

FLO-2.3.2   Recognize that functional and structural tests occur at any test level (K1)

FLO-2.3.3   Identify and describe non-functional test types based on non-functional requirements (K2)

FLO-2.3.4   Identify and describe test types based on the analysis of a software system's structure or architecture (K2)

FLO-2.3.5   Describe the purpose of confirmation testing and regression testing (K2)

Ref	Questions

25.	FLO-2.3.1. (K2)
	
	 Assume the following four possible types of test for an e-commerce software:
	
	     I. Test all possible requests on the database.
	
	     II. Test the system responses under increasing load.
	
	     III. Test the functionalities as they are added to the system.
	
	     IV. Verify the correct processing of normal customer orders.
	
	 Which of the following sentences is true?
	
	 A. I is a change-related test, II is a non-functional test, III is a functional test, IV is a structural test.
	
	 B. I is a structural test, II is a non-functional test, III is a change-related test, IV is a functional test.
	
	 C. I and II are structural tests, III is a change-related test, IV is a functional test.

	D. I is a non-functional test, II is a functional test, III is a change-related test, IV is a structural test.
26.	FLO-2.3.2 (K1) Which of the following sentence is correct? A. Functional tests are never executed at component level. B. Functional tests check the functions on the system. C. Functional tests can be executed at all test levels D. Functional tests apply only at system and acceptance test level, because the other levels focus on non-functional aspects only.
27.	FLO-2.3.3 (K2) Which of the following characteristics is a non-functional characteristic? A. Suitability. B. Accuracy. C. Maintainability. D. Regression.
28.	FLO-2.3.4.(K2) Assume you are testing an online banking system. You receive a draft of the technical specifications describing the architecture of the system at the level of interfaces to other applications. As soon as you receive that document, you design tests to cover all messages and interface exchanges, to process simultaneously end-to-end tests and the system-of-systems components during integration and system tests. What type of testing are you doing? A. Structural tests. B. Integration tests. C. System tests. D. Functional tests.
29.	FLO-2.3.5 (K2) What is the use of retests (or confirmation tests) and regression tests? A. Regression tests check that defects have been corrected in the software, while retests confirm that no new defects have been introduced in the software. B. Retests (confirmation test) check that defects have been fixed in the software, while regression tests confirm that no new defects have been entered in the software. C. Regression tests and confirmation test are synonyms, they ensure that no new defect have been introduced during maintenance activities. D. Regression tests can be executed at all test levels, during the maintenance of software.

30.	Terms (K1)
	What is the use of code coverage?
	A. To determine which areas of the code have been executed by a set of tests.
	B. To measure the code executed during static analysis of code.
	C. To measure the number of lines of code executed by a sequence of tests.
	D. To make sure that the testers test the whole software.
31.	Terms (K1)
	What is black-box testing?
	A. A test design technique based on an analysis of functional or non-functional specifications of a software component without referring to its internal structure.
	B. A specific test technique where the hardware component is tested in the dark, to avoid damage by ultra-violet rays of light-sensitive components.
	C. An identification of expected test results so that they can be compared to actual test results during test execution.
	D. An informal test technique where the tests are designed by the tester based on the results of previous tests, while considering the software as a black box.

Section 2.4. Tests and maintenance (K2)

FLO-2.4.1   Compare maintenance testing (testing an existing system) to testing a new application with respect to test types, triggers for testing and amount of testing (K2)

FLO-2.4.2   Recognize indicators for maintenance testing (modification, migration, and retirement) (K1)

FLO-2.4.3   Describe the role of regression testing and impact analysis in maintenance (K2)

Ref	Questions
32.	FLO-2.4.1 (K2)
	What test activity is more important during maintenance tests than during the test of new developments?
	A. Structural tests.
	B. Confirmation tests.
	C. Regression tests.
	D. Performance tests.

Ref	Questions
33.	FLO-2.4.2 (K1) Assume the following situation: I. During development a maintenance request is approved. II. Software is modified to comply with new regulations. III. An application is moved to a server that has another OS than the current server. IV. Data from an obsolete system are archived for subsequent analysis. What sequence is true? A. I and II are true, III and IV are false. B. II and III are true, I and IV are false. C. III and IV are true, I and II are false. D. II, III and IV are true, I is false.
34.	FLO-2.4.3 (K2) Which sentence is true? A. Impact analysis allows estimation of the maintenance workload by identifying the components impacted by the changes. B. During new developments and maintenance, impact analysis helps us identify which regression tests to execute. C. During maintenance tests, impact analysis enables identification of which confirmation tests to execute. D. During maintenance tests, impact analysis enables us to estimate which regression tests to execute.
35.	Terms (K1) What is maintenance testing? A. A way for the customer to evaluate the efficiency of third-party maintenance contracts. B. A test of changes applied to an operational system or the verification of the impact of changes to the system's environment. C. Test of an already-tested program to ensure that changes applied to it have not generated side effects. D. The corrective actions of tests when a software evolves and is maintained.

Chapter 3

Static Techniques
(FL 3.0)

Test techniques can be split into dynamic and static techniques.

The main advantage of static techniques is that they do not require the application of a functioning system or software: they can be applied to documents and parts of software. Thus they can be executed long before dynamic techniques, which require a functioning system or software for execution.

The second advantage of static techniques is that they are often cheaper than dynamic techniques, and that their return on investment is much higher. Defects being identified earlier, their fixes are cheaper, and they often are not introduced in the software at all, being found in specification documents.

Static techniques cover two large sets of activities:

– reviews, whether formal or informal;

– static analysis, with or without tools.

3.1. Static techniques and the test process (FL 3.1)

We saw previously that it was possible to split test techniques into two categories: dynamic techniques, which require functioning software, and static techniques, which do not require functioning software.

FLO-3.1.1 Recognize software work products that can be examined by the different static techniques (K1)

Static techniques can be applied to numerous deliverables, such as software components, whether or not they can compile; high-level or detailed level specifications; lists of requirements; contracts; development plans or test plans; and also to numerous other deliverables. Static tests can thus be executed very early in the development cycle.

Software components, regardless of whether they can compile, can be examined with reviews (code reviews) or with static analysis. The other items, such as documentation, requirements and specifications, test design documents, test cases and test procedures, even test data, can also be submitted for review. Development plans, test plans, processes, and business activities can also be the subject of reviews.

FLO-3.1.2 Describe the importance and value of considering static techniques for the assessment of software work products (K2)

The ratio between the costs of the static techniques and the number of defects identified (return on investment) is very high; much higher than the ratio for dynamic testing. This is due simultaneously to generally reduced costs and to quick and multiple benefits:

– the time required to execute a review is much shorter that the time to design and execute a test. Indeed, the design of a test requires the tester to read and analyze the test basis; then to implement the adequate test techniques and design the test case, the test data; then to execute the test case on executable code. Static techniques do not need anything other than reading and analyzing the test basis (the component being tested) and can be executed before the code is compiled;

– the effort to gather and analyze metrics linked to static techniques is slow, as it applies to a smaller number of elements (metrics) than during dynamic tests;

– process improvement aspects are simultaneously a cost and a benefit, because they enable a more rational usage of resources (resources are always limited) associated with the software development.

The benefits associated with static test techniques are:

– reduction in duration and increased efficiency in defect detection. This is because static techniques identify defects instead of failures, while dynamic techniques identify failures, and then someone – the developer or the tester – must identify the defect;

– reduction in the test duration to find the same number of defects, because defects detected in reviews, which can occur long before the execution of dynamic tests, need not be found during dynamic test execution;

– an increase in developer productivity, as they are able to identify any inconsistency or ambiguity in specifications earlier, and thus avoid the introduction of defects in the code;

– an increase in tester productivity, because defects that are already identified will not need to be identified later during dynamic testing, and testers will be able to focus on more important defects, or those that can only be detected via dynamic testing;

– an increase in deliverable quality that will continue throughout the life of the software, including during maintenance.

Static test techniques, reviews and static analysis, are proven effective solutions to increase the quality of software.

FLO-3.1.3 Explain the difference between static and dynamic techniques, considering objectives, types of defects to be identified, and the role of these techniques within the software life cycle (K2)

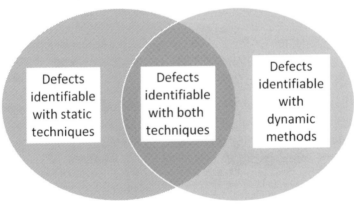

Figure 3.1. *Static and dynamic techniques and defects*

Some software defects are only identifiable through the use of static test techniques, such as naming conventions for variable or functions names, programming rules, or internal documentation. Other defects are only identifiable with dynamic techniques, such as response time and performances. Some defects are identifiable by both dynamic and static techniques, such as the aspects of data initialization or the number of parameters exchanged between two modules.

The main differences between the static and dynamic techniques are:

– the aspects identified (failures for dynamic test techniques, and defects for static test techniques);

– the moment when detection occurs (potentially before compilation for static test techniques, and after compilation – even after integration – for defects identified by dynamic test techniques) and the time left for fixing the defects between defect detection and planned time to market;

– the efficiency of the techniques depending on the type of defect; and

– the stakeholders involved with each of the techniques.

The aspect that is similar between the static and dynamic techniques is the objective to increase efficiency by avoiding increased defect fixing costs.

3.2. Review process (FL 3.2)

Many standards can be applied with regards to reviews. International Software Testing Qualifications Board (ISTQB) suggests the use of the IEEE 1028-2008 [IEE 08b] standard. Other standards can apply in other contexts, such as: ECSS-M-ST-10-01C for the management of reviews in the space industry.

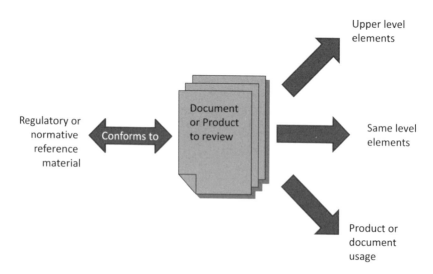

Figure 3.2. *Types of objectives per level of review*

Usually review objectives can be of four types:

– verification of compliance with the higher-level documents that were used to create it (e.g. requirements, specification, contract, etc.);

– verification with regards to project documents at the same level (e.g. test case specifications, test data, source code, component interface, etc.);

– verification with regards to standards and norms, recommended best practices, to ensure conformity of the product subject to the review or static analysis;

– verification with regards to usage and fitness for use, such as to design more detailed components.

3.2.1. *Types of reviews*

IEEE 1028-2008 identifies many types of reviews:

– *management reviews*;

– *technical reviews*;

– *inspections*[1];

– *walk-throughs* and

– *audits*.

Reviews can be grouped according to their level of formalism, from the less formal to the most formal. All reviews have a product or process to which they apply.

3.2.1.1. *Informal reviews*

Some reviews are totally informal, such as a discussion at lunch, in the hallway, or near the coffee machine. These reviews can focus on technical or management issues and are characterized by:

– the lack of a formal process;

– documentation of the result that varies depending on the participants;

– varying efficiency depending on the participants.

Informal reviews can include the principle of pair programming, peer review, and technical or management meetings to solve a specific point.

---

1 A good reference book on inspections is [GIL 93].

3.2.1.2. *Management reviews*

The goal for management reviews is to follow the progress, define the status of plans and schedule, or to evaluate the efficiency of the management approaches used and their adequacy to the objectives. Management reviews identify conformance and deviations to management plans or procedures. Technical knowledge may be necessary to successfully manage such types of reviews. Evaluation of components or objects may necessitate more than one single meeting, and meetings can fail to address all the different aspects of the product or process subject to review.

Management reviews can be applied to the following processes (among others):

– acquisition and delivery processes;

– development, usage, and maintenance processes;

– configuration management processes;

– quality assurance processes;

– verification and validation processes, peer-reviewed processes, and audits;

– problem management and resolution processes, and defect-management processes;

– continuous process-improvement processes, and infrastructure management processes;

– training and coaching processes.

Management reviews can be applied to the following products (among others):

– defect reports;

– audit reports;

– backup and recovery plans, restoration plans;

– technical and business requirements and specifications;

– hardware and software performance plans;

– installation and maintenance plans;

– progress reports;

– risk-management plans;

– configuration-management plans;

– quality-assurance plans;

– project-management plans;

– test documentation (strategy and policy, test plans, test specifications, test conditions, test procedures, test cases, test logs and reports, test data, etc.);

– validation and verification plans, acceptance plans;

– migration strategies and plans;

– development process descriptions;

– test and development architecture; etc.

3.2.1.3. *Technical reviews*

The goal of technical reviews is to evaluate, with a team of qualified persons, a software product, to determine whether it is suitable for its planned use and identify deviations from applicable standards and specifications. These reviews provide evidence for management about the technical status of a project; they can also provide recommendations and evaluate alternatives. Technical reviews may need more than one meeting, and do not have to cover all the aspects of the product being evaluated.

Technical reviews can apply to the following products (among others):

– specifications and requirements for software;

– software and system specification documents;

– test and user documentation;

– maintenance and user manuals;

– system or software version and release creation procedures;

– installation procedures;

– delivery notes;

– software or system-development process descriptions;

– software or system architecture descriptions.

3.2.1.4. *Inspections*

The goal of inspections is to detect and identify defects in a product. An inspection is a systematic examination by peers of a product that does one or more of the following activities:

– verify that the product fits its specifications and its requirements;

– verify that the product has the required quality attributes;

– verify compliance by the product to the applicable rules, standards, norms, specifications and guidelines;

– identify discrepancies with regards to the three aspects above;

– obtain adequate data (such as defects and load data);

– provide information that can improve and document inspection processes;

– request or grant waivers for violation of standards where applicable;

– uses the data as the input to project-manage decisions as needed.

In general, inspections are made up of two to six participants (including the author), led by an impartial trained facilitator (trained in inspection techniques). Determination of remedial or investigative action for an anomaly is a mandatory element of software inspection, although the resolution does not have to occur in the inspection meeting. Collecting data for the purpose of analysis and improvement of software-engineering procedures is another mandatory element of software inspections. An inspection can be applied to the following products (among others):

– software and system requirement specifications;

– software and system design descriptions (detailed or not);

– source code and algorithms;

– test documentation (test plans, test specifications, test cases, test procedures, etc.);

– user documentation, installation, and user manuals;

– maintenance manuals;

– procedures for creating new versions of the system or software;

– installation procedures;

– release notes;

– system or software process development description;

– marketing and publicity documentation;

– software architectural descriptions.

3.2.1.5. *Walk-throughs*

The main purpose of a systematic walk-though is to evaluate a software product. This type of review can be held with the goal of educating the audience regarding the product. The main objectives of a walk-through are:

– find anomalies;

– improve the product;

– consider alternative implementations;

– evaluate conformance to specification and standards;

– evaluate the usability and accessibility of the software product.

Walk-throughs can be applied to the following products (among others):

– software and system specifications and requirements;

– high-level and detailed specifications of the software or system;

– source code and algorithms;

– test plans and procedures;

– user documentation;

– maintenance manuals and procedures;

– installation procedures and methods to create releases;

– release notes;

– licenses;

– software and system-development process descriptions;

– software architecture descriptions.

3.2.1.6. *Audits*

The purpose of audits is to provide an independent evaluation of the conformance of a product or process to applicable standards, rules, norms, guidelines, plans, specifications, and procedures.

Audits can be applied, among others, to the following products:

– backup and recovery plans;

– contingency plans;

– contracts;

– installation plans and procedures;

– user operations and maintenance manuals;

– risk-management plans;

– configuration management plans and procedures;

– source code, algorithms, and component development documentation;

– quality assurance plans, project management plans, verification and validation plans;

– reports from other reviews (technical reviews and walk-throughs);

– other deliverables.

Usually, audits start with a meeting where the auditors (those who execute the audit) and the audited organization (that undergoes the audit) examine and agree on the audit scope and organization. When specified in the audit plan, the auditors can provide recommendations that will then be part of a separate document.

3.2.2. *Roles and responsibilities during reviews*

FLO-3.2.1 Recall the activities, roles, and responsibilities of a typical formal review (K1)

Roles and responsibilities vary depending on the type of review and the level of granularity of the component subject (object) studied.

3.2.2.1. *Management reviews*

For management reviews the following roles are defined:

– manager, the person for whom the management review will be undertaken and will decide on achievement or not of the review goals;

– review leader, who takes care of the administrative aspects of the review, its planning and its preparation, review meeting execution and makes sure that the objectives are reached and the deliverables are provided;

– recorder (or secretary), who documents the defects, the actions, decisions, and recommendations provided by the review team;

– the management staff, who are assigned to the review execution and will actively participate in the review;

– the technical team, which provides the required information to the management staff to enable them to reach their objectives and;

optionally:

– customer representatives or users, whose mandate is defined before the review by the review leader;

– other team members (e.g. quality assurance), whose role will be defined by the team leader before the review meeting.

3.2.2.2. *Technical reviews*

For technical reviews, the following roles are defined:

– manager, for whom the technical review will be undertaken and who decides whether the objectives have been reached or not:

– review leader, responsible for the administrative aspects of the review, its planning, preparation, and execution, and who ensures that the objectives are reached and the expected deliverables provided;

– recorder, who documents defects, actions, decisions, and recommendation provided by the review team;

– technical reviewers, assigned to the execution of the review and who will actively participate in the review;

optionally:

– members of the management team who can participate in the technical review in order to identify aspects that may need management involvement to be resolved;

– other team members and stakeholders (managers, technical team, customers, and users) whose role will be defined before the review by the review leader.

3.2.2.3. *Inspections*

For inspections, the following roles should be defined:

– inspection responsible, in charge of planning and organizing the tasks associated with the inspection. This individual defines the parts of the product (documents, source code, etc.) that will be inspected during the review meeting, be responsible for the orderly operation of the review, and make sure its objectives are reached, and ensures that inspection data are collected and inspection products are delivered;

– recorder, who documents the defects, actions, decisions, waivers, and recommendations provided by the inspection team;

– reader, who leads the inspection team through the software or system in a logical and complete fashion, interpreting and paraphrasing the product sections and highlight its important aspects;

– author, who is responsible for ensuring that the product reaches the entry criteria for the review, contributing to the review based on his/her comprehension of the product, and implementing the required updates to reach the specified review exit criteria;

– inspectors, who identifies and describes the anomalies in the software product. Inspectors are selected based on their expertise and should be selected to provide different points of view and cover pertinent viewpoints on the product.

3.2.2.4. *Walk-throughs*

The following roles should be defined for walk-throughs:

– walk-through leader, who leads the meeting, managing the administrative tasks related to the review (e.g. documentation distribution, meeting preparation) and ensures the walk-through meeting(s) are conducted in an orderly manner. The walk-through leader prepares the statement of objectives to guide the team in the walk-through and makes sure that the team is able to reach decisions or identify actions for each issue or discussion point, and ensures that the deliverables of the walk-through are provided;

– recorder, who documents anomalies, actions, decisions, waivers, and recommendations by the team, and also notes the different comments provided during the meetings on defects, omissions, contradictions, suggestions for improvement, or alternative approaches;

– author, who presents the product during the walk-through meeting;

– team members, who prepares and actively participates in the walk-through meeting by identifying and describing the defects in the product.

3.2.2.5. *Audits*

The following roles are defined for audits:

– lead auditor, responsible for the audit, including administrative tasks, and who ensures that the audit is executed efficiently and that it reaches its objective. The lead auditor is responsible, among others, for:

- preparing the audit plan,

- assembling the audit team,

- making decisions regarding how the audit will be conducted and how audit decisions will be processed,

- preparing the audit report,

- informing on the apparent ability or inability for any of the individuals who execute the tasks,

- negotiating with the audit initiator any incoherence or discrepancies that may impair the ability to satisfy audit exit criteria,

- recommending corrective actions;

– recorder, who documents anomalies, actions, decisions, waivers, and audit team recommendations;

– auditors, who examines the products defined in the audit plan, documenting their observations in an independent, objective, and non-biased way;

– initiator, who is responsible for the decision to execute an audit, decide on the objectives and extent of the audit, of the products or processes to audit, evaluation criteria used in the audit, including applicable standards, guidelines, plans, specifications, and procedures, who decides on who will execute the audit, revises the audit report, and decides which follow-up actions will be required, and distributes the audited report;

– audited organization, which provides a liaison for the auditors and provides all information requested by the auditors. When the audit is completed, the audited organization should implement corrective actions and recommendations.

3.2.3. *Phases of reviews*

FLO-3.2.1 Recall the activities, roles, and responsibilities of a typical formal review (K1)

The CFTL-ISTQB foundation syllabus v2011 identifies the following phases of formal reviews:

1. Planning:

– defining the review criteria;

– selecting the personnel;

– allocating roles;

– defining the entry and exit criteria for more formal review types (e.g. inspections);

– selecting which parts of the documents to review;

– checking entry criteria (for more formal review types).

2. Kick-off:

– distributing documents;

– explaining the objectives, process, and documents to the participants.

3. Individual preparation:

– preparing for the review meeting by reviewing the document(s);

– noting potential defects, questions and comments.

4. Examination/evaluation/recording of results (review meeting):

– discussing or logging, with documented results or minutes (for more formal review types);

– noting defects, making recommendations regarding handling the defects, making decisions about the defects;

– examining/evaluating and recording during any physical meetings or tracking any group electronic communications.

5. Rework:

– fixing defects found (typically done by the author);

– recording updated status of defects (in formal reviews).

6. Follow-up:

– checking that defects have been addressed;

– gathering metrics;

– checking on exit criteria (for more formal review types).

The following sections describe the phases as proposed by the IEEE 1028-2008 standard for each type of review.

3.2.3.1. *Management reviews*

Management preparation: during this phase, management ensures that the following activities are executed:

– plan time and resources required for reviews, including support functions;

– provide funding and facilities required to plan, define, execute, and manage the reviews;

– ensure training level and knowledge level is adequate to understand the process or product being reviewed;

– ensure that the planned reviews are executed;

– act in a timely manner on the review team recommendations.

Planning or kick-off phase: during this phase, the review leader:

– identifies, with appropriate management support, the review team;

– assigns specific responsibilities to the review team members;

– schedules and announces the meeting;

– distributes review materials to participants, allowing adequate time for their individual preparation;

– defines a timetable for review material distribution, return of comments, and forwarding of the comments to the author for disposition.

Individual preparation phase: each reviewer individually examines the product or process submitted to review, before the review. Defects and questions identified during this phase should be documented and should be sent to the review leader for disposition.

Review meeting: during the actual review meeting(s) the participants should:

– review the objectives of the management review;

– evaluate the product or process submitted for review, based on the defined objectives;

– evaluate the state of the project, including the plans and schedules;

– review the defects identified by the participants before the review;

– generate a list of action, identifying, and emphasizing the risks;

– documenting the review meeting;

– other objectives can also be accomplished such as: risk analysis, identification of recommended solutions identified, or other issues that require attention.

Closing activities for the review: after the review meeting, it will be necessary to ensure that actions decided are executed and closed, and that the end of review report exists and identifies:

– the product or process that was reviewed;

– the members of the review team;

– the goals of the review;

– the specific inputs to the review;

– the actions that were identified and their status (open or closed), the person responsible and the target date (if the action is still open) or closure date (if the action is closed);

– the list of defects identified by the review team.

The review output report is delivered to management and applicable stakeholders, and subsequently archived. It may be useful to gather metrics applicable to the review, to evaluate its efficiency and effectiveness.

3.2.3.2. *Technical review*

Management preparation: management ensures the following activities are carried out:

– plan time and resources required for reviews, including support functions;

– provide funding and facilities required to plan, define, execute, and manage the reviews;

– provide training and orientation on review procedures applicable to a given project;

– ensure that reviewers are available with an appropriate level of skills, expertise, and knowledge sufficient to comprehend the software product under review;

– ensure that planned reviews are conducted;

– act on review team recommendations in a timely manner.

The review leader (also called moderator) will be responsible for the following activities:

– identify, with appropriate management support, the review team;

– assign specific responsibilities to the review team members;

– schedule and announce the meeting place;

– distribute review materials to participants, allowing adequate time for their preparation;

– set a timetable for distribution of review material, the return of comments, and forwarding of comments to the author for disposition.

As a part of the planning procedure, the review team determines whether alternatives are to be discussed at the review meeting or whether these alternatives should be discussed afterwards in a separate meeting, or left to the author of the software product to resolve.

Planning or kick-off phase: presentation of the review processes and of the product. These presentations describe the review process such as it is defined by the review leader, and provide a summary of the software product or system submitted for review.

Individual work phase: individual preparation phase where each participant will examine the software product and other inputs, before the actual review meeting. Defects detected during this examination phase must be documented and provided to the review leader who will classify them, to ensure that the meeting is run efficiently. The review leader should send these anomalies to the author for disposition.

The individual preparation phase is very important, and the review leader should ensure that participants prepare adequately for the review meeting. As a part of the planning procedure, the review team should determine whether alternatives are to be discussed at the review meeting. Alternatives may be discussed at the review meeting, afterwards in a separate meeting, or left to the author of the software product to resolve.

Review meeting: during the technical review, the review team will have one or more meetings with the objective to:

– decide on the agenda to evaluate the software product and its anomalies;

– determine whether:

- the software product is complete,

- the software product complies to rules, standards, guidelines, plans, specifications, requirements, and other procedures applicable to the project,

- where applicable, the changes to the product are correctly implemented and do not impact the specified area,

- the software product is suitable for its intended use,

- the software product is ready for the next activity,

- the findings of the inspection necessitates a change in the software project schedule,

- anomalies exist in other system elements, such as hardware, external or additional systems;

– identify anomalies and decide their criticality;

– generate a list of action items, emphasizing risks that are associated with these items;

– document the meetings.

Closing activities for the review: at the end of the technical review, it will be necessary to make sure that the actions decided upon are achieved and closed, and that the end of review report is available, identifying:

– the product or process that underwent the review;

– the members of the review team;

– detailed information on the product reviewed, including configuration data;

– specific inputs for the review (e.g. checklists, standards, etc.);

– review objectives and whether they were reached or not;

– list identified anomalies of the software product or system;

– list unresolved issues of the system, hardware, or specifications level;

– list issues raised with management;

– list actions identified and their status (open or closed), the individual responsible for each action, and the expected closing date (for open actions) or the actual closure date (for finished actions);

– an evaluation of the software or system product, and its compliance to applicable rules, standards, guidelines, plans, specifications, requirements and procedures, without waivers or deviations.

3.2.3.3. *Inspections*

Management preparation: management should make sure the following activities are carried out:

– anticipate the required time and resources for the inspections, including its supporting tasks;

– plan adequate financial resources and facilities to plan, define, execute and manage the reviews;

– provide training and coaching on the inspection procedures applicable to the project;

– make sure that reviewers are available, with the adequate level of knowledge and required expertise, and a sufficient understanding of the product under review;

– make sure the reviews are carried out;

– act on the basis of the recommendations from the review team.

The author provides the review leader with the required material, including the software product or system under inspection, and the standards, requirements, specifications and other documents used to develop the product.

The review leader will be responsible for:

– identifying, with management support, the members of the review team;

– assigning specific responsibilities to the members of the review team;

– planning and announcing the location and time of the review;

– distributing the material to the participants, leaving enough time for individual preparation;

– define a schedule for the distribution of the review material, return of comments, and transmittal of the comments to the author for disposition;

– specify the breadth of the inspection, including the issues inspected in order of priority in the documents and products;

– define the inspection rate for individual preparation and meetings. The inspection rate is the speed (in pages per hour of lines of code per hour) to which the product should be inspected.

Presentation or kick-off meeting: presentation of the product and inspection procedures. These inspections procedures describe the process that will be implemented and a brief presentation of the product that will be inspected. The inspection leader will specify how the product will be inspected (sequentially, hierarchically, according to the data flow or the control flow, or the call graph, whether bottom-up or top-down, etc.). The reader prepares sufficiently to present the product during the inspection meeting.

Individual work phase: the work phase during which each participant will individually examine the software product and other inputs, before the inspection meeting itself. Anomalies detected during this examination phase must be documented and sent to the review leader who classifies them in order to ensure an efficient use of time during the review. The inspection leader sends the anomalies to the author for disposition. Depending on the number of anomalies found and on their correction, the review leader can decide to postpone the inspection meeting.

Inspection meeting: at the start of the inspection meeting itself, the inspection leader describes the roles of each participant, clarifies the inspection objectives, and reminds the inspection team to focus on the product being inspected but not on the product's author. The members of the inspection team should focus their remarks to the scribe or the review leader, but not to the author, and defer the discussion of the identified issues to a subsequent meeting. The inspection will have different main parts:

– process of main aspects, focusing on the particular product and not on a specific aspect of this product;

– inspection of the software product and recording of anomalies, during which the reader will present the software product to the inspection team who will examine it exhaustively and objectively. The scribe notes the anomalies, their localization, description, and classification. The author can respond to questions and help detect anomalies, based on his/her comprehension of the product. If there is disagreement on a defect, the potential anomaly will be identified and marked for resolution at the end of the inspection;

– the review of the list of anomalies or potential anomalies identified will be discussed. The inspection leader will not allow the discussion to focus on how to solve the anomaly, but only on the exact definition of what constitutes the anomaly;

– the decision on the follow-up of the inspection, is intended to determine the disposition of the software product, which can be:

- accept with no further verification: the product is accepted as is or with only minor modifications,

- accept with rework verification: the product is to be accepted after the inspection leader or a designated person of the inspection team verifies the rework, to ensure the quality of the changes,

- reinspection: the software product cannot be accepted as is, and a new inspection takes place after correction of all the identified anomalies.

Closing activities for the review: after the inspection, the inspection leader will ensure that the identified actions have been closed. The inspection will be considered closed when the inspection report is delivered. It will contain at least the following information (non-exhaustive list):

– the project that created the software product under inspection;

– the member of the inspection team;

– the duration of the inspection meetings;

– the software product inspected;

– the size of the product inspected (e.g. number of pages of text);

– the specific inputs to the inspection;

– the inspection goals and whether they have been reached or not;

– the list of identified anomalies and their location, description, and classification;

– the disposition of the software product;

– any waivers granted or requested;

– the individual and total preparation time for the member of the inspection team;

– the total rework and correction time;

– a summary of the anomalies with the number of anomalies per category;

– an estimation of the planned rework effort and the planned completion date if the rework effort is significant;

– (optionally) an estimate of the savings by fixing the items found in inspection, compared to the cost of fixing the item later, assuming the anomalies were found later.

3.2.3.4. *Walk-throughs*

Management preparation: the walk-through leader conducts the administrative activities associated with the walk-through, and:

– plans the time and resources required for the walk-through meetings, including any supporting tasks;

– plans the financial resources and facilities to plan, define, and execute the reviews;

– provides training and coaching on review procedures for walk-through applicable to the project;

– makes sure that the walk-through team members are available, with the adequate level of knowledge and expertise, and sufficient understanding of the topics to understand the product submitted to review;

– makes sure the walk-through is executed;

– acts based on the recommendations of the review team.

The walk-through leader is responsible for the following actions:

– identifying the members of the team;

– planning the walk-through meetings and selecting their location;

– distributing the documents and supporting information to the participants, planning adequate time for individual preparation.

Overview presentation: an overview presentation can be provided by the author before or during the walk-through meeting.

Individual preparation: an individual preparation phase where all participants examine the software product and other inputs, before the actual walk-through meeting. Issues identified during this phase must be organized according to two criteria: general or specific.

Anomalies detected during the preparation phase should be documented and sent to the review leader who will classify them, to ensure an effective use of the review time. The walk-through leader should send these anomalies to the author for disposition. Depending on the number of anomalies identified and the rework time, the walk-through leader may envisage delaying the actual walk-through meeting.

The actual order by which the software product will be evaluated (sequential, hierarchical, data flow, control flow, top down or bottom up) will be defined by the author or by the walk-through leader.

Examination meeting: at the start of the meeting, the walk-through leader describes the roles of the participants, clarifies the objectives, and acts as a facilitator. The leader reminds the participants to focus on the product being reviewed, not on its author. Members of the team can address their questions to the author.

The author can present an overview of the software product undergoing review. This should be followed by a general discussion during which the walk-through team members can raise the general items identified during or after the preparation phase. During the walk-through meeting:

– the author or review leader undertakes an overall presentation of the software product;

– the review leader coordinates the discussion on the general defects;

– the author or review responsible presents the product and each of its parts;

– the members of the team identifies the anomalies that are specific to the section being examined;

– the scribe notes the recommendations and actions arising from the discussion of each anomaly.

Closing activities for the walk-through: after the meeting, the walk-through leader issues the output details of the walk-through meetings including:

– a detailed list of identified anomalies;

– the decisions and actions identified;

– any other information of interest.

The walk-through leader ensures that the decisions and actions identified during the meeting are executed and closed.

3.2.3.5. *Audits*

Management preparation: the hierarchical management ensures that the audit is executed as specified by the different applicable standards and procedures, respecting the regulatory, legal, life-contractual, or other obligations. This includes:

– planning adequate time and required resources for the audits, including supporting tasks, as planned by the applicable documentation;

– anticipating financial resources and facilities to plan, define, execute, and manage the audits;

– providing training and coaching on the audit procedures applicable to the project;

– ensuring an adequate level of expertise and knowledge to understand the product being audited;

– ensuring that the planned audit is executed;

– acting on the basis of the recommendations from the audit team.

The audit plan is written and specifies:

– the objective and scope of the audit;

– the audited organization, including its location and its hierarchy;

– the software product to be audited;

– the evaluation criteria, including applicable regulations, standards, guidelines, plans, specifications, and procedures used for evaluation;

– the responsibilities of the auditors;

– the examination activities (interview staff, read and evaluate documents, observe tests);

– the required resources for the audit activities;

– the scheduling of the audit activities;

– the requirements for confidentiality and confidentiality levels;

– the checklists to use;

– the report formats;

– the distribution of the audit report;

– the required follow-up activities.

If the audit applies to a sub-component of the product, a valid sampling method is used to define a statistically representative sample. The audit plan is approved by the audit initiator, but should allow for changes based on the results and items identified during the audit, subject to approval by the audit initiator.

Kick-off meeting: a kick-off meeting, between the audit team and the audited organization takes place at the beginning of the examination phase of the audit. The agenda of the meeting includes:

– the objective and scope of the audit;

– the products or processes subject to audit;

– the audit procedures and deliverables;

– the expected contributions from the audited organization (e.g. number of persons to interview, location, etc.);

– the audit schedule;

– the access to the facilities, information, and required documentation.

Preparation: the audit initiator notifies the audited organization hierarchy in writing before the audit, except in the case of unannounced audits. This notification defines the scope and objective of the audit, what is be audited, the auditors (members of the audit team), and the schedule of the audit, to enable the audited organization to ensure that the required personnel and material are available for the audit.

The auditors prepare for the audit by studying:

– the audit plan;

– the audited organization;

– the products or processes to audit;

– the applicable regulations, standards, guidelines, plans, specifications, and procedures to be used for the evaluation;

– the evaluation criteria.

The lead auditor, in addition, makes the necessary arrangements for:

– training and coaching by the members of the audit team;

– acquiring the material, documents, and tools required by the audit procedures;

– examination activities.

Examination: the examination activities consist of:

– collecting and evaluating evidence based on the audit criteria, where the auditors interview the audited organization members, collect evidence of conformance or non-conformance, examine documents, and observe the process. The auditors attempt all activities defined in the audit plan, undertake additional investigative activities if required to document all existing conformance or non-conformance;

– a closing meeting between the auditors and the organization submitted to the audit;

– preparation of the audit report.

Closing activities for the audit: the lead auditor organizes a closing review with the audited organization's hierarchy where the following items are evaluated:

– actual extent of the implementation of the audit plan;

– problems experienced during implementation of the audit plan;

– observations of the auditors;

– preliminary conclusions of the auditors;

– preliminary recommendations of the auditors;

– overall evaluation of the audit (whether the audit criteria were fulfilled or not).

The lead auditor will prepare the audit report as soon as possible after the end of the audit. All communications between the auditors and the audited organization pass through the lead auditor. The lead auditor sends the audit report to the audit initiator and the audited organization. The audit initiator is responsible for distribution of the audit report within the audited organization.

Correction of any anomalies identified is the responsibility of the audit initiator and the audited organization. They determine corrective actions to remove or avoid non-conformance.

3.2.4. *Success factors for reviews*

FLO-3.2.3 Explain the factors for successful performance of reviews (K2)

As reviews involve many people, any review that is not efficient will have an important impact in terms of project workload. It is thus important to ensure reviews are successful and efficient.

The following factors impact positively on the success of reviews:

– each review has clearly pre-defined objectives; this avoids misunderstandings between the review team members or about the review objectives (e.g. identification of defects instead of finding possible solutions);

– the persons involved are adequately experienced to attain the review's objectives; it is important to have good participants with the necessary skills and knowledge for the review level and objectives defined (e.g. developer for a code review, subject matter expert for a functional review, etc.). Otherwise the review objectives will not be reached;

– the techniques applied are adapted to reach the objectives, adapted to the types and levels of the software deliverables, and adapted to the level of competence of the reviewers. Otherwise, an incorrect application of techniques can occur with associated loss of time or incorrect results;

– the individual work is executed correctly so as not to waste the time of the other participants during the review meeting;

– defects found are accepted and expressed objectively, and personnel or psychological issues are resolved, so that reviews become positive experience for the authors. A review is not the place to settle scores and remember the roles of authors and reviewer could be reversed in the future;

– the review is executed in a spirit of openess and cooperation, where results are not used to evaluate participants, but only to evaluate the software product submitted for review;

– written notes are taken and serve as basis both for process improvement and to note defects or comments provided during the meetings;

– checklists or roles are used where appropriate, to increase the efficiency of defect detection. Checklist and defect taxonomy improvement at the end of reviews will enable improvement of future reviews;

– training is provided on review techniques, specifically for more formal reviews such as inspections and audits;

– the management supports an adequate review process (e.g. by providing adequate time for reviews – including individual activities – in the project schedule);

– the focus is on learning and process improvement.

In general, including testers in reviews contributes to the success of reviews and enables testers to learn about the product, its operation, and prepare better tests at an earlier stage.

An additional aspect for reviews is that, by including all stakeholders (or their representatives) in the specification document reviews, so that they can protect their individual interest, we can efficiently ensure exhaustivity of the specifications and anticipate discontent when the software product or system is delivered. The stakeholders that should be included are: management, customers, marketing, and users to obtain an understanding of the requirements; developers, architects, and technical specialists (network, databases, etc.) to ensure that requirements are feasible; testers to ensure requirements are testable; quality-assurance managers, configuration management specialists, etc. to anticipate the activities and modifications of process that could occur.

Even though results can vary on a case-by-case basis, formal reviews have demonstrated their efficiency since the invention of the inspection process (Michael Fagan at IBM) until today. Despite this, a large number of organizations do not apply efficient review techniques. According to Capers Jones [JON 07, pp. 426-430] one of the success factors of reviews for defect detection, is their proximity to the origin of defects. This avoids a period of chaos, linked to the detection of defects at the end of the design process.

3.2.5. Comparison of the types of reviews

FLO-3.2.2 Explain the differences between different types of reviews: informal review, technical review, walk-through, and inspection (K2)

IEEE 1028-2008 [IEE 08b, pp. 38-39] provides a detailed comparison of the different types of review, partially included in the table hereafter (Table 3.1).

Characteristic	Informal review	Technical review	Inspection	Walk-through
Goal	Identify defects and alternatives quickly and cheaply	Evaluate conformity with regards to specifications and plans, evaluate integrity of modifications	Find defects, check their resolution, verify the quality of the product	Find defects, identify alternatives, improve the product
Recommended size	Two or more persons	Three or more persons	From three to six persons	From two to seven persons
Directed by	Author	Principal engineer	Trained facilitator	Facilitator or author
Volume of material submitted to review	Moderate	Moderate to high, depending on the specific goals of the meeting	Relatively small and can be inspected in a single day	Relatively small
Deliverables	No mandatory deliverables, optionally a list of anomalies, alternatives and recommendations	Technical review documentation, list of actions with responsibilities and closure date	List of anomalies, synthesis, inspection documentation	List of anomalies, list of actions, decisions, follow-up propositions
Use of checklists	No	Optional	Yes	Optional
Management participation	No	Depending on the actual need	No	No

Table 3.1. *Comparison of review types*

Reviews, formal or not, have demonstrated their efficiency and effectiveness by:

– detecting anomalies early in the development process (specifically for informal reviews, inspections, and walk-throughs);

– increasing developer productivity through correction of requirements and specifications before the design; thus, avoiding the need to fix code that has already been written;

– increased productivity of testers, through a reduction of defects introduced in the code (defects that do not have to he detected, fixed, and retested), and an increase in available time during test campaign execution to identify more complex defects;

– an ability to identify gaps in requirements or specifications, and thus design and testing teams obtain identical understanding.

Some reviews, such as informal reviews and walk-throughs have a higher return on investment because they are cheaper to implement.

3.3. Static analysis by tools (FL 3.3)

FLO-3.3.1 Recall typical defects and errors identified by static analysis and compare them to reviews and dynamic testing (K1)

It is possible to use tools to execute some analysis on models or software products and thus identify defects. This is called "static analysis by tools".

The category of issues identified by this type of tools and analysis are frequently problems, defects, or topics that would be more difficult (if not impossible) to identify with other means.

The main goals of static tests with tools are to:

– obtain a better understanding of the software or system, or even model, by a study of its structure, so as to facilitate its testing;

– detect defects and problematic issues (such as syntax error) early, before test execution, so as to correct the software as early as possible;

– evaluate some aspects of software or model design, through the use of metrics (such as a high level of complexity) and adapt the testing effort based on this information;

– identify defects that would be undetectable by dynamic tests, such as maintainability issues, code documentation (comments in the code), compliance to naming rules for variables and functions, application modeling, and design, etc.

Many different tools are available to execute such analysis.

3.3.1. *Types of static analysis*

Beyond the static analysis of text documents, with syntactical or lexical correction in word-processing software, the main types of static analysis are:

– analysis of the software application model;

– analysis of the software application components;

– analysis of the software application structure.

3.3.1.1. *Modeling*

Software model analysis is based on the modeling of the software or system and the analysis of that model, on the principle that a model is usually easier to define, design and understand than a complete piece of software. Furthermore, some parts of the software (or even the whole system) is designed from models or modeling languages such as UML (unified modeling language).

Model validation enables early identification of defects, and thus prevention of their introduction in the software.

The important aspects to take into account when designing a model [JOR 09, pp. 6-9; UTT 07, pp. 60-66] are:

– the level of consistency, completeness, and clarity of the model. These aspects are difficult to implement – or even obsolete – if the software modeling is only done partially (many small models, each representing part of the software, but not integrated in an unique model), or depending on the type of software or system currently being developed (real time, parallel execution, reactive systems, etc.);

– an adequate size allowing the model to represent all the behaviors of the software, and an ability to "execute" the model, which is to create an engine that will execute (or exercise) the model. It is thus possible to detect sequences of events for which results were unforeseen (failures);

– a sufficient level of completeness to "provide" the level of understanding, which replaces the completeness objective that cannot be reached by the inherent complexity of the system being represented. One way to reach that goal is to use a representation model or notation model that supports that objective;

– an adequate level of understanding, which allows clear identification of the behavior of the model. This translates requirements and specifications into executable code, either directly or using specific formal specification languages.

It is necessary to note that the design of a model can be considered as a development task and a source of errors, thus models will need to be validated and verified.

Many different books explain modeling and provide useful sources of information, such as [JOR 09] and [UTT 07].

3.3.1.2. *Static code analysis*

Static analysis of software components' source code enables testers to check whether the code complies with applicable coding and naming rules. This analysis – often done with the help of specific tools – can be executed before or after the code is finished, which enables testers to:

– detect software defects early in the development cycle, and thus reduce development time and costs;

– improve code reliability by identifying the sections of code that were not covered by dynamic testing;

– identify components subject to defect clustering or responsible for the majority of the defects;

– anticipate and diagnose problems through graphical visualization of results and metrics;

– improve developers' coding practices and lower maintenance costs (through the creation of code that is easier to read, fix, and test);

– diagnose and anticipate problems by providing data supported by metrics and graphs;

– facilitate code refactoring, through identification of duplicate code or structures, etc.

This type of analysis is used in some context to evaluate the quality of the code and authorize – or not – its integration in higher-level components.

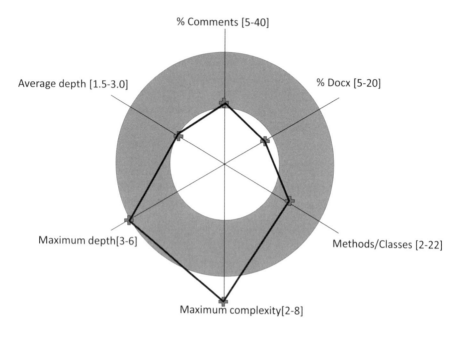

Figure 3.3. *Static analysis graph*

Static analysis provides metrics, such as the cyclomatic number (see section 4.4.2.2, page 184) and can be executed before a test phase to check the validity of the components, or after a test phase to evaluate the coverage reached and determine whether additional tests are necessary. Metrics used can be represented in graphs such as Figure 3.3. We see here that limits (ranges) are provided for all six metrics measured, and that some of these metrics are within the allowed range, while other metrics are outside the allowed range. This graph informs us of the type of corrections to implement in the code subject to analysis: specifically increase code documentation and reduce code complexity that is beyond the authorized maximum.

3.3.1.3. *Architecture analysis*

Analysis of software architecture enables identification of components that are frequently called and could be the root cause of transaction slowdown. Such an analysis can be executed after poor results from performance tests, to identify what needs to be implemented as changes.

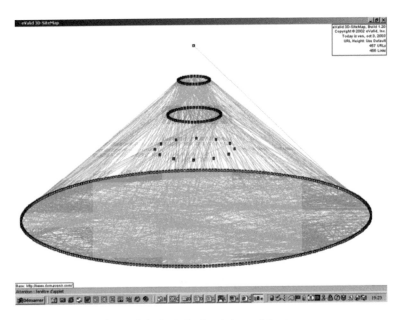

Figure 3.4. *Optimized website architecture*

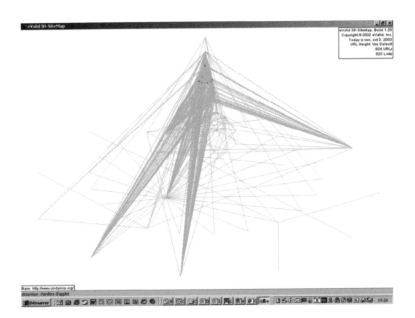

Figure 3.5. *Architecture that is not optimized*

Architecture analysis is also useful to ensure that the software application is maintainable, including for website development.

Comparison of Figures 3.4 and 3.5 enables the identification of one architecture that is more evenly balanced than the other, and that the number of levels – i.e. user actions necessary to reach the last level – is more reduced in Figure 3.4 than in Figure 3.5. This allow us to quickly identify that one site will be more maintainable and will most likely have better performance, than the other. The graphs of Figure 3.4 and Figure 3.5 were produced by a tool[2] developed based on Internet Explorer™, which analyzes and models the architecture of websites, and executes functional and performance tests.

Analysis of the architecture also enables identification of other aspects such as (for websites):

– missing or erroneous URLs that will produce 4xx errors;

– very large URLs that will slow down page loading;

– URLs with a small volume but for which the loading time is important, not a problem for dynamic pages, but problematic otherwise.

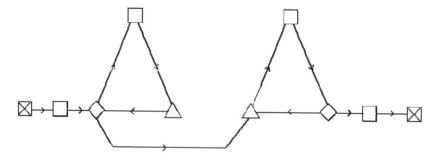

Figure 3.6. *Control flow*

This allows analysis of developed software so that it can be optimized and the user experience of the software improved.

Analysis of the architecture is not limited to component architecture, but can include modeling and analysis of the control flow (see also section 4.4)

---

2 eValid produced by Software Research Inc. in San Francisco [EVA].

3.3.2. *Types of defects that can be identified*

FLO-3.3.3 List typical code and design defects that may be identified by static analysis tools (K1)

Static analysis can identify the following main defects:

– referencing a variable with an undefined value;

– inconsistent or incoherent interfaces between modules and components;

– variables that are never used or declared incorrectly;

– code that cannot be accessed (dead code);

– mission or erroneous logic (potentially infinite loops);

– computations or constructions that are overly complex;

– programming standards violations;

– lack of respect of naming rules for variables and functions;

– security vulnerabilities;

– syntax violations in code and models, etc.

Obtaining all metrics and identifying all types of defects is not possible with a single tool. It may be necessary to use more than one tool to detect the types of defects mentioned above, and to apply them at the different test levels.

We have tools that can be used:

– at component level testing, before integration: control flow analysis, computation of the cyclomatic number, syntax validation, verification of naming and programming rules, generation of variable cross-references (definition and referencing of variables), data flow analysis;

– during component integration testing: comparing interfaces structures (messages and data structures);

– during system testing: call graphs, etc.

We have seen a number of metrics that enable us to evaluate a level of complexity of the software. These metrics – called Halstead metrics – include simple metrics such as:

– n1 = number of distinct operators (verbs) in the software;

– n2 = number of distinct operands (subjects) in the software;

– N1 = Number of occurrence of operators;

– N2 = Number of occurrence of operands.

From these metrics, Halstead developed a set of equations that allow measurement of the level of complexity of the vocabulary of the software. This is useful when measuring the portability of the software.

3.3.3. *Data flow analysis*

Data flow analysis consists of evaluation of the variables and verifying whether they are correctly defined and initialized before being used (referenced).

A variable is a computer memory area (a set of bytes and bits) to which a name is associated (the variable name). When the variable is not used, for example before the program is launched or after the program ends, the memory area is allocated to another program or to the system. It can thus contain any data, alphabetic or numeric. When the program needs the variable, a memory area is allocated, but is not always initialized. The content of the memory area is thus not guaranteed. To ensure that the memory area contains valid data, it is important to initialize it with an adequate value. Some programming languages automatically initialize variables when they are declared, other languages do not. Similarly some programming languages dynamically allocate variables (and their type, numeric or alphanumerical) during their identification, for example at their first use in the code. We could thus have two variables with similar names "NOM" and "N0M" (here the digit 0 instead of the letter O), that could be considered identical when read by the developer but that are defined as two different variables by the computer. We could also have the defect identified hereunder:

```
#include <stdio.h>
Main() {
int x;
printf (« %d »,x);
}
```

As the "x" variable is not initialized, its content is random.

It is also important to differentiate variables that have the same name but a different range in the software. Some variables ("global" variables) are shared by all functions and exist from the beginning to the end of the program, other variables exist only during the life (existence) of the sub-program and threads launched by the main program and can be shared ("public variables") or not ("private variables"), other have a still shorter existence, limited to the existence of the function when it is called by the program or sub-program.

Depending on the programming language and the definition of the variable (global, private, or public), we can have variable with the same name but different areas of applicability, when they apply to different areas of the memory.

Data analysis via data flow analysis are powerful detection methods that ensure that variables are correctly used, i.e. that each variable is correctly initialized before being referenced (used).

3.3.3.1. *Modeling data flow*

Modeling dataflow for a single variable is done by using a pairs of information corresponding to the state of the variable before the action and the action executed [COP 03, pp. 168-179]. There are three possibilities for the first occurrence of a variable:

1. ~d variable does not exist yet (indicated by a ~) and then defined (d), that means the program requests a memory area from the system;

2. ~u variable does not exist yet, and is then used (u). This is possible with some programming languages and can include initialization of the variable;

3. ~k variable does not exist and is then killed (k for "killed"), and the memory area is returned to the system for use by other programs.

It is clear that this applies for each and every variable, whether they are global or local, public, or private, and during their existence.

The first type of action (~d) is correct and corresponds to the initial definition of a variable and its initialization. The second type of action is incorrect, it is not normal to use an undefined variable. The last type of action is probably incorrect; destruction of a variable before using it is not a recommended programming practice. Sometimes the type of action ("r") can be used to represent the referencing of a variable (similar to "u").

Figure 3.7 illustrates dataflow analysis, which is similar to control flow, but focuses on the data and variables.

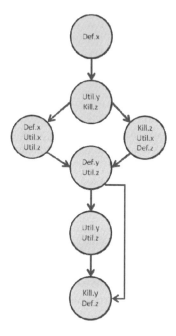

Figure 3.7. *Control flow and data flow*

We have three variables *x*, *y* and *z* that are (Def.), utilized (Util.), and discarded (Kill.).

Dataflow analysis allows us to identify the following pairs:

– dd = defined and defined again: not specifically wrong, but abnormal and could warrant the removal of the first definition;

– du = defined then used: nominal usage;

– dk = defined then discarded: not specifically wrong, but abnormal and could warrant the removal of both instruction;

– ud = used then defined, acceptable but suspect;

– uu = used then used again: nominal usage;

– uk = used then discarded: nominal usage;

– kd = discarded then defined: acceptable usage;

– ku = discarded then used: incorrect usage where a variable is discarded then referenced;

– kk = discarded then discarded again: possible programming mistake.

3.3.3.2. *Testing with dataflow analysis*

Let us take the three following data flows for each of the three variables:

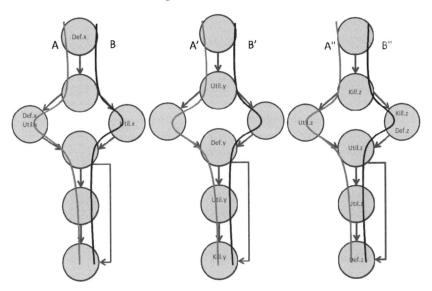

Figure 3.8. *Example of dataflow for three variables*

Dataflow analysis for each of the three variables allows identification of the following cases:

For the variable x	For the variable y	For the variable z
~d: correct	~u: major defect	~k: programming defect
dd: suspect, possible defect on path A	ud: acceptable, whatever the path (A' or B')	ku: important defect on path A"
du: correct in path A	du: correct	kk: potential error on path B"
du: correct in path B	uk: correct	kd: acceptable
	dk: suspect, possible defect on the alternate path to the last component	uu: correct in path AA"
		ud: acceptable

Table 3.2. *Defects in dataflow analysis*

3.3.3.3. *Limitations and assumptions*

Dataflow analysis focuses on the sequential use of data, not on their utility or how they are used. Using a variable in a division is as correct as using it in a string operation, and does not focus on the type of variable (numerical or alphabetical). The assumptions that we are making in dataflow analysis are that the code and the usage of variables are as they "should" be.

Dataflow analysis is not able to identify all defects related to data and variables. Some paths can be inaccessible and contain incorrect sequences. Moreover, real-time software, managed through interrupts or different execution priorities for its components can render dataflow analysis difficult if not outright impossible (such as when race conditions occur between processes and variables).

Using dataflow analysis is effective where code cannot efficiently be verified through reviews or inspections. This technique is cumbersome and requires testers with programming experience to understand code, control flow, and variables.

3.4. Added value of static activities

FLO-3.3.2 Describe, using examples, the typical benefits of static analysis (K2)

Return on investment of reviews and statistical analysis is very high; it is surprising that many organizations do not implement such activities or do not implement them efficiently. According to Caper Jones [JON 07, pp. 427-429, 435-469], "formal inspections have proven both to benefit overall projects costs and to shorten project schedule". The average reduction in duration is of 15% and the workload is reduced by about 20%, with an average of 200% more defects identified before delivery of the software.

It is sometimes difficult, in certain development cycles, such as agile methods and Scrum, to introduce the concept of formal reviews and static analysis and to obtain the full benefits expected from these techniques.

According to Tom Gilb [GIL 93, p. 19], inspections are twice as effective at detecting defects as walk-through. What is more, formal inspection allows reductions in the development duration – in mostly sequential development cycles – and in development costs, while having the positive impact of reducing maintenance costs throughout the life of the software. Here, we have an advantage that is not limited to a single development phase.

According to Marnie L. Hutcheson [HUT 03, p. 25] and Capers Jones [JON 07, p. 488], defect identification and removal efficiency for design reviews and code inspections vary between 45% and 68% even though they are in the 37% to 60% range for the sum of all formal test activities.

Static activities, whether reviews (formal or informal) or static analysis, enable a large increase in software and system quality at a very low cost. Their impact goes beyond simple defect detection, because it can be felt throughout the whole life cycle and maintenance of the software.

3.5. Synopsis of this chapter

Let us summarize what was learned in this chapter.

In section 3.1 we learned the importance of static testing activities, the differences compared with dynamic testing, the deliverables on which they can be applied, and the potential advantages that can be obtained from static testing. You should also understand the glossary definition of the following terms: dynamic test, static test.

Section 3.2 covered the different types of reviews as defined in the IEEE 1028-2008 standard, with their inputs, deliverables, processes, and participants. We saw the different levels of formalism, from the most formal – audit – to the less formal – walk-through and management reviews – and we identified the pertinent factors that ensure the success of reviews. You should also be familiar with the following glossary definitions: entry criteria, formal review, informal review, inspection, metric, moderator, peer review, reviewer, scribe, technical review, walkthrough.

Section 3.3 detailed the different processes of static analysis with tools, covering modeling, static code analysis, architecture, dataflow analysis and defects that can be identified using such techniques. Glossary terms to remember are: complier, complexity, control flow, data flow, static analysis.

Section 3.4 summarized the advantages and added value of static techniques that have demonstrated their use and important efficiency.

3.6. Sample exam questions

Section 3.1. Static techniques and test processes (K2)

FLO-3.1.1   Recognize software work products that can be examined by the different static techniques (K1)

FLO-3.1.2   Describe the importance and value of considering static techniques for the assessment of software work products (K2)

FLO-3.1.3   Explain the difference between static and dynamic techniques, considering objectives, types of defects to be identified, and the role of these techniques within the software life cycle (K2)

Ref	Questions

36.	FLO-3.1.1. (K1)
	
	Consider the following software deliverables:
	
	    I. Test plan.
	
	    II. Detailed system specifications.
	
	    III. Source code.
	
	    IV. Test scenarios.
	
	    V. Contractual requirements.
	
	Which of the following is correct?
	
	A. All these products can be subject to review.
	
	B. Only II and III can be subject to review.
	
	C. Only II, III and V can be subject to review.
	
	D. Only I, III and IV can be subject to review.

37.	FLO-3.1.2 (K2) You are the tester on a large project. You are invited to participate in a system specification review, as representative of the test team. What major benefit can the test team obtain from such a review? A. A reduction in test duration and effort. B. A reduction in the number of defects entering the test phase. C. A reduction in the number of defects delivered to customer. D. A reduction of the testing costs.

Ref	Questions
38.	FLO-3.1.3 (K2) You have installed the software to test on your computer after a modification. You execute the software by going through each screen to check the validity of each message (including error messages). What technique are you using? A. Exploratory testing. B. Regression testing. C. Static testing. D. Dynamic testing.
39.	Terms (K1) What is an inspection? A. A process evaluation executed by management, controlling the execution, status of plans, confirming requirements and systems allocation, or evaluating the efficiency and effectiveness in reaching an objective. B. A step-by-step presentation by the author of a document in order to gather information and obtain consensus on its content. C. An independent evaluation of a product or process to ensure its conformity to standards, rules, guidelines, specifications and/or procedures, based on objective criteria. D. A type of review based on visual examination of documents to detect defects, following a strict formalism and always based on documented procedures.

Section 3.2. Review processes (K2)

FLO-3.2.1   Recall the activities, roles, and responsibilities of a typical formal review (K1)

FLO-3.2.2   Explain the differences between different types of reviews: informal review, technical review, walk-through, and inspection (K2)

FLO-3.2.3   Explain the factors for successful performance of reviews (K2)

Ref	Questions
40.	FLO-3.2.1 (K1) Consider the following activities: I. Selection of exit criteria. II. Correction of defects found. III. Definition of the sections of the document to review. IV. Identification of defects. V. Logging and classification of defects. VI. Assignation of roles to members. In which order do these activities occur in a formal review? A. I, VI, III, IV, II, V. B. III, I, VI, IV, V, II. C. VI, I, III, IV, V, II. D. VI, I, III, IV, II, V.
41.	FLO-3.2.2 (K2) What is the main difference between an inspection and a walk-through? A. In an inspection the author presents the document step-by-step and manages the review. B. A walk-through is a type of pair programming, while an inspection is applicable on any type of product. C. In a walk-through the author presents the document step-by-step and manages the review. D. There is no difference between the two types of reviews.
42.	FLO-3.2.3 (K2) To have successful reviews, it is crucial that the participants be motivated to find defects in the product submitted for review. Why? A. To identify as much defects as possible as quickly as possible, because it will be cheaper for the organization and more efficient for all. B. So that the authors can correct more defects, even if for them the review is very stressful. C. So that each participant can be humble, because it is better to work in an organization where egos have no place. D. Because it will enable the use of metrics to evaluate authors and reviewers.

43.	Terms (K1)
	What is a peer review?
	A. A test technique where you vary pairs of values in equivalence classes.
	B. A programming technique where you associate a tester with a developer so that defects are identified as early as possible.
	C. A technical review executed by one or more colleagues in order to identify defects and provide improvements.
	D. A systematic evaluation of the acquisition, development, delivery, management, and maintenance processes related to software.

Section 3.3. Static analysis with tools (K2)

FLO-3.3.1   Recall typical defects and errors identified by static analysis and compare them to reviews and dynamic testing (K1)

FLO-3.3.2   Describe, using examples, the typical benefits of static analysis (K2)

FLO-3.3.3   List typical code and design defects that may be identified by static analysis tools (K1)

Ref	Questions
44.	FLO-3.3.1 (K1)
	What are the main differences between dynamic tests and static analysis?
	A. Dynamic tests do not require execution of the code, while static analysis requires it.
	B. Static analysis and dynamic testing find the same type of defects.
	C. Static analysis does not require the execution of the code being analyzed, while dynamic testing does.
	D. Static analysis finds failures while dynamic testing finds defects.
45.	FLO-3.3.2 (K2)
	Consider the following aspects:
	I. Early defect detection.
	II. Measurement of tester efficiency via metrics.
	III. Early information on complex component via metrics.
	IV. Prevention of defects.

	V. Identification of missing requirements. Which of the following is correct? A. All those aspects are advantages linked to the use of static analysis. B. I, II and V are advantages linked to the use of static analysis. C. I, III and IV are advantages linked to the use of static analysis. D. II, IV and V are advantages linked to the use of static analysis.
46.	FLO-3.3.3 (K1) Which of the defects below can be identified by static analysis? A. Lack of code for a planned use case. B. Detection of a module called too frequently. C. Discrepancy in the color coding of graphical interfaces. D. Potential buffer overflow leading to a security vulnerability.
47.	Terms (K1) What is complexity? A. The number of independent paths in a program, representing the complexity of the program. B. The degree by which a component has a design and/or internal structure difficult to understand, maintain, and verify. C. A degree of measurement of the difficulty to design a software, defining the complexity of the development. D. The percentage of defects found before delivery, which represents the complexity of testing.

Chapter 4

Test Design
Techniques (FL 4.0)

To better illustrate the process of test design, let us take an example. This example is very common (see [BIN 00, pp. 5-9] and [MYE 79, pp. 1-3]). A software receives three integers, separated by commas, representing the length of the sides of a triangle. The software must provide the type of triangle, or a message if the three values do not represent a triangle.

How many tests should we consider?

It is important to remember that a valid triangle must respond to two conditions: no side may be equal to zero, and each side must be smaller than the sum of the other two sides. This means that a triangle with the sides **a, b** and **c**:

    s= (a + b + c) / 2

Then **s** >**a** and **s** > **b** and **s** > **c**.

A triangle can be equilateral (three sides of equal length), isosceles (two sides of equal length), or scalene (no two sides are equal).

We could envisage the following test process:

– let us identify the test conditions, that is, the reasons why we test, the aspects we want to check;

– once we have identified the test conditions, we replace the types of values with real values (integers in our case), and determine the results we should obtain.

Identification of the information mentioned in the specifications (the different inputs and outputs planned) allows us to test the following conditions (valid and invalid outputs):

– a valid equilateral triangle, where the three sides are equal: **a, a, a**;

– a valid isosceles triangle, where the two first sides are equal: **a, a, c**;

– a valid scalene triangle that responds to the specifications above;

– a form that is not a triangle, for example where the third side is the sum of the two other sides: **a, b, (a+b)**.

We can detail these conditions:

– combination of **a, b, a** and of **b, a, a**, which provide two other conditions for an isosceles triangle, one with a different value in second position, the other with a different value in first position.

We can also detail the cases where we have a form that is not a triangle with (among others):

– three combinations where one value is zero, with the first, second or third value being zero (0, b, c), (a, 0, c), (a, b, 0);

– the case where there is more than one zero value (three: 0, 0, 0) or the three combinations of two zero values: (a, 0, 0), (0, b, 0) or (0, 0, c);

– the other combinations of one side equal to the sum of the other two (b+c, b, c), (a, a+c, c);

– the combinations where one side is larger than the sum of the two others, with the larger side in first, second, or third position.

We can also define error where the input data does not respond to specifications such as:

– non-numeric value (alphabetic or special character) in first, second, or third position;

– less than three input values;

– more than three input values;

– real numeric values (with decimal point) for each of the positions;

– negative values for each of the positions, etc.

Once we have defined our test conditions, we can replace the theoretical values (a, b, c) with real values responding to the same criteria in order to have test cases.

We can combine test cases together to create test procedures or scenarios.

4.1. The test development process (FL 4.1)

FLO-4.1.1 Differentiate between a test design specification, test case specification, and test procedure specification (K2)

We saw in the previous example that test design is different from test case design: one focuses on a type of response from the software, while the other focuses on how the software responds to a specific sub-set of data.

The same type of difference exists between the specification of a single test case and the combination of multiple test cases in a *test procedure* or a test scenario.

Frequently a test with a single value is designed, then the data is generalized to a range of data that has the same behavior. The other mode of design, where a range of values is identified, then specific values for testing are selected is also frequent.

4.1.1. *Terminology*

FLO-4.1.2 Compare the terms test condition, test case, and test procedure (K2)

The International Software Testing Qualifications Board (ISTQB) glossary proposes the following definitions:

Test condition: an item or an event of a component or system, which could be verified by one or more test cases, e.g. a function, transaction, quality attribute, or a structural element.

A test condition is thus one of the reasons for testing, an objective to reach, validate or verify.

Test case: a set of input values, execution preconditions, expected results, and execution post conditions, which are developed for a particular objective or test condition, such as exercising a particular program path or verifying compliance with a specific requirement.

A test case is thus an example of a test condition, which is testable separately from the others and for which we have all the information necessary to determine compliance with the result of this test execution in comparison to the expected results. A test case model has been suggested by the IEEE 829 and is described in Chapter 8.

Test procedure specification: a document specifying the sequence of actions necessary for the execution of a test. Also known as test script, test scenario, or manual test script.

A test procedure is a combination of manual or automated test cases, frequently used to represent how users could use the software. A template for test procedures, proposed by the IEEE 829 standard is available in Chapter 8 page 327.

4.1.2. Traceability

FLO-4.1.3 Evaluate the quality of test cases in terms of clear traceability to the requirements and expected results (K2)

Whatever the technique or method being used to undertake the test, we will always need to answer questions such as "how far are you in your testing?", "when will you have finished?", or more pointed questions such as "how did you test requirement EX-2570.2, and what are the results?" Responses to such questions should not be "I'll check and call you back", but should be available at the tip of your fingers; otherwise you might lose the confidence placed in you by developers, project leaders, and customers.

One solution is to implement traceability from requirements and specifications, to the test cases and their execution, via the test conditions. This will enable you to have complete clarity in your tests and what still needs to be done.

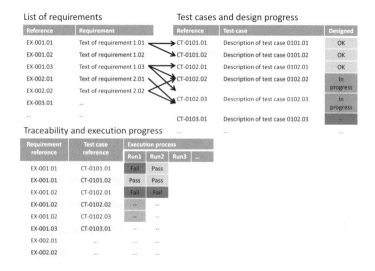

Figure 4.1. *Traceability and coverage follow-up*

To implement this traceability, it is necessary to reference each of the requirements, each of the specifications, and create tracking tables where you can clearly identify the links between the test conditions, test cases, and test case execution.

Figure 4.1 illustrates how to implement traceability from the requirements to the test cases and how to quickly respond to the questions that were asked.

In a first step, we will store our requirements in a table, splitting compound requirements into single requirements. This will enable us to have the simplest requirements by splitting them according to the sub-requirements present in the phase. Requirement "*EX-001 software will allow the addition and removal of users*" could be split in "*EX-001.01 software will allow the addition of users*" and "*EX-001.02 software will allow the removal of users*" and in "*EX-001.03 software will allow user access*" (it is necessary to allow user access before removing them).

In a second step, we will list all our test cases and give them a reference.

In a third step we will implement traceability, in a table that will have the individual requirements and the test case(s) related to this requirement. This will allow us to create, in a file, the representation of the arrows linking the requirements to the test cases.

In the different lists, we can add indicators showing the progress of the different tasks; for example, whether the test cases have been designed or not (in the test case table) or the result of the test case execution in the traceability and execution control. This solution allows you to identify at a glance what has been done, and what remains to be done for each requirement. It is evident that it is also necessary to measure what remains to be done in terms of test cases, duration of test execution (and design), as the design, implementation, and execution of some tests can take longer than others.

Bidirectional traceability between requirements, test cases, and their execution enables the measurement of test processes and the identification of the impact when a test case covers more than one requirement (test case CT-0102.02 and CT-0103.01 in Figure 4.1). Horizontal and vertical traceability both need to be taken into account.

Implementing traceability is often facilitated with the use of test tools (see Chapter 6), and can be time-consuming when implemented manually. The benefits and increased visibility from traceability implementation fully justify the – sometimes important – investment in a manual traceability scheme.

Maintenance of traceability tables is very time-consuming if the requirements and specifications are not stable; in such cases the use of tools is recommended.

FLO-4.1.4 Translate test cases into a well-structured test procedure specification at a level of detail relevant to the knowledge of the testers (K3)

Test design requires knowledge of the domain and of software, as well as knowledge of test techniques. Knowledge of how systems and software behave is also useful. It should be noted that a number of assumptions and limitations are applicable according to the techniques used. Such constraints are also applicable for test case and test procedure specifications.

It is necessary to ensure that the persons who will execute the tests – now or in the future – will have the adequate level of detailed information to understand the impacts, ins and outs of the test cases and procedures to enable execution. This implies different constraints depending on the type of test, level of test, and testers.

Depending on the type of tests, either we would require documentation to define pre-conditions, input data, and the start-up environment, as well as test objectives; or we would require testers with knowledge of the software, its usage, and the operational context, so that the information may be known without having specific text documentation. The first option (detailed input data) applies to more systematic testing, while the second is more applicable to exploratory testing.

Depending on the test level, we need to know how software and systems work (for example in component testing and component integration testing), while at other test levels – such as system testing or acceptance testing – knowledge of the business is more important.

In order to have maintainable test suites that are easily adaptable to software or system changes, it is necessary for testers to have a good knowledge of the different test techniques and of the vocabulary used. This, together with constantly updated documentation, allows you to maintain a test efficiency level throughout the life of the software or system. These different considerations allow us to understand the importance of the assumptions and limitations imposed by the test design techniques.

4.2. Categories of test design techniques (FL 4.2)

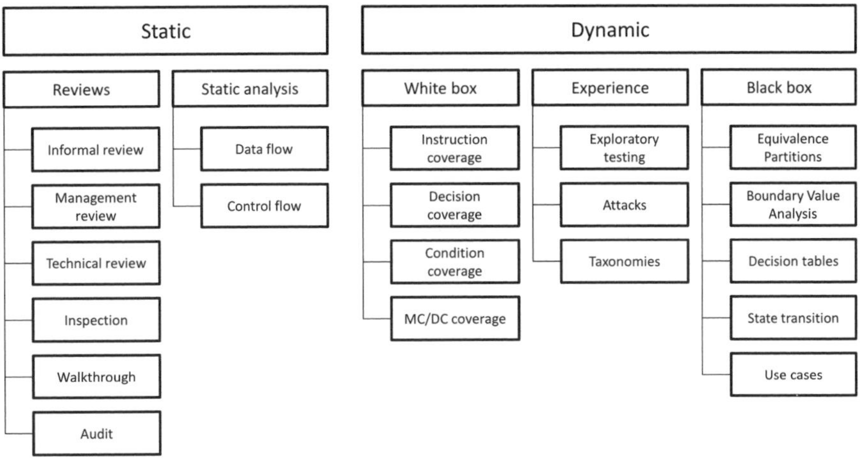

Figure 4.2. *Test techniques*

Beyond static testing, there are many dynamic testing categories:

– those based on the software or system specifications;

– those based on the software or system structure, or a model thereof;

– those based on the experience of the testers, their knowledge of the business and of potential defects.

To each of these groups of techniques are associated assumptions and limitations that need to be taken into account when these techniques are used.

4.2.1. *Black box, white box, or gray box*

FLO-4.2.1 Recall reasons that both specification-based (black-box) and structure-based (white-box) test design techniques are useful and list the common techniques for each (K1)

Many approaches are available for testing software:

– focusing on the requirements and the specifications at the basis of the software, and consider the software as correct once all the requirements and all the specifications have been verified. This approach is called "black box" because the software is considered as a black box, and the focus is on the interfaces as described in the specification documentation – or visible by simple observation – without bothering about the internal structure (code) of the software. It is similar to testing a car only through the driver interfaces (steering wheel, buttons, pedals, etc.). The black-box approach is also called the "specification-based approach". By definition it does not use information pertaining to the internal structure of the software or system;

– considering the software as a set of lines of code, instructions, and components, and assuming that once all these structural components have been verified and validated, the software should work properly. This approach is called "white box", contrary to "black box", because we focus on the internal structure of the software instead of only on its interface specifications. It is similar to testing a car only by checking each of its components (tires, accelerator, brakes, etc.). The white-box approach is also called the "structure-based approach" as it is based on the internal structure of the software.

Glass box: some testers considered that a box, whether white or black, does not enable the content to be seen. They propose the term "glass box" instead of "white box" based on the assumption that glass is transparent and allows the structure inside the box to be seen. There are different types of more or less transparent glass, tinted, pebbled, and sanded glass, i.e. opaque and not transparent, that do not enable clear vision of what is behind the glass. Accordingly in this book, we will speak of "white box" and "black box" techniques.

Usually the tester has some knowledge of the structure of the software and can determine its major components. Thus the tester does not have strictly "black" or "white" box knowledge and will design tests using both types of aspects. We will then talk of "gray-box" testing.

Whichever test category is envisaged, it is necessary to remember that a single test technique or a single test category is not enough to ascertain a level of quality.

For example: let us take the formula $\sqrt[z]{1/x}$ (translated in programming language as sqrt(1 / x)). It is necessary to have a minimum of three values for variable "x" to test this instruction: a positive value, which will give a valid result, a negative value, which should result in a defect (imaginary value error), and a zero value, which should give another type of defect (divide by zero error). A single test will thus not detect all types of defects.

We must thus design tests with different techniques, methods, and categories.

4.2.2. *Experience-based techniques*

Testing based on the experience of the tester covers both business domain experience (i.e. using the system or software as an experienced user to achieve a business goal), and software and/or systems tester experience (i.e. searching for defects and failures, reporting them, checking whether they are fixed).

In general, these techniques are based on an analysis of the – hardware and software – application context, on a study of the architecture, interactions between functionalities and characteristics, and types of users of this software application.

Experience-based techniques build on the specific expertise of each of the testers, and will allow testers to use their imagination and creativity to design effective and useful tests.

4.2.3. *Test characteristics*

FLO-4.2.2 Explain the characteristics, commonalities, and differences between specification-based testing, structure-based testing, and experience-based testing (K2)

Generally, a test has an objective of providing evidence that a characteristic is present (or absent). This characteristic will be identified with more or less ease with a test technique, depending on the characteristic.

The usual characteristics of specifications-based techniques are:

– use of formal or informal models to specify problems and software components, and use of these models to systematically derive test conditions and test cases, and

– measurement of a level of coverage based on an analysis of the functionalities, risk, and use of the software.

The usual characteristics of structure-based techniques are:

– use of the software code and architecture for the design of test conditions and test cases, and

– measurement of a coverage level of the code (or of the architecture) based on the execution of existing tests, followed by the design of additional tests to increase the coverage.

The usual characteristics of experience-based techniques are:

– use of the tester's knowledge to design tests cases,

– use of external reference models (list of possible defects, etc.) to design test cases to identify presence or absence of this defects of a certain type in the software,

– design of test cases taking into account the knowledge of the different stakeholders (developers, designers, testers, users, experts, etc.) and the knowledge of the context, environment and usage of the software.

4.2.4. *Limitations and assumptions*

Each of the characteristics identified above is based on a number of hypothesis (assumptions) and has associated limitations.

Testers should know the different techniques in order to use them efficiently and know when they are appropriate.

4.2.4.1. *Specifications-based tests*

Black-box tests are based on the requirements and specifications to determine whether the software is correct or not. The main hypothesis is thus that the requirements are complete and correctly cover the wishes as expressed by users and customers.

If customer requirements have not been correctly identified, reported, and understood, the software that will implement these requirements will not fit the actual needs. If the software designer added unspecified functionalities (Easter egg, backdoors, etc.) these aspects will not be identified.

4.2.4.2. *Structure-based tests*

In structure-based tests, also called white-box tests, the underlying hypothesis is that the program code (or architecture) corresponds to the customer requirements and the contractual or regulatory applicable standards.

If the software designer did not fulfill these requirements, such as omitting some requirements or adding unspecified additional functions (Easter egg, backdoors, etc.), these aspects will not be identified (except by a detailed code analysis not usually part of structure-based tests).

4.2.4.3. *Experience-based tests*

For experience-based tests, the main hypothesis is that the testers have adequate business (user and customer related) knowledge, and are able to design tests that fulfill the needed functionalities. The techniques grouped under this category simultaneously require an understanding of the external (functional) aspects and internal (programming architecture, hardware, and interfaces) aspects of software and systems, as well as an ability to quickly detect any potential dysfunction – minor or not – and its impact for the user.

If the tester is a beginner or lacks expertise in the specified domain, or if the software or system is not based on established or known paradigms, it is frequent that the defects identified will not correspond to the most important risks to identify.

Experience-based tests frequently allow quick identification of defects, which is impressive for non-specialists. This is, however, very dependent on the experience of the individual testers.

4.3. Black-box techniques (FL 4.3)

Black-box techniques are based on the specifications, documentation, and interface descriptions of the software or system. It is also possible to use models (formal or informal) representing the expected behavior of the software to design tests.

Usually black-box type test techniques are applied to the user interfaces, and require interfacing the software via introduction of data and gathering of outputs, either from the screen, reports, or printouts.

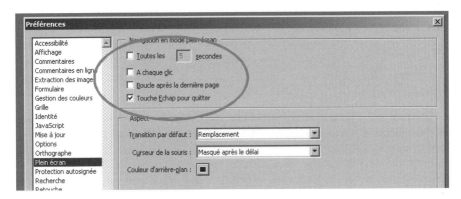

Figure 4.3. *Example of fields*

A tester will thus interact with the software by inputting data, acting on switches, buttons, or other interfaces. Selection of the input data and the order of data entry or actions can lead to a gigantic combined number of actions as suggested by the following example suggested by Cem Kaner during a conference:

How many test cases are necessary to test all the possible values in the fields within the circled area of Figure 4.3, namely: four check boxes and one two-positions field.

At first sight the calculation is easy:

Four fields with two possible states each: two to the power of four (2^4) that is 16 cases, to which you need to add one field of two positions for seconds, varying from 00 to 99, i.e. 1600 potential test cases.

However, this calculation is erroneous: we can identify that the field has one digit and a space, so that this "seconds" fields is made up of two alphanumerical positions, and that anything can be input, such as letters, special characters, spaces, etc. Thus, if our system is a 16 bit computer, we will have 2^{16} (i.e. 65,536) possibilities for each position, for a combinatory explosion of 4,294,967,296 test cases, which needs to be multiplied by the 16 test cases for the check boxes, which gives us a total of 68,719,476,736 different test cases. If we execute these tests at a rate of one test per second, we have a total duration of 2,177.5 years. For 32 or 64 bit systems, the duration is even larger.

We rapidly understand that it is necessary to reduce this duration to a more manageable time scale. Thus we have to implement techniques to reduce the number of test cases requiring execution, without reducing the scope of our tests.

4.3.1. *Equivalence partitioning (FL 4.3.1)*

FLO-4.3.1 Write test cases from given software models using equivalence partitioning, boundary value analysis, decision tables, and state transition diagrams/tables (K3)

The previous example demonstrated the need to reduce the number of test cases, but this reduction has to be implemented without losing efficiency and coverage.

Equivalence partitioning is a simple technique, applicable for any and all variables present in the software, whether input or output values, alphabetical, numerical, or other. It is based on the principle that all values from a same equivalence partition will be processed the same way by the same instructions.

During test case execution, we will select a representative from each of the identified equivalence partitioning.

The interest of equivalence partitioning is that it allows us to reduce the number of possible test cases in a systematic way without losing instruction or functional coverage.

Another interest of equivalence partitioning is the associated reduction in the combinatorial explosion between the different variables and the associated reduction of test cases it implies.

In an example we took previously ($\sqrt[z]{\dfrac{1}{x}}$ square root of $1/x$) we identified three series of data, three equivalence partitions:

– all positive numbers will be processed the same way and should give correct results;

– all negative numbers will also be processed the same way, and provide the same result; that is a failure because the square root of a negative number is an imaginary number;

– the zero value will be processed separately, and give a "zero divide" error. It would be a partition with a single value.

We thus see three different partitions, some with a set of values reduced to a single value. We have one "valid" partition, providing valid results, and two "invalid" partitions providing invalid results or failures.

Equivalence partitioning can be applied to all variables, whether input, output or internal variables, numeric or non-numeric variables, covering ranges of values or even a finite list of values, but also to other aspects such as the size of fields or typology of fields (description of field characteristics).

What are the equivalence partitions for dates, specifically for the days, months, and years? Typically, for days it is 01-31. However, this does not correspond to a valid partition for days, not all of these values will be processed the same way as some verifications will need to be executed based on the number of the day (and on the processes[1] associated with the "day" variable). There are many equivalence partitions:

– 1-28, which will be processed similarly for all the months of the year;

---

1 Such as "PreviousDay" and "PreviousMonth", which would create a specific equivalence partition for the value "01".

– 29, which will be processed differently for the month of February for leap years, considered invalid for February of non-leap years and will be present for all other months;

– 30, which will be processed for all months except February;

– 31, which will be processed only for certain months.

We also have to take into account the invalid partitions, such as less than 1 or larger than 31, or non-numeric values or even non-integer values.

For months, the usual response is 1-12, but should be separated in three valid partitions:

– 1, 3, 5, 7, 8, 10, 12, i.e. months of 31 days;

– 2 for February, which for leap years will have 29 days and 28 days otherwise;

– 4, 6, 9, 11, i.e. months of 30 days.

We will also have invalid partitions, as for the days.

For years, we will have leap years and non-leap years, with the particular invalid equivalence partition for year 0. We can, depending on the context, go even further in the level of detail and excluded the days that were removed (October 5-14, 1582) to synchronize the lunar calendar to the Gregorian calendar in use since October 15, 1582.

NOTE: In the above example we took into account the interactions between variables (days, months and years), and ended up with more partitions than otherwise.

We can represent the valid and invalid equivalence partitions as follows:

Input/output	Valid equivalence partitions	Invalid equivalence partitions
Day	1-28	Less than 1
	29	Greater than 31
	30	Non-numeric
	31	Empty
		Non-integer
Month	1, 3, 5, 7, 8, 10, 12	Less than 1
	2	Greater than 12

	4, 6, 9, 11	Non-numeric
		Empty
		Non integer
Year	1582-9999	Less than 1,582
	Non-leap years	Greater than 9,999
	Leap years not multiple of 100	Non-numeric
	Leap years multiple of 100	Empty
	Non-leap years multiple of 100	Non-integer
Discrete values	January 19, 2038	October 5, 1582 – October 14, 1582
Output values	January 2, 1582 – December 31, 9999	Before January 1, 1582
		After December 31, 9999

Table 4.1. *Valid and invalid equivalence partitions*

The value of January 19, 2038 is a specific value because BIOS clocks on PC/AT compute the time as 1 second increments on a 32 bit counter, from January 1, 1970 onwards. On January 19, 2038 at 03:14:08, this counter will go beyond 4,294,967,295 (maximum value for a 32 bit field) and will reinitialize the time to 00:00:00 with a date initialized to December 13, 1901. See also [PAG 09, pp. 83-86]

In the example illustrated in Figure 4.3, we can identify the following equivalence partitions:

– numeric values between 01 and 99, where the leading zero is present;

– numeric values between 1 and 9 (inclusive), with a leading or trailing space;

– alphabetic value of one or two positions, including accented characters;

– negative numeric values (–1 to –9);

– special characters (&, ~, §, *, space, null, etc.) in one or two positions;

– characters coded in two positions (Chinese, Japanese, kanji, etc.);

– etc.

We will thus have reduced the number of conditions and test cases to a manageable number.

Once the data are segregated in valid and invalid equivalence partitions, it may be necessary to analyze the data and break it down further into sub-partitions or sub-classes. To help us identify these sub-classes, we can use:

– ranges of data: a contiguous set where each value between the minimal and maximal value provide a result of the same type (valid or invalid depending);

– sets of data: where each data point in the group responds the same way, but where the data points do not need to be specifically contiguous;

– unique data points: there the data in the class are processed differently that all other partitions (such as zero in the square root of $1/x$ example $\sqrt[z]{1/x}$) or Boolean values;

– discrete values: where one specific value is mandatory or forbidden, such as the presence of a "@"character is forbidden in an SMTP email address or domain name (because the "@" character links the address to the domain name).

Equivalence partitions can also be applied to alphanumeric or time-related values (before or after an event). For alphanumeric values, partition identification can cover the way data are introduced (i.e. will a name with a leading or trailing space be considered identical as the same name without the space?) and the size of the variable.

4.3.1.1. *Testing with equivalence partitioning*

Equivalence partitioning applies to all input values and it may be necessary to process combination of input values to check the validity of the data. Equivalence partitioning can be used at all test levels: at component test level the variables will be single input or output variables; at component integration level we will look for interface data and messages; at system test level and acceptance test level we will mostly have input and output values related to business processes.

Testing invalid equivalence partitions is as necessary as testing valid equivalence partitions, even if the test of such partitions seem to have less value. For example, on commercial websites, it is necessary to ensure that the number of items ordered is a positive number and not a negative one. Purchase of a negative number of items would result in crediting the customer's credit card, instead of debiting that card. Such a defect led to a loss of more than 150,000 USD for a large online sales store before the defect was identified and fixed.

Testing of valid and invalid equivalence partitions is done, after selection of the test conditions; for all valid partitions a representative for each equivalence partition is selected; for each invalid partition a representative for a single invalid partition is selected and combined with representatives for all other valid partitions. This is to be able to anticipate the type of response expected (and thus create an effective test case). For example, if we select the date 14-21-0000, we are unable to anticipate the error message we must obtain (except for "incorrect date" of course), because we do not know which partition – i.e. day, month or year – will be processed before the other.

Testing equivalence partitioning is not limited to values, but can also cover size of variables. We can have the case of a 106-year-old person who was asked to justify absence from school, just because the age was limited to a two-digit field instead of a three-digit field, and was thus considered to be 6 years old instead of 106 years old.

We can note that equivalence partitioning does not cover the data at the edges (boundaries) of the partitions. This is because equivalence partition tests aim to identify defects applicable to a set or range of values, while boundary value analysis looks for defects at the edges of these equivalence partitions. Defects identified with each of these techniques are of a different nature. Using both techniques simultaneously can lead to missing certain defects, or mis-implementing either or both of these techniques. It is more reasonable to concentrate on one technique at a time and thus one type of defect at a time. Equivalence partitioning is a simple technique that serves as starting point for numerous techniques, including boundary value analysis.

Equivalence partitioning enables us to limit the number of test conditions implemented to a manageable amount of potential test values. When implementing tests, when we will need specific values as test case input data, we will select one representative from each of the equivalence partitions. We will determine the expected output values and thus be able to have both input and output data necessary for the creation of a correct test case.

4.3.1.2. *Limitations and assumptions*

The efficiency of equivalence partitioning depends on the correct identification of the different partitions for each of the variables. The principle is that all members of the partitions be processed the same way. This identification of the equivalence partitions (also called equivalence classes), depends on the knowledge by the tester of the application and business context. Thus, increasing the tester's knowledge of the application context will reduce the risk of incorrect use of the technique, and thus the risk of not identifying critical risks or executing redundant tests.

Splitting data in valid and invalid partitions is important. Partitioning that is too large (such as valid days in one partition of 1 to 31, instead of five partitions) will produce a reduced number of partitions and an increased risk of missing defects, or generating false-positive or false-negative results. An over-analysis and a separation into a larger number of partitions than required will increase the number of test cases for each variable and the combination of these test cases will be overwhelming.

Some values can be considered as similar to Boolean values, and thus require only two partitions (i.e. the gender of a person could be noted as M or F). However, the software could have default values (such as "space" or "null") that would correspond to a lack of information, and this does not correspond to either of the partitions, which may lead to incorrect values being stored and defects being missed. The test of these default values should be anticipated, sometimes as separate partitions.

Reliability management theories indicate that it is only seldom that a single defect causes the failure of a whole system; it is more commonly a combination of defects that causes the failures. Equivalence partitioning enables the identification of unique defects instead of combined defects, which will force us to use multiple techniques if we want to identify such combinations of defects.

4.3.1.3. *Advantages of equivalence partitioning*

Equivalence partitioning requires more time than the selection of previously problematic values (i.e. historic values that led to defects). When applied correctly, it:

– forces the tester to execute detailed analysis of the input and output data characteristics and values;

– increases efficiency of tests by a reduction of the number of test cases;

– provides clear evidence concerning the sub-sets of data tested and how they were tested (via traceability from specifications to test conditions);

– helps identify forgotten cases;

–systematically increases the efficiency of tests to reduce the remaining risks.

Equivalence partitioning is not a silver bullet, and its efficiency depends directly on the abilities of the testers and their knowledge of the context and of the system being tested.

4.3.2. *Boundary value analysis (FL 4.3.2)*

FLO-4.3.1 Write test cases from given software models using equivalence partitioning, boundary value analysis, decision tables and state transition diagrams/tables (K 3)

The way the software processes data at the edges of the equivalence partitions can be different from the expected behavior. Whether during specification or coding, problems frequently occur at the boundaries of the equivalence partitions.

A study of the boundary values is a well-known technique with the objective to analyze the behavior of the software at the edges of the partitions. If it is used with equivalence partitioning for linear variables, this technique can identify problems at the boundaries of previously identified partitions. We can use this technique to identify defects such as:

– incorrect use of relational operators ($<, >, =, \neq, \geq, \leq$),

– one-off errors with identified limits,

– problems in loops and iterations,

– incorrect types of variables (or variable size) used to store data,

– artificial constraints linked to data and types of variable.

Horsepower	Up to 5000 km	From 5001 to 20000 km	Over 20000 km
3 CV	d x 0,387	(d x 0,232) + 778	d x 0,271
4 CV	d x 0,466	(d x 0,262) + 1 020	d x 0,313
5 CV	d x 0,512	(d x 0,287) + 1 123	d x 0,343
6 CV	d x 0,536	(d x 0,301) + 1 178	d x 0,360
7 CV	d x 0,561	(d x 0,318)+ 1 218	d x 0,379
8 CV	d x 0,592	(d x 0,337) + 1 278	d x 0,401
9 CV	d x 0,607	(d x 0,352) + 1 278	d x 0,416
10 CV	d x 0,639	(d x 0,374) + 1 323	d x 0,440
11 CV	d x 0,651	(d x 0,392) + 1 298	d x 0,457
12 CV	d x 0,685	(d x 0,408) + 1 383	d x 0,477
13 CV and more	d x 0,697	(d x 0,424) + 1 363	d x 0,492
d represents the distance covered			

Figure 4.4. *Expense reimbursement for kilometers traveled in France in 2010 for tax purposes*

If we look at the table for expense reimbursement per kilometer traveled in France in 2010 (instruction 5 F-12-10 in Bulletin Officiel des Impôts n°37 dated March 22, 2010), presented in Figure 4.4 for each "puissance administrative" (administrative horsepower) we can identify three partitions: distance smaller or equal to 5,000 km, between 5,001 and smaller or equal to 20,000 km, and above 20,000 km.

A comparison of the boundary values of these partitions allows us to see that it may be interesting for taxpayers to declare 1 km more (or less) traveled by car. For instance, for a 5 CV vehicle, it is more economically efficient to declare a traveled distance of 5,000 km (i.e. 2,560 Euros of expenses to deduce from your income) instead of 5,001 km (2,558 Euros due to rounding). The same decision can be identified, for the same distance, for vehicles of 10, 12, and 13 horsepower. On the other hand, for other horsepower values, it is more interesting to declare 5,001 km instead of 5,000. This single kilometer gives you 3 Euros instead of a couple of cents otherwise. If we execute the same calculations at the boundaries around 20,000 kilometers, the same types of vehicles are penalized the same way.

Other boundary value examples can be applied for dates, such as the lack of year zero (the year of Jesus Christ's birth is considered as year "1"– 1 A.D. – and the year before as year "–1" or 1 B.C.), or for numeric values of variables (limitation of integer values in a 16-bit machine in the range –32,768 to +32,767) or the size of alphanumeric fields (smaller or not to 4,096 characters for example).

Another type of boundary value can be varying in the absolute, but constant at a moment in time (size of window in pixels, millimeters, or inches).

For valid ranges of values (linear equivalence partitions) identified previously with the equivalence partitioning technique, we can look at the behavior at the boundaries of these valid classes: we will talk of valid boundaries. We have also the ability to take values outside of the valid classes – in effect in invalid classes – and we will talk then of invalid boundary values. A formal definition of boundary value is "the value at the edge of a partition, or one increment on either side of that value", where "increment" is the smallest step between two contiguous values.

In our preceding example (square root of $1/x$), beyond the three partitions (or classes), we can identify the limits of the valid partition, that is – if variable x is an integer – the values MININT and MAXINT.

4.3.2.1. *Test with boundary values*

Values used for boundary value testing are part of equivalence partitions. There are two levels of coverage:

– weak coverage, where the limits is the boundary value and the smallest increment inside the equivalence partition; and

– strong coverage, where – beyond the values of weak coverage – the values at the smallest increment beyond the partition are also evaluated.

Strong coverage of boundary values corresponds of valid equivalence partitions is close to weak coverage of boundary values for all equivalence classes (valid and invalid).

Beyond boundary values of input value ranges, it is also important to test the loops inside the software, instructions such as "while", "until", and "for … next". This enables us to ensure that the first and last iterations of all loops are processed correctly (boundaries of the loops).

Vectors and matrix processing is also important, especially as some programming languages consider that a 15 element table (or vector) starts at zero and finishes at 14, or starts at 1 and finishes at 15 in other languages. A programmer switching from one language to another may easily get the pointers wrong.

4.3.2.2. *Limitations and assumptions*

Boundary value analysis is not applicable to Boolean values or finite list of values, but mostly to linear ranges.

When we execute boundary value analysis on equivalence partitions, the primary assumption is that the equivalence partitions identified are correct. If we incorrectly computed the equivalence partitions, we will of course find incorrect boundary values and potentially miss some defects.

As boundary value analysis is applicable after equivalence partition, all assumptions and limitations applicable to equivalence partitions are also applicable to boundary value analysis.

4.3.2.3. *Advantages of boundary values*

Boundary value analysis is a technique that applies at all test levels, and can require access to the code (for loops boundaries and variable types description). In general, boundary value analysis is executed after equivalence partitioning and applies to the values input via the application interfaces (both graphical and non-graphical interfaces).

Values in the equivalence partitions are sorted to identify the upper and lower boundaries of these partitions.

It is also possible to use this technique for non-functional, such as performances, load, stress, etc.

4.3.3. *Decision tables (FL 4.3.3)*

We have seen that equivalence partitions and boundary value analysis do not take into account interactions between variables, processing each variable independently. Most variables interact with one another, and these interactions lead to different actions. One solution would be to execute the Cartesian product of equivalence partitions (and of boundary values depending on what is required), to represent them in tables to analyze the result of the different combinations.

FLO-4.3.1 Write test cases from given software models using equivalence partitioning, boundary value analysis, decision tables, and state transition diagrams/tables (K 3)

Decision tables are an efficient way to capture a number of requirements or to represent the inner design of a software application. They can also be used to design test conditions and test cases. Decision tables are useful to represent complex management rules.

The decision table technique is extremely efficient and too seldom used in the industry.

Implementation of decision tables requires a number of phases:

1. Identification of the conditions and partitions associated with these conditions;

2. Computation of the number of combinations in the table and introduction of the data to fill in the identified combinations;

3. Verification of the possible combinations and reduction of combinations where it is possible;

4. Verification of the combination coverage;

5. Identification of results or resulting actions.

We will illustrate decision tables with an example: when is an individual allowed to drive a car on public streets in France, taking into account only the age, obtainment of the theoretical and practical exam, and the presence of an authorized accompanying adult in the case of learning to drive accompanied by a qualified driver. We will not take into account other criteria such as alcohol level, physical disabilities, or vehicle insurance, previous driving convictions, use of unauthorized substances, etc.

Identification of the conditions

The first aspect of the implementation of a decision table is the identification of the interacting conditions and rules. In our example the following conditions interact:

– age of the driver, with three associated partitions, namely:

   - age below 16 years old,

   - between 16 and 18 years old,

   - 18 years old or more;

– whether the driver successfully passed the theoretical exam (or not);

– whether the driving instructor or an authorized driver is present or absent;

– whether the individual successfully passed the practical driving exam.

Computation of the number of combinations and data input

The number of combinations is easy to compute:

– three partitions for age

– two partitions for theoretical exam: obtained Yes or No

– two partitions for the presence of the authorized driver: present Yes or No

– two partitions for the practical and thus driving license: obtained Yes or No.

For a total of 24 combinations ($3 \times 2 \times 2 \times 2$).

	01	02	03	04	05	06	07	08	09	10	11	12	13	14	15	16	17	18	19	20	21	22	23	24
Age A:<16 16<B<18 C: 18	A	A	A	A	A	A	A	A	B	B	B	B	B	B	B	B	C	C	C	C	C	C	C	C
Theory OK?	O	O	O	O	N	N	N	N	O	O	O	O	N	N	N	N	O	O	O	O	N	N	N	N
Accompanying driver present?	O	O	N	N	O	O	N	N	O	O	N	N	O	O	N	N	O	O	N	N	O	O	N	N
License obtained?	O	N	O	N	O	N	O	N	O	N	O	N	O	N	O	N	O	N	O	N	O	N	O	N
Driving authorized?	N (a)	N (a)	N (a)	N (a)	N (a)	N (a)	N (a)	N (a)	N (b)	O	N (b)	N	N (b)	N (d)	N (b)	N (d)	O	O	O	N	N (c)	N (d)	N (c)	N (d)

Table 4.2. *Expanded decision table*

The decision table will thus have 24 columns and five lines (one per condition plus one per action) as described in Table 4.2.

Introduction of the actions, that is the last line, allows us to determine the result of the combination of conditions. Different cases can be identified:

1. When driving is not allowed due to non-fulfillment of the pre-requisite for the theoretical exam, and driving accompanied with an authorized driver (or not);

2. Cases when driving accompanied by an authorized driver is possible;

3. Cases when driving accompanied or not is possible;

4. Theoretically impossible cases due to applicable legal pre-requisites.

Verification of the possible combinations and reduction of combinations where possible

Some combinations are not possible:

– all combinations (a) where the age is below 16 years old are impossible, we can thus group these eight columns in a single one without losing any coverage level. This allows us to go from 24 to 17 columns;

– all combinations (b) where the driving license is obtained and the age is below 18 years old are impossible because of the law stating that the exam can only be taken by someone 18 years old or above. This allows us to combine these columns into a single one;

– all combinations (c) where the theoretical exam has not been obtained and where the practical exam has been obtained are likewise impossible as success at the theoretical exam is a pre-requisite for the practical driving exam. This would allow us to merge these columns into a single one;

– all combinations (d) where the age is not important if the theoretical exam and practical exam have not been obtained, whether an authorized accompanying driver is present or not.

We see that the combination verification and reduction phase allows us to reduce these 24 combinations to a significantly more reduced number. These different applicable combination reductions sometimes apply to the same columns.

	01	09	10	12	14	17	18	19	20	21
Age A: <16 16<B<18 C: 18	A	B	B	B	–	C	C	C	C	C
Theory OK?	–	–	Y	Y	N	Y	Y	Y	Y	N
Accompanying driver present?	–	–	Y	N	–	Y	Y	N	N	–
License obtained?	–	Y	N	N	N	Y	N	Y	N	Y
Driving authorized?	N (a)	N (b)	Y	N	N (d)	Y	Y	Y	N	N (c)
Weight	8	4	1	1	4	1	1	1	1	2

Table 4.3. *Reduced decision table*

Reduction of combinations applies only for columns where applicable conditions and results are identical. Non-applicable conditions (i.e. conditions where the result does not matter) are replaced by "–" in these combinations. We keep only one column representing the combination and remove all other columns with this combination, taking care to note the weight of this combination (the sum of the combined columns). The weight of each non-combined column is "1".

Verification of combination coverage

The sum of the weight of all remaining columns in the decision table must remain equal to the number of combinations computed previously. This allows us to make sure that we covered all combinations.

In the example above (Table 4.3), the sum of the weights in the last line, valued at 24, corresponds to the number of identified columns when computing the number of possible combinations. This comparison allows verification that you have not forgotten columns and enables us to select the columns to test first (those with the largest weight, to be most efficient).

Identification of results or resulting actions

In some cases the actions planned can be ambiguous or undefined. It is then necessary to turn towards the stakeholders at the origin of the specification to identify the expected behavior.

4.3.3.1. *Testing with decision tables*

Designing test conditions with the decision table technique enables reduction of the number of test cases that need to be designed – after reduction of the number of columns in the decision table – without reducing the coverage of the equivalence partitions identified.

This method allows identification of combinations of conditions that might not have been foreseen by the software design team.

4.3.3.2. *Limitations and assumptions*

Assumptions associated with decision tables focus mostly on the correct identification of the equivalence partitions and values to take into account. A second assumption is the impact of unique defects instead of combined defects. As we usually only take into account valid partitions, the impact of defects on invalid partitions and combination of invalid partitions is not assessed, and defects could remain after implementation of this test design technique.

In terms of limitations, the number of columns and lines quickly becomes important if we combine all equivalence partitions for all variables and if we add the boundary values.

4.3.3.3. *Advantages of decision tables*

This method is useful for complex management rules as it combines equivalence partitions, identification of boundary values, and uses these techniques as inputs for test case design.

The present author used decision tables with up to 216 columns to model complex management rules to identify potential failure in the processes of an aerospace project. This allowed identification of three failure states that had not been previously identified.

4.3.4. **Other combinational techniques**

Testing all combinations of values for all variables (combination of all equivalence partitions for all variables) leads to an enormous number of test cases, which are impossible to execute in a reasonable time frame. It is thus necessary to use other, quicker techniques.

Beyond decision tables, other techniques can be applied to combinations of values:

– n-tuples testing, where pairs (or n-tuples) of values are tested simultaneously;

– orthogonal arrays.

Test of n-tuples: this technique is used to reduce the combinatorial explosion of decision tables and is based on the assumption that it is the interaction of pairs (or n-tuples if there are more than two variables) of values – valid or invalid – that lead to defects. This allows reduction of the combinations by only testing pairs (or n-tuples) of values. The principal assumption is that the necessary combination to identify defects is n and not n+1.

Orthogonal arrays testing: this technique is based on a statistical selection of data vectors (arrays), each having values that are different from all other vectors. Statistically, all the equivalence partitions are thus covered by the sum of values present in the different arrays, which allows you to cover a very large combination of input values (equivalence partitions) with a limited number of test cases, and thus cover all partitions with a reduced number of test cases. The principal drawback of this method is that the coverage of the range of values, more precisely the combination of each type of input value with the other types of input value, is not guaranteed (and thus defects could be missed).

For a more detailed analysis of these techniques, which are not part of the ISTQB foundation level exams, see [COP 03, pp.66-91].

4.3.5. *State transition testing (FL 4.3.4)*

FLO-4.3.1 Write test cases from given software models using equivalence partitioning, boundary value analysis, decision tables, and state transition diagrams/tables (K 3)

Many systems and electronic components have a number of stable states and transitions from one stable state to another stable state. These machines are called "finite state machines". State transition testing is based on the fact that the same action will give different results depending on the initial state for this action. This reasoning can apply for physical and logical systems, as well as for state of transactions. The actions that lead from one state to another are called transitions. It should be noted that transitions do not have to modify the state of the system.

This technique is based on the following steps:

– identify the different stable states of the system, including temporary states, including the initial and final states;

– for each state, identify the transactions, events, conditions, and actions that can be executed in this state;

– model the system as a graph (or drawing) or as a table, in order to use it as oracle;

– for each combination of state, event, and condition, verify the actions and resulting states.

The advantage of this technique is that the model defined can be as detailed or as generic as necessary. Where a part of the system is more important (or more complex), it is possible to model that part in more detail; where the system is less important, it is possible to use a lower level of detail.

Identification of the valid states and transitions allows identification of invalid or non-authorized transitions from that state. It is thus possible to verify that the possible actions from that state do not allow execution of invalid transactions. Identification of invalid transitions and actions must be envisaged to ensure that such transitions and states are indeed impossible.

Analysis of valid and invalid transitions, from all possible states of a system enables the design of test conditions, and sometimes identification of transitions that were not anticipated.

We will use the following means of representation to show the state diagrams and state transitions:

– a state is represented as a circle or oval: State

– a transition from one state to another is represented by an arrow going from the initial state to the resulting state (which can be the same as the initial state), with a description of the action executed, whether it is a manual action or an automated (i.e. system) action: 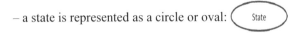 Transition

– the initial state is identified by an arrow to that state that comes from a point outside the graph:

– the representation of the final state is obtained by an arrow that leaves that state to reach a circle:

To illustrate the principle of state diagrams, we can use the example of a telephone with handset and dial. If we want to test all transitions and all states, we must first identify all states and all actions that can be executed from each of these states. We have a number of easily identifiable states such as "idle" and "in conversation", "numbering", etc. It is possible to identify temporary states that must exist based on the way the system works, such as the state "verify number validity" which, when a new digit is entered, checks whether the number is valid or not. This state must exist to explain how we can reach valid phone numbers with two, three, eight, or more digits.

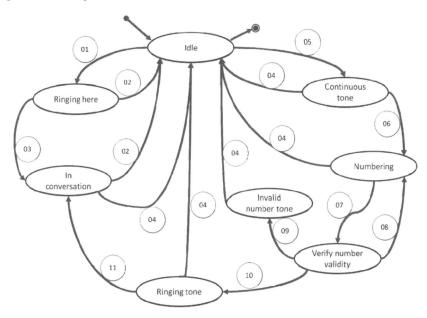

Figure 4.5. *State transition diagram for a telephone*

We can identify the following state transitions:

01 Reception of a call, which leads to the transition from "Idle" state to "Ringing here" state;

02 The caller can hang up, which brings us back to the "Idle" state, whether the handset was picked up or not;

03 We can pick up the handset, which brings us to the "In conversation" state;

04 We can hang up the handset, leading us to the "Idle" state, and this action can be executed from a large number of states;

05 We can pick up the handset, going from the "Idle" state to the "Continuous tone", which indicates the set is waiting for us to enter a number;

06 Entering the first digit enables us to pass from the "Continuous tone" state to the "Numbering" state, whereby the "Continuous tone" disappears;

07 Is the introduction of additional digits, which leads us to the temporary state "Verify number validity";

08 Allows us to return from "Verify number validity" state to "Numbering" state to introduce additional digits;

09 Moves us from "Verify number validity" state to the "Invalid number tone" signifying that the number dialed is invalid (i.e. does not correspond to a valid phone number);

10 Moves us from the "Verify number validity" state to "Ringing tone", where the phone rings at the correspondent's location;

11 Transitions us from the "Ringing tone" state to the "In conversation" state.

If we want to exhaustively test this system, go through each state and each transition, we will have to go from the "Idle" state via other states back to the "Idle" state.

This will give us the nine possible sequences described hereafter (A, B, C, D, E, F, G, H, J) that can be represented in a table format (Table 4.4) or in graph form (Figure 4.6).

Ref	Current state	Event	Action	Resulting state
A	Idle	01 Reception of a call	Start ringing	Ringing here
A	Ringing here	03 Pickup handset	Initiate the conversation	In conversation
A	In conversation	04 We hang up	Terminate call	Idle
B	Idle	01 Reception of a call	Start ringing	Ringing here
B	Ringing here	03 Pickup handset	Initiate the conversation	In conversation
B	In conversation	02 Caller hangs up	Terminate call	Idle

Ref	Current state	Event	Action	Resulting state
C	Idle	01 Reception of a call	Start ringing	Ringing here
C	Ringing here	02 Caller hangs up	Terminate call	Idle
D	Idle	05 We pick up handset	--	Continuous tone
D	Continuous tone	04 We hang up	Terminate call	Idle
E	Idle	05 We pick up handset	--	Continuous tone
E	Continuous tone	06 First digit	Initialize number	Numbering
E	Numbering	04 We hang up	Terminate call	Idle
F	Idle	05 We pick up handset	--	Continuous tone
F	Continuous tone	06 First digit	Initialize number	Numbering
F	Numbering	07 Next digit	Concatenate digit to number	Verify number validity
F	Verify number validity	09 Invalid number	--	Invalid number tone
F	Invalid number tone	04 We hang up	Terminate call	Idle
G	Idle	05 We pick up handset	--	Continuous tone
G	Continuous tone	06 First digit	Initialize number	Numbering
G	Numbering	07 Next digit	Concatenate digit to number	Verify number validity
G	Verify number validity	08 Wait for next digit	--	Numbering
G	Numbering	07 Next digit	Concatenate digit to number	Verify number validity
G	Verify number validity	10 Valid number	Start the call	Ringing tone
G	Ringing tone	04 We hang up	Terminate call	Idle
H	Idle	05 We pick up handset	--	Continuous tone
H	Continuous tone	06 First digit	Initialize number	Numbering
H	Numbering	07 Next digit	Concatenate digit to number	Verify number validity

Ref	Current state	Event	Action	Resulting state
H	Verify number validity	08 Wait for next digit	--	Numbering
H	Numbering	07 Next digit	Concatenate digit to number	Verify number validity
H	Verify number validity	10 Valid number	Start the call	Ringing tone
H	Ringing tone	11 We pick up handset	Initiate the conversation	In conversation
H	In conversation	04 We hang up	Terminate call	Idle
J	Idle	05 We pick up handset	--	Continuous tone
J	Continuous tone	06 First digit	Initialize number	Numbering
J	Numbering	07 Next digit	Concatenate digit to number	Verify number validity
J	Verify number validity	08 Wait for next digit	--	Numbering
J	Numbering	07 Next digit	Concatenate digit to number	Verify number validity
J	Verify number validity	10 Valid number	Start the call	Ringing tone
J	Ringing tone	11 We pick up handset	Initiate the conversation	In conversation
J	In conversation	02 Caller hangs up	Terminate call	Idle

Table 4.4. *State transition table representation*

To this table we can add test case references and traceability information that will enable us to provide follow-up information to control test activities. This table can also be used as an input table for an automated test tool that would execute each action and check the resulting state (oracle).

The different states and transitions can be represented in a graphical form as shown below (Figure 4.6):

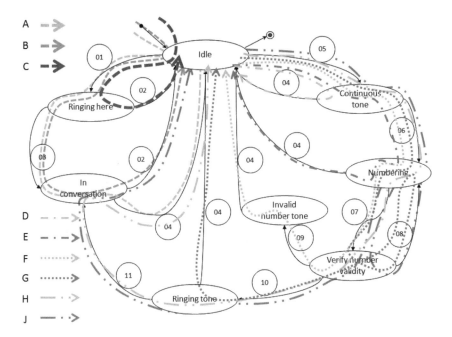

Figure 4.6. *State transition diagram*

4.3.5.1. *Testing with state transition*

A graphical representation of states and transitions quickly becomes cluttered and difficult to visualize if the graph has too many states or transitions. It is then necessary to group many different sub-states and their transitions in separate graphs showing the operation of the sub-system, with its inputs and outputs. The higher-level graph is thus simplified.

A table representation enables a simpler tracing of tests and better control of test process, and can simplify representation when there are numerous states and transitions.

To identify potentially forgotten actions, it is possible to explore the system by trying all possible actions at all the possible states. Unidentified transactions should then be impossible (and if not should be reported and evaluated).

4.3.5.2. *Limitations and assumptions*

The main assumptions with state transition testing are that we have identified all states and all transitions. Any possible "un-identified" state or transition can lead to potential defects being left for the customer to find.

State diagrams and state transitions are useful tools to capture some types of requirements, specifically those applicable to states and associate transitions between states, because they allow identification of transitions and states to test. We have seen that some states can be identified as necessary, even if they are not formally identified.

State transition graphs are not applicable to stateless systems.

4.3.5.3. *Advantages of state transition testing*

State transition testing allows testers to become familiar with the software or system and to design tests representing valid and invalid processing.

State graphs and state transition graphs can also help design the system, identifying unplanned states during design, or unplanned combinations of actions or transitions. It can thus be used as an exploration tool.

We can extrapolate the states of a real-time system to represent the states of a document or of transactions, and thus use this method to test non-real-time systems such as workflows and processes.

4.3.6. *Use case testing (FL 4.3.5)*

Use cases are a representation of the expected behavior of a system as it should respond to the requests of users external to the system. The level of modeling detail can vary for use cases, which usually involves transactions from initiation until termination, and includes other factors besides the system, such as sub-systems or other software applications.

The sum of all the use cases is used to describe the way the system or software works. This is the case in agile development methods when specifications are provided in the form of use cases or user stories.

FLO-4.3.3 Explain the concept of use case testing and its benefits (K 2)

Use case testing is a technique that can identify a sequence of transactions within a system. This is similar to a sequence of directed state transitions, where the transitions are executed by actors – human or not – from one initial state of the system to the end (resulting) state. Contrary to the state diagrams and state transitions, use cases focus more on user functionalities at the system level instead of at the sub-system level.

The principle is to identify the actors – human or system software – that interact by providing input and output information in response to each user action (transition). Users' interactions with the system or the software are sequential steps, gathered in scenarios.

Let us study two types of use cases:

– business use cases, which represent the system as a black box, and identifies the user actions with a terminology similar to the one used in their business. This representation will describe a process that provides added value to the user and describes what the process does or generates;

– system use cases, describing the system (or software) in terms of technical functionalities, specifying functions, services, and sub-systems provided, and thus what the system will do in response to actor's solicitations.

Some modeling languages – such as UML (unified modeling language) – are used to represent the transactions and the actors. UML is used to model and document software in a standard way and allows visualization of the main components of the system architecture.

4.3.6.1. *Testing with use cases*

Testing with use cases is frequently done by defining a number of nominal cases, corresponding to nominal operation of the system of software and authorized use cases. This represents about 60% of the cases. It will then be necessary to derive scenarios or extensions corresponding to degraded operation, or possible fault patterns, based on variations of nominal operation.

One of the major components in use cases is the selection of test data. We could use techniques previously mentioned (equivalence partitions or boundary values, or even decision tables) to select test values.

Use cases can be grouped in scenarios. It is recommended that at least one test from each main scenario (nominal use cases) is included to make sure that the software or system functionalities are validated. Depending on the criticality of the software (its integrity level) the other scenarios, corresponding to degraded operation, should be tested if they can lead the system or software to a critical state.

Use case representation can be identical to state transition.

4.3.6.2. *Limitations and assumptions*

As use cases are similar to the way users will interact with the system, this technique is frequently used during acceptance tests.

This test technique is usable wherever user transactions are clearly defined. If transactions are not correctly defined, it is impossible to correctly identify all valid or invalid use cases and acceptance tests could be refused by the users and customers. As these tests are executed at the end of the test campaign, and at the end of the development phase, the costs might be huge.

It is clear that it is impossible to exercise all combinations of use cases and valid and invalid data, thus it is important not to overestimate the quality of the software or system after using this technique: a large number of defects may remain hidden.

4.3.6.3. *Advantages of use case testing*

Use cases are readily comprehensible by users, and thus are frequently used during acceptance tests, and during system tests. They can be the basis of automation techniques such as action words and keyword-driven testing.

Use cases are also used when creating requirements and specifications. It is an approach that allows implication of users in requirement gathering and process definition.

4.3.7. *Limitations and assumptions*

During tests based on specifications and on requirements, we evaluate the software with reference to the specifications, requirements, or documentation and we do not question these inputs. The main assumption is thus that the specifications and requirements are correct. If, for any reason, this assumption is not true, the quality of the tests and of the software will be impacted.

4.4. Structure-based techniques (FL 4.4)

Beyond activities based on functionalities and specifications, representing the system as a black box, we have the possibility to test it by designing tests based on the structure and source code of the software or system to test.

These activities require programming knowledge, limited to the ability to read and understand the programs, languages, and the programming techniques used. The tester is not required to be able to correct or design code during the ISTQB certification exams.

Software programs and systems are made up of executable instructions (source code) that can be translated (compiled or interpreted) by the computer. The executed code (object code) is written in a binary language that the computer understands. Developers and testers focus only on the source code.

A software source code is thus made up of executable instructions: operators and verbs of action and variables on which those verbs apply. It is recommended that non-executable comments (in natural language) are included in the source code to document the code and explain the purpose of specific parts of the software.

Some instructions allow comparison between values or variables and the result of this comparison will cause the software to continue its execution differently depending on the result of these comparisons. The actual comparison will occur during software execution. The graphical representation of such instructions (called decisions) is drawn as a lozenge and the possible results – branches issued from the decision – are represented by the links that exit from the lozenge.

Figure 4.7. *Representation of a decision*

Instructions without decisions are represented by rectangles. To ease representation, if more than one instruction follows another without any branching instruction (without any decision), they are represented by a single rectangle.

Figure 4.8. *Representation of instructions*

Program representation, called control flow, can be different depending on the habits of the programmers, and is frequently used to define the program algorithms. We can represent the code in Figure 4.9 by one of the two control flow representations of Figure 4.10.

```
int factorial (int x) {
    int result = -1;
    if (z >= 0) {
        result = 1;
        for (int i=2; i <= z; i++) {
            result = result * i;
        }
    } else {
    }
    return result;
}
```

Figure 4.9. *Code of function "Factorial"*

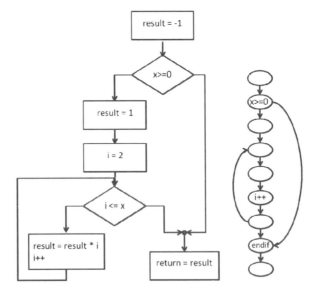

Figure 4.10. *Control flow for function "factorial"*

4.4.1. *Statement testing and coverage (FL 4.4.1)*

FLO-4.4.1 Describe the concept and value of code coverage (K 2)

When executing tests based on the structure of the software, the principal concept is to verify each and every executable instruction (instructions and decisions) and, assuming they are all correct, the software is considered correct.

For this we shall simulate the execution of the instructions and verify which instructions are executed by the control flow for the software. This will enable us to identify the necessary values for the different variables so that we can cover each of the instructions.

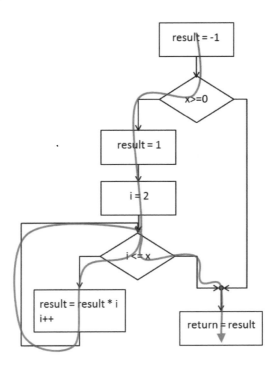

Figure 4.11. *Instruction coverage*

We see that instruction coverage for Figure 4.9 gives us the graph in Figure 4.11. This graph shows us that for variable "x" we must have a value that is greater or equal to zero, which will lead us to the left-hand branch, so that we can initialize the variable "result" (result=1) and the "for" loop that includes initialization of counter "i" and, depending on the result of the comparison between "i" and "x" the execution of the multiplication of the value of "result" by "i" and the storage of the result in variable "result".

In the graph of Figure 4.11, the lack of instructions on the right-hand side of the first decision (x≥0), allows us not to consider this branch.

We can thus go through the control flow with a single path and cover all the instructions.

We can understand that the level of coverage of the software is relatively low, and that it might be important to also cover "empty" branches.

4.4.1.1. *Testing with instruction coverage*

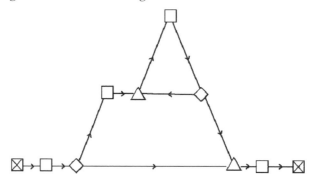

Figure 4.12. *Control flow – horizontal representation*

In order to design new tests with the instruction coverage technique, it is necessary to correctly model the software control flow. This can be done manually by the tester, requiring the ability to read and understand programming languages, or the development team can provide the control flow – if it was designed – or automated tools can be used to analyze the control flow and present it in a graphical format. The representation can then be presented as in Figure 4.12, where triangles represent the end of decisions ("if" instructions), the place where the two alternatives merge and the program control flow continues as a single flow.

Analysis of the code (or instruction) coverage during program execution frequently requires the introduction of additional instructions – traces – that will identify the sections of the code that have been executed. This activity, called instrumentation, will:

– slow down code execution, because more instructions will have to be executed;

– complicate the fixing of defects in the code because:

- if the code that includes these tracing instructions is a copy of the reference code, both the reference code and the copy need to be fixed;

- if the instrumentation was generated automatically from the reference code, the reference code will have to be fixed, then the instrumented code must be regenerated.

```
10 ...                          A ──
20 if a>0 {x=x+1 ;}  B ········
30 if b>0 {y=y+1 ;}  C ─·─
40   ...                        D ───ı

10 ...
20 if a>0 then {x=x+1 ;}
25 endif
30 if b>0 then {y=y+1 ;}
35 endif
40   ...
```

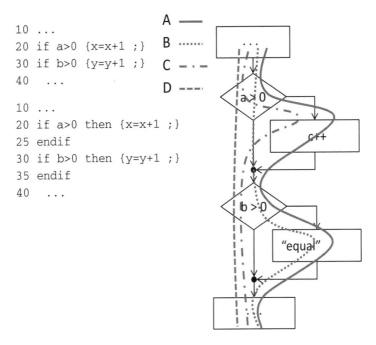

Figure 4.13. *Example of alternatives*

Decisions can be represented differently depending on the programming language and on the presence or lack of alternatives. In Figure 4.13, the two portions of code represent the same thing, even if in the first section the "then" instructions are not present and if in the second section the "endif" instructions are present to identify the end of the "if" instructions. Some simple rules enable the identification of the end of instructions or groups of instructions. Depending on the language, the instructions in a branch are grouped between brackets ({ ... }), preceded or not – for the first alternative by a "then" instruction.

The second alternative is preceded by the instruction "else", which can be absent if there is no second alternative. If a second alternative is present, it is important to identify the place where this second alternative ends and normal program execution resumes. This is sometimes identified by an "endif" instruction, or by the closing bracket of the alternative (}). In Figure 4.13, the two instructions from the first portion of the code and the four lines of the second portion of the code are translated by the four paths (A, B, C, D) that represent the combination of each possible alternative.

To reach 100% instruction coverage (also called code coverage), only path A is required. Thus, we understand that we may need a more complete coverage measure than simple instruction coverage.

4.4.1.2. *Limitations and assumptions*

Two main assumptions impact all structure base tests:

– the assumption that the source code reflects what the specifications requested, and do not include extraneous instructions (Easter egg), nor lack any necessary instruction;

– the analysis does not limit itself to an evaluation of the structure of the code (its architecture) but also includes evaluation of the decisions and their relationships with one another.

We could have the code Figure 4.14.

```
05 ...
10 if a = b {
15                 Call Function_A ;
20                 } else {
25     if a < b {
30                 Call Function_B ;
35                 } else {
40       if a > b {
45                 Call Function_C ;
50                 } else {
55                 Call Function_D ;
60                 }
65   ...
```

Figure 4.14. *Linked conditions*

To have complete instruction coverage, we would need to have four test cases as described in Figure 4.15. However, if path D seems possible, it will never be executed because the three decisions are mutually exclusive (a is either equal, or smaller or larger than b) and the call to Function D will never occur.

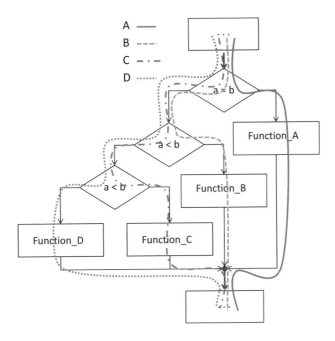

Figure 4.15. *Control flow for linked conditions*

Other limitations acting on the structure, and thus the aspects of instruction coverage, apply for object-oriented languages where there are classes of objects and functions (methods) that are associated with them. These functions can be inherited at code execution, and undergo modification during these inheritance (polymorphism). As a polymorphism is executed in real time, the code that is effectively never executed was instrumented and the information received by instrumentation may not correspond to the actual execution.

Another set of important limitations is that most of the error conditions (such as those associated with potential hardware errors) are difficult to implement in practice. They represent exceptional problems such as a lack of internal memory, or of disk space, unreadable files, lost connections, etc. These exceptions are difficult – or even impossible – to simulate and thus could very well remain untested. It would thus be in these cases that the software would have unexpected – because untested – behaviors. Tools[2] exist to intercept some of these system calls and simulate exception conditions.

---

2 Such as [HOL] available freely with [WHI 03].

4.4.1.3. Advantages of instruction coverage

Instruction coverage enables testers to have, via code instrumentation and execution of planned functional test cases, an evaluation of the coverage level reached by the tests designed using black-box techniques. This allows the design of additional tests to exercise areas of the software that were not executed and thus increase the level of coverage. Another important aspect is the ability to identify dead code, i.e. code that will never be executed, or identify infinite loops. This can lead to software fixes.

Instruction coverage is required in the aerospace industry for all software where a failure would have major consequences (Category C software according to DO178B standard).

4.4.2. Decision testing and coverage (FL 4.4.2)

FLO-4.4.2 Explain the concepts of statement and decision coverage, and give reasons why these concepts can also be used at test levels other than component testing (e.g. on business procedures at system level) (K 2)

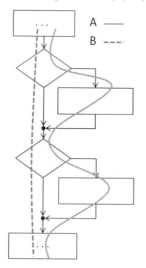

Figure 4.16. *Branch coverage*

It may be necessary to cover empty branches of decisions. Figure 4.16 shows us that instead of a single test case, it is necessary to have a minimum of two test cases

(A and B) to cover all the branches. This will cover alternatives that were not covered with instruction coverage.

4.4.2.1. *Testing with branch and decision coverage*

Instead of only exercising branches with instructions, we will take each of the "true" and "false" alternatives (branches) of each decision, whether or not there are instructions in these branches. We will thus have a more important number of test cases.

Instructions, such as "case of", will have one test for each possible exit as displayed in Figure 4.17.

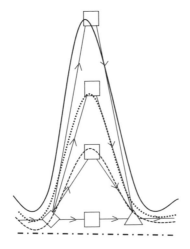

Figure 4.17. *Control flow instruction "case of"*

Decision coverage and branch coverage is identical as there are as many branches as there are decisions.

4.4.2.2. *Cyclomatic complexity*

Branch coverage (Figure 4.16) does not correspond to the coverage of the combinations of branches, called path coverage (shown in Figure 4.13).

The analysis of all the independent paths of a graph enables us to establish a level of complexity for the architecture of the graph. This complexity is called the "cyclomatic number"[3], or cyclomatic complexity, and is computed according to the following formula:

$$M=v(G)=e-n+2\times p.$$

where:

$V(G)$ is the cyclomatic number for graph G

e is the number of edges

n is the number of nodes

p is the number of connected components of the graph (usually 1).

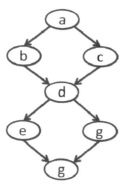

Figure 4.18. *Control flow with two conditions*

In Figure 4.18, formula computation would give $e=8$, $n=7$, $p=1$, and $M=8-7+2\times1=3$. This number is equal to the number of binary decisions plus 1. This cyclomatic number can also is computed as the number of enclosed regions of the graph after the extremities of the graph have been linked together. In Figure 4.18, linking node 'g' to node 'a' will create an additional enclosed region, and a cyclomatic number of 3.

Complexity analysis enables the computation of the number of independent non-recursive paths that can, in a linearly combination, generate all possible paths in a software component. This complexity is used at two levels:

– for maintainability analysis of the source code, as any increase in complexity will have an impact on code maintainability. It is recommended not to have a cyclomatic value above 10 to keep the code readable and understandable. (Note,

---

3 Introduced by McCabe in 1976.

however, that it does not change the cyclomatic value of a complex algorithm if this complex algorithm is split into smaller components); and

– to evaluate the number of test cases required to cover the control flow graph for this software. This enables evaluation of the number of test cases – designed by a sub-contractor to cover all the paths of a software – that are coherent or not. If it is close to the cyclomatic number, it is possible that all paths have been covered.

A detailed analysis of the cyclomatic number is available in [KAN 03, pp. 315-318]

4.4.2.3. *Limitations and assumptions*

Assumptions and limitations associated with branch coverage and decisions are similar to the assumptions and limitations associated with instruction coverage.

The assumptions associated with the cyclomatic number, branch coverage, and decision coverage are linked to the content of the decisions (the conditions) and whether these conditions are linked or not. If conditions (and decisions) are linked, it is clear that some branches will not be executed.

4.4.2.4. *Advantages of branch and decision coverage*

The advantages of branch coverage and decision coverage are the same as those for instruction coverage. As branch coverage and decision coverage are more complete that instruction coverage, the evaluation of the number of paths can allow an estimation of the workload required to design and execute the test cases on this section of the software.

Branch coverage and decision coverage automatically ensure that instruction coverage is attained. The opposite is not true: instruction coverage does not guarantee decision coverage or branch coverage.

Decision coverage is required in the aerospace industry for all software where a failure would have dangerous consequences (Category B software).

4.4.3. *Other structure-based techniques (FL 4.4.3)*

FLO-4.4.3 Write test cases from given control flows using statement and decision test design techniques (K 3)

We have seen that the combination of each of the branches from every decision allows the design of different paths. This is also the case when the software includes loops and iterations. In this case, each iteration or loop can be executed once, or any number of times up to the maximum number of iterations possible. This level of coverage, called path coverage, is more complete than branch coverage, and is usually unattainable except for trivially simple programs.

4.4.3.1. *Decisions and conditions*

Decisions are the result of true/false instructions that include conditions. These conditions can be simple:

```
if a = b then x=x+y;
```

or more complex:

```
if (a = b) or (c > d) then y=x+2
```

In the second decision, we have two conditions (a=b) and (c>d) each of which can be true or false independently. A combination of the results from each of these conditions will determine the result (true or false) of the decision, and thus the branch that the software will execute.

There are four logical operators when analyzing complex conditions:

– AND, where both conditions must be true for the result to be true,

– OR, where one of the two conditions must be true for the result to be true,

– XOR (exclusive OR) where one – and only one – of the condition must be true for the result to be true,

– NOT (negation) that is the negation of a condition and inverts the result.

A combination of the logical operators and the use of parenthesis to ensure that conditions are processed in a correct order enables testers to design decision tables and anticipate the result.

Conditions				
Condition 1 (Cond.1)	T	T	F	F
Condition 2 (Cond.2)	T	F	T	F
Cond.1 AND Cond.2	T	F	F	F
Cond.1 OR Cond.2	T	T	T	F
Cond.1 XOR Cond.2	F	T	T	F
NOT (Cond.1 AND Cond.2)	F	T	T	T
NOT (Cond.1 OR Cond.2)	F	F	F	T
NOT (Cond.1 XOR Cond.2)	T	F	F	T

Figure 4.19. *Boolean decision table*

Figure 4.19 shows the results obtained when two conditions (Cond.1 and Cond.2) are compared and the resulting decision.

Decision coverage executes each decision in true and false, and condition coverage executes each condition in true and false. Depending on the combination of conditions used, the coverage can be identical or not. In Figure 4.20, we can see that the paths A and D simultaneously fulfill decision and condition coverage, while paths B and C only provide condition coverage but not decision coverage.

4.4.4. MC/DC coverage (FL 4.4.3)

As we have seen above, condition and decision coverage are not identical.

If we use the sum of all conditions and all decisions, the number of test case to execute would be too large. A hybrid coverage type has been designed: modified condition and decision coverage (MC/DC).

The principle of this type of coverage covers all paths and decisions, by having coverage of each decision (corresponding to branch coverage) and coverage of each condition. Constraints are that (a) each entry point and exit point is covered, and (b) that each condition within a decision demonstrates its impact on the result of the decision.

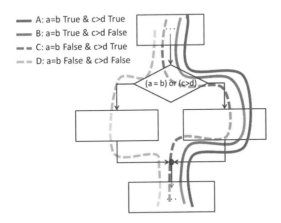

Figure 4.20. *Decision and condition coverage*

In Figure 4.20, MC/DC is obtained with paths A and D, or with paths B, C, and D. In the first instance, paths B and C are extraneous; in the second instance, paths B and C cover the conditions and path D covers the remaining decision.

4.4.4.1. *Testing with MC/DC*

Selection of the test cases (and test data for variables) to reach 100% MC/DC requires 100% decision coverage for each decision in the software module, then you must demonstrate that each condition that may independently impact on the result has been covered. A condition impacts the result of the decision if, by varying only the result of that condition and keeping the value of the other conditions constant, the result of the decision is able to be changed.

4.4.4.2. *Limitations and assumptions*

Testing a software structure with 100% MC/DC generates a heavy testing workload, and should be reserved for critical or complex code sections.

This type of structural coverage is also impacted by all hypotheses associated with structural coverage.

Moreover, MC/DC, like all structural coverage, only takes into account the conditions and decision. Equivalence partitions required to ensure the quality of the instructions are not covered because these instructions do not influence the decisions or conditions. Thus the instruction "$y=\text{sqrt}(1/x)$", which requires a minimum of three test cases ("x" positive, negative or equal to zero) is considered to be adequately covered by a single value, whether the coverage level is instruction or code coverage, branch or decision coverage, condition or MC/DC.

4.4.4.3. *Advantages of MC/DC*

MC/DC is required in the aerospace industry for any software where a failure could have catastrophic consequences (Category A software). Because of the required effort needed to reach MC/DC, it should be limited – in an industrial context – to software modules that are critical and of limited size.

4.4.5. *Limitations and assumptions of structure-based testing*

When executing tests based on structure, we will identify defects directly from the structure of the software. We will not compare the software to the requirements, specifications, or other documentation. The hypothesis is that the code we evaluate corresponds to what the developer should have designed.

4.4.6. *Coverage level and exit criteria*

FLO-4.4.4 Assess statement and decision coverage for completeness with respect to defined exit criteria (K 4)

Evaluation of exit criteria in the frame of structure based tests requires many evaluations:

– what is required in terms of coverage level? Instruction coverage, decision or branch coverage, conditions coverage, or MC/DC will have an impact on the number of tests to execute and thus on the workload;

– what should be covered? Depending on the software and its context, it may occur that the exit criteria are less stringent than regulatory requirements;

– have we identified all the instructions that must be included or understood as decisions or conditions? Decisions are not limited to "IF – THEN – ELSE" but include "WHILE", "UNTIL", "FOR – NEXT", "CASE – OF", etc. Conditions can include exclusive "OR", and "AND" based on identical results (true when both conditions are identical).

It is necessary to know the differences and similarities of structure-based techniques, to clearly identify the important aspects and understand the impact they can have on the exit criteria.

It is also necessary to keep in mind the different hypotheses and assumptions associated with structure-based techniques, so as not to assume – erroneously – completion of exit criteria.

4.5. Experience-based techniques (FL 4.5)

FLO-4.5.1 Recall reasons for writing test cases based on intuition, experience, and knowledge about common defects (K 1)

Recently, experience-based techniques have gained in acceptance as they allow identification of defects without requiring exhaustive and systematic testing. Different approaches are proposed, from the concept of attacks proposed by James A. Whittaker [WHI 03, pp. 3-16], to defect taxonomies proposed by Cem Kaner *et al.* [KAN 99, pp. 363-436], including exploratory testing [WHI 10, pp. 16-19]. Taxonomies and attacks focus on functional aspects and some non-functional aspects such as security [WHI 04, pp. 3-13, 38, 56, 82 and 102].

These techniques can be added to systematic test techniques (black box and white box) and can complement them when these systematic techniques cannot be correctly applied (such as when there are resource or time constraints).

4.5.1. *Attacks*

The principle is to attempt to "attack" the software via its interfaces: user interfaces (inputs, outputs, data and computations) or its system interfaces (file and database interfaces, software or the operating system interfaces) to identify defects and failures.

The method consists of designing a potential failure model for each type of interface and to apply attacks to try and expose these potential failures. The possible attacks proposed are:

– via the user interface;

– via computations and the data used;

– via system interfaces.

4.5.1.1. *User interfaces*

Attacks via the user interfaces include:

– exploration of the input value domain:

  - introduction of input value that force the display of each error message,

  - introduction of values that force the software to use default values,

  - exploration of the allowed data types and character sets,

  - force input buffer overflows,

  - find input data that interact and test their combination,

  - repeat the same values or series of values a large number of times;

– exploration of the output value domain;

– force generation of different outputs for each input value;

– force generation of invalid output values;

– force change of properties for output values;

– force screen refresh.

4.5.1.2. *Data and computation*

Attacks via data and computation include:

– exploration of the data storage system:

  - apply input data with varied initial conditions,

- force the data structure to store too much or not enough data,

- explore other ways to modify the internal constraints applicable to the data;

– computations and characteristics interactions:

- experiment with invalid operators or combination of operators,

- force a function to execute itself recursively,

- force the results of computations to be too large or too small,

- find characteristics that share the data or interact incorrectly.

4.5.1.3. *System interfaces*

Attacks via faults based on system interfaces include:

– attacks based on the device:

- fill the device to maximum capacity,

- force the device to be busy or unavailable,

- damage the device;

– attacks based on the files and file systems:

- assign an invalid file name,

- modify access permissions,

- modify or corrupt the content of a file;

– attacks based on the operating system:

- inject failures that force execution of exception management code,

- inject defects that can be easily created in the test environment,

- inject defects that can occur in real-life usage.

4.5.2. *Defect taxonomies*

Defect taxonomies are list of defects or failures that have already occurred or that could occur in the software or system. Some of these defects can occur in your environment, and to envisage them can ensure that they are indeed present or absent.

It is recommended that taxonomies be improved by adding defects and failures that are identified in the software and systems or from other lists of defects available commercially, on the Internet or from colleagues. Some defect taxonomies are inapplicable and thus do not need to be tested.

Proposed defect taxonomies can be associated with types of defects such as:

– user interfaces defects;

– defect management and exceptions;

– defects associated iwth boundary values, including concurrent modification of variables (modification of the same data by two different actions at the same time);

– computational errors;

– initial and subsequent states;

– control flow errors;

– incorrect usage or interpretation of data;

– load, stress, or volume problems;

– interaction of components on the same set of data;

– hardware errors and interaction (including network);

– problems associated with version and configuration management,

– errors associated with tests. This is important because the quality of tests is seldom verified.

4.5.3. *Error guessing and ad hoc testing*

Error guessing and ad hoc testing, contrary to attacks, defect taxonomies, and exploratory testing, is not based on any systematic practice or technique, but on estimation (guessing) by the tester of the location of possible defects. This method is frequently synonymous with unplanned, undirected tests, without defined goals or objectives and without clear progress control.

This is not a recommended method.

4.5.4. *Exploratory testing*

According to James Bach [BAC 03, p. 2] exploratory testing is "simultaneous learning, test design, and test execution". In other words exploratory testing is any test where the tester actively controls the test design during its execution and uses the information acquired to design other (better?) tests".

This definition does not mean that a tester doing exploratory testing only has the software application to design the tests, on the contrary: any design documentation is usable, including any test documentation and the results of previous tests.

It is thus clear that exploratory tests are strongly influenced by the tester's context, and must be adequately documented in order to enable reproduction of any identified failures. Usage of tools, such as those that record the tester's actions, is authorized in these types of tests.

James Whittaker [WHI 10, pp. 39-64] proposed two scales of exploratory tests: small-scale tests that help design local tests, and large-scale tests to help test strategy and planning.

4.5.4.1. *Scenario-based exploratory testing*

Exploratory testing is used in addition to pre-planned test scripts or test scenarios. Scenarios are frequently defined in the frame of systematic tests, whether they are derived from requirements, from descriptions of the software characteristics, or user stories.

One example of exploratory processes that can be implemented is:

– creation of a mental model of the system's behavior;

– design of one or more tests demonstrating incorrect behavior of the model;

– execution of these tests, observation of the behavior, and analysis of the results;

– repetition of this process until the model is proved or demonstrated defective.

Exploratory tests are frequently executed in short time periods (sessions) from 60 to 90 minutes, and are based on agreements (or charts) defining the characteristics to test. Sessions limit the duration of exploration of one characteristic, in order to allow exploration of other characteristics with the same level of detail.

Charts are a kind of guide – not a script to follow blindly – defining the important aspects to verify for a characteristic, documentary references, types of defects to look for, tactics to implement, and associated risks. Charts can be designed by the test manager, or a test analyst, in order to cover all major characteristics of the software.

The management principle is to assign a chart – or one agreement – to a tester for a session, then to synthesize the session (and its results) during a short discussion between tester and test manager. This has for objective to (a) report defects, (b) identify aspects or components that might need further exploration, and (c) to report on the perceived reliability of the software. Such meetings do not lend themselves to implementation of this technique to large-scale testing teams.

Exploratory testing applies:

– when time constraints do not allow systematic or exhaustive test techniques implementation;

– when it is not necessary to ensure detailed traceability between requirements, specifications and test cases;

– when tests do not have to be re-executed, because each execution would depend on the tests executed before;

– to allow testers to analyze features or aspects that have been identified as problematic (such as when defect clustering occurs for a component).

4.5.5. *Limitations and assumptions*

Experience-based techniques are based on the following assumptions and limitations:

– executable code is available and running with a minimal level of reliability. All exploratory techniques are dynamic techniques, and require an adequate test environment (including test data);

– for techniques based on lists or taxonomies of defects: on the existence of published lists of defects applicable in your context. If there are none, it will be difficult to use such taxonomies;

– for techniques based on attacks: on the identification of attack profiles that are coherent. This enables selection of the most probable attack profiles;

– for techniques bases on exploration: on the abilities of the testers, whether it is with regards to the business context, or the technical context or specific experience with test techniques.

Contrary to other techniques, exploratory testing is not able to prevent defects, because they do not implement formalized and repetitive techniques.

4.6. Choosing test techniques (FL 4.6)

FLO-4.3.2 Explain the main purpose of each of the four testing techniques, what level and type of testing could use the technique, and how coverage may be measured (K 2)

An exhaustive use of all the different dynamic techniques leads to a combinatory explosion of the test cases that are to be designed, implemented, and executed. It is necessary to pragmatically use each of the identified techniques, to take into account their limitations, and to remember all the assumptions and hypotheses.

There is no single "best" technique, only techniques that are better or less adapted to the context.

FLO-4.5.2 Compare experience-based techniques with specification-based testing techniques (K 2)

Structure-based techniques allow – if used in conjunction with comparison to the specification – detection of useless or malicious code. However, they are complicated and not really applicable to large software applications.

Specification-based techniques are the only techniques able to identify missing code, but will be unable to identify extraneous code.

Some techniques are more adapted to one test level than another, to one type of defect than another, to one context than another.

FLO-4.6.1 Classify test design techniques according to their fitness to a given context, for the test basis, respective models and software characteristics. (K2)

Selection of the most appropriate technique(s) will depend on the context of the project. We can define project internal factors, such as:

– the software development model used and available design documentation, such as the presence of use cases, decision tables, or state transition graphs;

– the level of experience of the testers, and the number of testers available, which will influence test effort and the level of experience envisaged;

– the experience of the development teams, and the type of test activities that they implement – or not – before providing the software to the testers, will influence the number of defects that will be transmitted to the test team, and thus impact the level of effort required for reviews in the design phase, the level of test, and of defect correction in the testing phases;

– the test objectives, whether they are a filter before delivery, or a development support activity (through defect prevention);

– the type of potential defects, which will help us select techniques appropriate to identify such defects.

We can also identify factors that are external to our project, such as:

– risks associated with the use of the software or system, which will simultaneously determine the breadth and depth of tests, as well as the adaptation of the objectives to these risks;

– contractual or regulatory constraints defining the applicability of some techniques;

– the type of system, which will influence the techniques implemented, such as the use of boundary value analysis in financial applications;

– the time frame and budget, which will influence – constrain – the test effort and force the selection of quicker techniques over more exhaustive or systematic ones.

One possible solution is to base testing on the test levels and execute a large number of component tests. Another possible solution is to limit testing based on identified risks for each functional or technical (i.e. non-functional) aspect associated with a test level.

Selecting adequate test techniques must be seen from a strategic point of view, with the activities spread over the whole software development process (including static and dynamic activities), and attempting to find defects as early in the process as possible.

4.7. Synopsis of this chapter

Let us see what was learned in this chapter.

Section 4.1 enabled us to identify the differences between test cases, test procedures, and test conditions, and understand how they are documented. You should be able to implement traceability between requirements or specifications, and test cases, design test conditions, and translate them in test cases and test procedures drawn up on the basis of standards, with the level of detail appropriate for the level of experience of the testers. You should know the definition of the following glossary terms: test case specification, test design, test execution planning, test procedure specification, test script, and traceability.

Section 4.2 explained the advantages of structure-based and specification-based test approaches, and provided techniques for each of these approaches. You should be able to explain their characteristics, similarities, and differences. You should know the glossary definition for the following terms: black-box test design technique, experience-based technique, test design technique, white-box technique.

Section 4.3 detailed the specification-based techniques. You should be able to design test cases based on equivalence partitioning, on boundary value analysis, on decision tables, state transition, and use cases. You should know the definition of the following glossary terms: boundary value analysis, decision table tests, equivalence partitions, state transition tests, use case tests.

Section 4.4 detailed structure-based techniques. You should be able to draw the data flow and the control flow of a software component, and to design test cases covering instructions, decisions, conditions, and modified conditions. You should understand the importance of code coverage. You should know the definition of the following glossary terms: code coverage, decision coverage, instructions coverage, structural testing.

Section 4.5 allowed you to identify the reasons favoring tests based on tester intuition and experience, and described a number of usable techniques to use without knowing the structure or specifications of the software. You should know the definition of the following glossary terms: exploratory testing, (fault) attack.

For each of the techniques mentioned in this chapter, you should be able to mention their advantages, disadvantages, limitations, and assumptions.

Section 4.6 allowed you to identify considerations when selecting techniques, such as context, risks, type of defect, specification description, and development models.

4.8. Sample exam questions

Section 4.1. The test development process (K3)

FLO-4.1.1   Differentiate between a test design specification, test case specification, and test procedure specification (K2)

FLO-4.1.2   Compare the terms test condition, test case, and test procedure (K2)

FLO-4.1.3   Evaluate the quality of test cases in terms of clear traceability to the requirements and expected results (K2)

FLO-4.1.4   Translate test cases into a well-structured test procedure specification at a level of detail relevant to the knowledge of the testers (K3)

Ref	Questions

48.	FLO-4.1.1 (K2)
	
	Consider the following test deliverables and their objectives:
	
	    I. Test condition specification.
	
	    II. Test case specification.
	
	    III. Test procedure specification.
	
	    IV. Specifies a sequence of test actions.
	
	    V. Specified the expected results of tests.
	
	    VI. Specifies sequences of test cases.
	
	Which of the following correctly links the deliverable with its objective?
	
	A. I is linked with IV, II is linked with V, III is linked with VI.
	
	B. I is linked with V and VI, II and III are linked with IV.
	
	C. I is linked with VI, II is linked with V, III is linked with IV.
	
	D. I is linked with VI, II is linked with IV, III is linked with V.

49.	FLO-4.1.2 (K2)
	
	You are testing an online commercial web-site:
	
	    I. One of the issues to check is the ability to process credit cards for payment settlement.
	
	    II. You obtain a list of accepted credit cards.
	
	    III. You document the actions to implement to test payment settlement.
	
	Which of the following sentence is correct?
	
	A. I is linked to test conditions, II is linked to test cases, III is associated with test procedures.
	
	B. I, II and III should be included in the test plan.
	
	C. I, II and III should be included in the test design documents.
	
	D. I is associated with test cases, III is associated with test conditions, II is associated with test procedures.

50.	FLO-4.1.3 (K2)
	
	Consider the following extract from a test case:
	
	The following values are invalid inputs for the field "number of items":
	
	    – negative value (i.e. "–1");
	
	    – zero ("0");
	
	    – non-integer value (i.e. "1.5");
	
	    – non-numeric (letters, special characters, spaces, etc.);

	– numeric value above the maximum authorized value;
	– numeric value above 99,999;
	– missing value (no data).
	From the user manual and online help (to identify maximum values for a purchase and appropriate error message depending on applicable conditions), verify that the appropriate error messages are displayed, and that it is possible to correct the field and to continue once an acceptable value is entered.
	What element from a test case is defined in this test case extract?
	A. Expected result,
	B. Execution pre-conditions,
	C. Traceability to requirements,
	D. Execution post-conditions.
51.	FLO-4.1.4 (K3)
	For an experienced tester, with business topic experience, which approach would be more efficient and effective to define test procedures in a project where time constraints are high?
	A. High-level definition of test conditions and general steps to implement them.
	B. Each step is described with lots of details.
	C. A high-level definition of the test conditions and a meeting with other testers to detail the steps.
	D. A detailed documentation of all the test cases and a recording of all the test steps executed during the tests.
52.	Terms (K1)
	What is a test condition?
	A. An input value, an expected result, a pre-condition and a post-condition.
	B. The steps to execute to have the system in a defined state.
	C. A specific state of a system, before execution of a test.
	D. Something that can be tested.

Section 4.2. Categories of test design techniques (K2)

FLO-4.2.1   Recall reasons that both specification-based (black box) and structure-based (white box) test design techniques are useful and list the common techniques for each (K1)

FLO-4.2.2   Explain the characteristics, commonalities, and differences between specification based testing, structure-based testing, and experience-based testing (K2)

Ref	Questions
53.	FLO-4.2.1 (K1)
	What justifies the use of a software structure-based test approach?
	A. Structure-based tests find defects instead of failures.
	B. Structure-based tests do not need tools because code can be read without tools.
	C. The coverage level can be measured and additional tests can be designed to increase the coverage level if needed.
	D. Modeling from the specifications enables you to design tests systematically.
54.	FLO-4.2.2 (K2)
	You design tests on the basis of business and use cases. What type of approach are you implementing?
	A. A specifications-based approach.
	B. A structure-base approach.
	C. An experience-base approach.
	D. An effective approach.
55.	Terms (K1)
	Which technique selects test cases on the basis of an analysis of the internal structure of a system?
	A. Black-box technique.
	B. White-box technique
	C. Gray-box technique.
	D. Experience-based technique.

Section 4.3. Specification-based or black-box techniques (K3)

FLO-4.3.1   Write test cases from given software models using equivalence partitioning, boundary value analysis, decision tables, and state transition diagrams/tables (K3)

FLO-4.3.2   Explain the main purpose of each of the four testing techniques, what level and type of testing could use the technique, and how coverage may be measured (K2)

FLO-4.3.3   Explain the concept of use case testing and its benefits (K2)

Ref	Questions
56.	FLO-4.3.1 (K3) A field accepts integer values from 1 to 99 representing a number of books to purchase. Consider the following numbers: I. 0 II. –5 III. 1 IV. 64 V. 99 VI. 100 VII. 256 Which of the following propositions is true? A. I, III, V and VI are boundary values, while II, IV, VII are respectively representatives of invalid too low, valid, and invalid too high equivalence partitions. B. III, IV and VII are boundary values, I, II, V and VI are representatives respectively of invalid too low, invalid too low, valid, and invalid too high equivalence classes. C. Only III, IV and V are part of one of the three equivalence partitions. D. The seven values are boundary values and members of the equivalence partitions.
57.	FLO-4.3.1 (K3) Which of the following tables could be an example of a decision table for a financial application at system test level? A. A table containing combination rules for input data in two fields of a screen. B. A table containing the rules for interfaces between components. C. A table containing mortgage rate computation. D. A table containing the rules for a chess game.
58.	FLO-4.3.1 (K3) You are testing an online commercial system that accepts four types of credit cards (Visa, Amex, MasterCard, and Diners), each with its own rules for defining valid and invalid number, as payment method. Part of the decision table for purchase settlement is as follows: **Condition** Invalid card Yes No No Purchase approved No No Yes

Action			
Transaction rejected	Yes	Yes	No
Payment processing	No	No	Yes

Combination invalid card and payment processing cannot occur. How many tests should be executed to completely cover the combination of equivalence partitions of this part of the table and of the types of cards?

A. 3

B. 6

C. 9

D. 12

---

59. FLO-4.3.1 (K3)

Consider the state chart below:

What is the minimum number of test cases to test all the paths of this state diagram, knowing that all the tests should start and finish at the starting state "Engine at stop"?

A.2

B. 3

C. 4

D. 6

---

60. FLO-4.3.2 (K2)

What is the rule for minimum coverage of a decision table?

A. Cover each combination of conditions

B. Cover each possible action

C. Cover each possible column

D. Cover each condition in true or false

---

61. FLO-4.3.2 (K2)

Consider the following test techniques and test levels.

   I. Equivalence partitioning.

	II. Decision tables.
	III. MC/DC.
	IV. Component testing.
	V. Integration testing.
	VI. Acceptance testing.
	Which of the following is correct?
	A.I is usable in VI, II is usable in V, III is mostly usable in IV.
	B.I is usable in V, II is usable in IV, III is mostly usable in VI.
	C.I is usable in IV, II is usable in VI, III is mostly usable in V.
	D.I are II usable in IV, V and VI, III is usable in IV.
62.	FLO-4.3.3 (K2)
	What is a typical advantage of use case-based tests?
	A. It identifies defects in each equivalence partition.
	B. It identifies defects at the boundaries of equivalence partitions.
	C. It identifies defects in transitions of specified states.
	D. It identifies defect in business-based actions.
63.	Terms (K1)
	What are state-transition based tests used for?
	A. To check that valid and invalid transitions are tested for all the states of an embedded software or system.
	B. A To verify that valid and invalid transitions are tested for all the states of a software.
	C. To verify that valid transitions are tested for all the states of a component or system.
	D. To validate that all transitions between states are correct.

Section 4.4. Structure-based or white-box techniques (K3)

FLO-4.4.1   Describe the concept and value of code coverage (K2)

FLO-4.4.2   Explain the concepts of statement and decision coverage, and give reasons why these concepts can also be used at test levels other than component testing (e.g. on business procedures at system level) (K2)

FLO-4.4.3   Write test cases from given control flows using statement and decision test design techniques (K3)

FLO-4.4.4   Assess statement and decision coverage for completeness with respect to defined exit criteria (K4)

Ref	Questions
64.	FLO-4.4.1 (K2) You are in charge of component testing of new functionalities added to an existing system. You want to increase black-box coverage with tests based on the structure of the components as they are added. Which structural coverage measure is best applicable at this level? A. Decisions coverage. B. Conditions coverage. C. Call graph coverage. D. Functional menu coverage.
65.	FLO-4.4.2.(K2) You are testing financial software and have just finished specifications-based tests. An analysis of the coverage reached indicates that 50% of the code has not been exercised by the tests you have designed. Based on this coverage information what decision could you take? A. You add tests to obtain 100% instructions coverage, because it will enable you to cover all the code. B. You decide that the coverage level is sufficient, the unreachable code being used to process improbable error cases. C. You add tests to obtain 100% decisions coverage because this will enable you to cover all the code. D. You add test cases to obtain 100% conditions coverage as this will enable you to cover all the code.
66.	FLO-4.4.2 (K2) You are testing a Category A airborne software, and just finished specifications based tests. An analysis of the coverage level reached indicates that 20% of the code has not been executed by the test cases you designed. Based on this coverage information what decision should you take? A. You decide to add tests to reach 100% instructions coverage. B. You decide to add tests to reach 100% decisions coverage. C. You decide to add tests to reach 100% conditions coverage. D. You decide to add tests to reach 100% modified conditions and decisions coverage.

Ref	Questions
67.	FLO-4.4.3 (K3)

Consider the following function:

```
int factorial(int n)
/* factorial computation with recursivity*
 * the function calls itself *
 * Mathematical description        *
 * n! = n*((n-1)!)                 *
 * Factorial of 0 and 1 equals 1.  */
{
int f=-1;
 if (n < 0) {
fprintf(stderr, "factorial: negative argument.\n");
} else if ((n == 0) || (n == 1)) {
  f=1;
  } else {
  f=n*factorial(--n);
  }
 return(f);
}
```

Assume you have a test environment that allows you to provide values to the "factorial" function (the inputs) and check the returned values (the outputs). Which sequence of tests will give you *100% decisions coverage with the smallest number of tests?* Consider that the input is the first value and the output the second value.

A. 0, 1; 1,1; 2, 2.

B. –1, –1; 1, 1; 5, 120.

C. –1, –1; 0, 1; 1, 1; 3, 6.

D. –1, –1; 0, 1; 4, 12.

Ref	Questions

68.	FLO-4.4.4 (K4)
	Consider the following function:
	
	``
	int factorial(int x) {
	int result = -1;
	  if(x >= 0) {
	    result = 1;
	    for(int i=2; i <= x; i++) {
	      result = result * i;
	    }
	  } else {
	  }
	  return result;
	}
	``
	
	Which sequence of input and output values will allow you to reach *100% instructions coverage* with the smallest number of tests? Consider that the input value is the first value of each pair, and that the output value is the second value of each pair.
	
	A. –2, –1 ; 0, 1 ; 1, 1 ; 5, 120
	B. –2, –1 ; 0, 1 ; 4, 24
	C. 0, 1 ; 3, 6
	D. 2, 2

Ref	Questions
69	FLO-4.4.4 (K4)
	Consider the following function:
| | ```
int factorial(int x) {
int result = -1;
  if(x >= 0) {
    result = 1;
    for(int i=2; i <= x; i++) {
      result = result * i;
    }
  } else {
  }
  return result;
}
``` |
	Which sequence of input and output values will allow you to reach *100% decisions coverage* with the smallest number of tests? Consider that the input value is the first value of each pair, and that the output value is the second value of each pair.
	A. –2, –1 ; 0, 1 ; 1, 1 ; 5, 120
	B. –2, –1 ; 0, 1 ; 4, 24
	C. 0, 1 ; 3, 6
	D. 2, 2
70	Terms (K1)
	What is branch coverage equivalent to?
	A. MC/DC.
	B. Conditions coverage.
	C. Decisions coverage.
	D. Instructions coverage.

Section 4.5. Experience-based techniques (K2)

FLO-4.5.1   Recall reasons for writing test cases based on intuition, experience, and knowledge about common defects (K1)

FLO-4.5.2   Compare experience-based techniques with specification-based testing techniques (K2)
```

Ref	Questions
71.	FLO-4.5.1 (K1) Why is it useful to undertake exploratory testing? A. This can find defects in specifications. B. This does not require specific training to have results. C. They take less time than structural test and black-box tests. D. It provides a useful complement to structural and specification based tests.
72.	FLO-4.5.2 (K2) In which way are experience-based techniques different from specification-based techniques? A. They depend on the understanding by the tester of the software context. B. They depend on the available documentation and the results of previous tests, instead of the software specifications. C. They require testers experienced in both technical and domain aspects. D. They depend on the individual understanding instead of the documentation of what the software is supposed to achieve.
73.	Terms (K1) What do we call the technique where the tests are designed based on results from previous tests? A. Ad hoc testing. B. Exploratory testing. C. Experience-based testing. D. Useless testing.

Section 4.6. Choosing test techniques (K2)

FLO-4.6.1   Classify test design techniques according to their fitness to a given context, for the test basis, respective models, and software characteristics (K2)

Ref	Questions
74.	FLO-4.6.1 (K2) You are testing the software of an artificial heart that will be inserted in patients to replace their failing organ. What types of tests should you envisage? A. Full coverage of requirements, complemented by experience-based tests. B. Full code coverage and full requirements coverage. C. Full decisions coverage and full requirements coverage. D. Full decisions, modified conditions and decisions coverage, full requirements coverage, and additional exploratory testing.

Chapter 5

Test Management
(FL 5.0)

Good test management is very important because it allows a rational and efficient use of resources that are always limited, as well as correct coordination of test activities with design and marketing activities for software and systems.

5.1. Test organization (FL 5.1)

It is better to avoid reinventing the wheel and re-designing a new organization test for each new development project. It is more efficient to define – at organization level – the expected objectives of software testing, the independence level of *testers* and the general aspects, or even the great principles and policies that will direct software and system testing within the company.

These principles should be described in a document presenting the organization "test policy". Such a document is applicable for all designed software or systems and can be referenced in the contractual documents delivered to customers, in a similar manner to the quality assurance plan.

5.1.1. *Independence levels*

We previously have noted (Chapter 1, section 1.5.1) the importance of a certain level of independence between test teams and development teams. There are several levels of independence:

– total lack of independence: when developers are the only ones testing their codes. Designers will often review the material produced before delivery; however, they might miss important defects, which will be found again in production;

– a limited level of independence whereby someone in the same team and with the same role as the designer is assigned to review the produced software. This is frequently called "pair programming" and/or "peer review" and enables more defects to be found than the previous independence level. These two first levels rely on individuals having a development and not a test background or specialization, and there is no specific requirement for test knowledge. Thus the tests they will execute may be less thorough;

– one person or a small group of individuals, specialized in software testing and associated to the development team, focusing on testing the components produced by the development team. Such an organization is found in so-called "agile" teams and in the Scrum model. The disadvantages of such an organization are (a) the co-optation of testers to execute development tasks, thereby reducing their testing efficiency; (b) hierarchical dependency with regards to the same project leader – sometimes an ex-developer – which makes it difficult to clearly protect the quality expectations on the produced code; (c) the skill level of the testers cannot easily increase, because these testers are often alone and thus unable to benefit from coaching from other, more experienced testers;

– a specialized software testing team within the same organization, but not in the same hierarchical chain as the development team. This parallel organization of design and quality follows the independence level recommended by numerous international standards and give testers wider career opportunities and allows them to benefit from the coaching and support from other, more experienced testers;

– a specialized software testing team in a separate economic entity (other company, freelance consultants, etc.), which concentrates all its economic activity on software testing and quality improvement. This includes service companies and consultants specialized in various aspects of testing (i.e. performance, security, or usability testing, etc.).

Selecting the independence level between the testers and development teams will impact the way testers will be able to act, their objectives, and their constraints during test campaigns.

Reasons in favor of a certain level of independence are, as indicated by Boris Beizer [BEI 95, pp. 242-244]:

– to protect testers and provide a certain objectivity level;

– to ensure that different configurations are compatible;

– to validate the performances and capacity of software systems;

– to evaluate the network and bandwidth;

– to ensure correct localization, i.e. the adaptation of the software to different languages and national specificities; and

– to reduce risks and increase the reliability of critical safety software (Category A software according to DO178B/ED12B for aeronautics, integrity level 1 according to IEEE 829-2008).

FLO-5.1.1 Recognize the importance of independent testing (K1)

It is important to have a certain level of independence between testers and developers. Usually, testers have a different vision of the software application to developers, and independently verify the developers' hypothesis and assumptions.

Testers and developers also have different objectives:

– developers: to design software quickly;

– testers: to ensure that the software is defect-free and that the users are satisfied.

Introducing independent test teams also has some disadvantages:

– developers could lose sight of their responsibility to deliver quality software, by transferring the responsibility of quality assurance to the testing team;

– tests can, if they are not correctly proportioned, become a bottleneck in software delivery;

– introducing an additional distance between the teams could lead to communication problems and thus to loss of information.

Each of the different independence levels has their own advantages and drawbacks.

FLO-5.1.2 Explain the benefits and drawbacks of independent testing within an organization (K2)

The advantages of reduced independence and of a closer proximity with development teams are:

– knowing in advance which components were complex, difficult to design, or led to problems during their design enables testers to examine these parts in more detail, thus anticipating defect clustering;

– anticipation of late deliveries, and fast information transfer when a delay occurs;

– verification of the hypotheses and assumptions made during the definition, specification, and implementation of the software;

– better understanding of potential problems and easier exchanges of information with development teams.

The disadvantages associated with reduced independence are, amongst other things:

– if the developer is the only person testing the software, it results in an increased bias where the author is simultaneously judge and jury;

– if the tester is the only person on the team testing the software, there is a possibility that the tester is co-opted as developer and fails to execute testing tasks.

The drawbacks related to an increased independence are amongst other things:

– problems related to the lack of communication between the test and development teams;

– dependence of the testers on developers and any comparison resulting from it (usually at the expense of the tests);

– contract interfaces between teams and an incomprehension of the tasks of each team;

– viewing test teams as a bottleneck that postpones delivery to the market without really providing any added value.

It is important, when introducing testers into an organization, to analyze these various aspects and to ensure the identification and distribution of the tasks, roles, and responsibilities.

5.1.2. *Roles and responsibilities*

FLO-5.1.4 Recall the typical tasks of test leaders and testers (K1)

Two typical roles are present in test projects: the role of test manager and that of the tester.

The role of test manager or "test project leader", covers test planning, test control, and test reporting activities. In small-scale teams, the test leader also executes requirements analysis and test design activities. Amongst the tasks of test leaders, the International Software Testing Qualifications Board (ISTQB) syllabus includes:

– coordination of the test strategy and test plan with the development project leader and other stakeholders;

– definition or adaptation of the *test strategy* to fit the project and the *test policy* of the organization;

– providing a testing viewpoint to other project activities, such as component integration planning, in order to adapt test activities to the planned project activities and, where possible, to adapt project activities to test activities;

– the test organization – by considering the context, objectives, and risks – including choosing the right test approaches; estimating time, effort, and tests costs; acquiring resources; and defining test levels and test cycles; the test approach and objectives as well as planning defect management;

– the specification, preparation, or even implementation and execution of tests, as well as the evaluation and control of test execution;

– planning modifications depending on the test results and progresses (sometimes documented in a test progress report) and the implementation of necessary actions to solve any problems;

– configuration management setup and adequate traceability implementation;

– introduction of adequate measures to evaluate the progress of testing and product quality;

– selection of what should be automated, to what degree, and how;

– selection of test tools, and organizing training sessions for testers to learn how to use the selected tools;

– decisions regarding test environment implementation;

– establishing test reports and summary presentations based on data gathered during testing.

"Testers" will generate tests (transforming test conditions into test cases), design test data (test input data, as well as expected test result data), execute the tests, and ensure the correspondence between actual data (resulting from execution of the software on the input data) and the expected data. In case of discrepancy between the two, the tester generates an anomaly report, which determines whether it is a software failure or a defect in the test specification or execution. The tester decides whether a correction should be implemented.

The following are some of the tasks undertaken by testers:

– reviewing test plans and contributing to them. This is very important, as testers will implement the test plan and they must be able to completely subscribe to it, as unrealistic expectations are demotivating;

– analyzing, reviewing, and evaluating the testability of user requirements, specifications and models;

– creating test specifications from the information found in the test data base;

– implementing the test environment in coordination with the system administrator and network managers;

– preparing and obtaining test data;

– implementing tests at all levels, executing and logging tests, evaluating results and reporting the gaps with expected results;

– using administrative and test management tools, as well as test execution or coverage tools, depending on the needs;

– automating tests (sometimes with the help of developers and/or experts in test automation);

– measuring component and system performances (when applicable);

– reviewing tests developed by others, by noting the identified defects;

– managing all these elements as configuration items, so as not to lose any data.

In some cases, developers and designers can also execute test activities. Typically, developers will execute component test and integration tests; while individuals executing acceptance tests will be business experts and users, and operational acceptance tests will be run by operators.

NOTE: In agile development cycles or when basing design on the "agile manifesto", testers could be designing tests before the software is created. Such a way of doing things is more a specification activity than a testing activity: a specification is what the developer should create, while a test is the evidence that a result has been reached or not.

5.1.3. *Human and contract aspects*

FLO-5.1.3 Recognize the different team members to be considered for the creation of a test team (K1)

Test activities are numerous and varied. Depending on the project size, they will be executed by one or more individuals with specialized roles, which are gathered together within a test team.

Test teams – as development teams – are made up of individuals who have different abilities, knowledge, and roles.

There are planning, prediction, monitoring, and execution roles.

At the foundation level, ISTQB defines two main roles:

– a *test leader* (or test manager) role;

– a technician role, executing the tests: a *tester* role.

In very small test teams, the same individual could take on different roles one after the other, throughout the project life.

In large teams, specialization is more marked. We will have:

– test analysts, whose specialization concentrates on one or more functional or non-functional aspects;

– technical test analysts, who are specialists in certain specific aspects, such as performance testing, security, or maintainability testing, or even some more specific aspects;

– technical specialists can also operate as test team support, whether they are database experts (to design the test data), or business experts (to ensure that test cases are correctly adapted to the user needs). Specialists in requirement management, usability (ergonomics and graphical user interfaces (GUIs)) or configuration management can also be associated with test teams depending on the specific team needs.

Including subcontractors in your test team, on a one-off basis via short-term consultancy contracts or for a longer period, such as staff augmentation, can generate specific problems, in terms of the knowledge acquired, differences in remuneration, and in the way in which they work.

5.2. Test planning and estimation (FL 5.2)

Test managers (project leaders, test leaders, test managers, etc.) must estimate the test workload, and organize and plan the activities over time. This means that the company's test policy needs to be put into practice, to identify the necessary resources and justify their use or acquisition.

This delicate and complex task is applied to a constantly evolving target: the software is being developed and the quality of the product and the effective end date of the project is unknown. The following factors influence the workload:

– process-related factors: constantly executing tests, changing management, process maturity, development and test processes, previous test phases, planned and actual levels of defects and corrections;

– hardware factors: tools, system tests, test environment, project documentation, similarity with other projects;

– human factors: tester abilities and expectations, support from development teams, relationships between teams;

– other delaying factors: complexity of the software, large number of stakeholders, too many new features, geographic distribution, delicate logistics, fragile test data;

– the correct understanding of the estimation techniques and other aspects that may influence results.

To illustrate this last point, let us take an example and make a diagram.

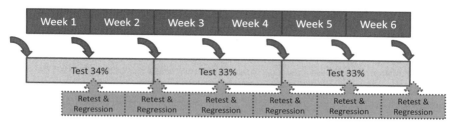

Figure 5.1. *Uniform test distribution*

Let us imagine that we have a 6 week period to test the software. If we distribute the testing activities uniformly over this period, 33% of the software will be tested in 2 weeks. If, at the end of each week, we receive a corrected version of the application, we will be forced to execute re-testing (confirmation tests) and non-regression tests on this version of the software. This will take time (re-initializing environments, impact analysis, re-execution of selected tests), during which we will not be able to test new functionalities as initially planned. We will end up accumulating delays that will impact future activities. This scenario will repeat for each new delivery during these 6 weeks, generating an increased workload for the test team, delays in planning, and a financial impact and stakeholder dissatisfaction (hierarchy, development team, customers, and users) towards the test team.

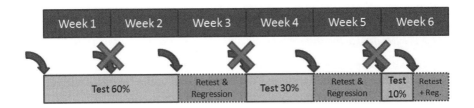

Figure 5.2. *Non-uniform test distribution*

If we break down our 6 week period in three 2 week periods, we could process 60% of the software during the first 2 week period (week 1 and week 2), then we could test an additional 30% of the functionalities during week 4 and the last 10% during week 6. During the other weeks we will execute non-regression testing and confirmation tests (re-test).

This will have several impacts:

– the necessity to disregard some patch delivery arriving unexpectedly during test periods;

– the necessity to limit the number of tests that can be executed during the periods allocated for testing new or modified functionalities;

– the last delivery, in the middle of week 6, should be a strong candidate for delivery; the period for re-test and regression testing is there to ensure that implemented corrections do not generate new, previously unknown defects. Not testing that candidate version extensively is very high risk.

We can notice that:

– understanding the techniques and their impacts on results strongly influences test organization;

– a selection of the most pertinent test cases and an evaluation of the coverage actually reached are important to ensure that the objectives have been reached by the end of week 2 (i.e. 60% coverage of the planned objectives). This will imply that some minor requirements or specifications might not be tested, in order to concentrate the tests first on critical issues, then on major ones and finally on the important ones, on the basis of the previously carried out risk analysis;

– the necessity of good coordination between the development and test teams is paramount, so that testing is not interrupted by unexpected deliveries.

5.2.1. *Planning and evaluation activities*

FLO-5.2.1 Recognize the different levels and objectives of test planning (K1)

We have seen previously that there are different test levels each with their own specific objectives. In addition to the activities related to the testing of the software that must be delivered, test managers define and lead their organization's test policy and test objectives, identify and manage risks, constraints and other activities to be carried out depending on the criticality (expected integrity level) of the software. These abstract activities are helpful for the integration of testing in the usual organization practices, and will eventually help to improve the quality of the delivered processes and software.

Test activity planning for software can be evaluated on several levels:

– long-term, at the overall software application level, whatever the version or release date. This helps to prioritize the processing of functional or non-functional quality characteristics (see ISO/IEC 9126-1:2001). The goal here is to organize testing activities according to long-term risks;

– at the level of the software application version that is currently being prepared, with its different test levels (component, integration, system and acceptance testing), so that tests are spread between the different levels according to the efficiency of the different techniques. The goal here is to ensure the broadest coverage by distributing the tasks amongst the different levels, sometimes with different objectives, while maximizing coverage;

– at the level of the current delivery, so that, depending on the current project constraints, the most important tests are carried out as early as possible. The goal here is to both measure the necessary level of quality and to avoid investing in less efficient tests. Amongst other things, this allows us to include smoke tests and sanity tests on dedicated workstations, in order to evaluate the correct operation of the basic functionalities of the software before distributing that version on all the tester's workstations. Smoke tests are a sub-set of the tests used to quickly check the quality of deliverables before investing in more extensive testing activities.

FLO-5.2.3 Differentiate between conceptually different test approaches, such as analytical, model-based, methodical, process/standard compliant, dynamic/heuristic, consultative, and regression-averse approaches (K2)

There are many test approaches. Each of them with their own advantages and disadvantages. The ISTQB foundation level syllabus identifies the following approaches:

– analytical;

– model-based;

– standard or process-based;

– dynamic and heuristic;

– consultative;

– regression adverse.

Analytical test approach implies an analysis of the test base, specifically requirements and contract documents, general and detailed design documents, user manuals and other available documentation, so as to identify the different aspects to verify and validate. There will thus be a significant aspect of analysis and design of test conditions. Depending on the focus on functional and non-functional characteristics, test execution activities may vary. This approach enables us to anticipate tool usage, depending on the objectives that have to be reached.

The model-based test approach relies on modeling the behavior of the software and its interfaces before designing test conditions. Functional aspects often prevail over non-functional ones. Modeling methods may not be adapted to the requirements, specifically if these requirements are not clearly expressed. Test tools are frequently used in such an approach.

The methodic test approach is based on methods, standards, and processes the use of which results in internal or external compliance to standards. How the standards are applied, the level of detail, and their applicability to the context strongly depends on whether or not the testers are familiar with the application of these standards. Applying standards can be an efficient solution if it takes into account the overall objectives, but can also be considered as too complicated if applied without thinking.

A dynamic or heuristic test approach such as the one proposed with exploratory testing, is applicable mostly when analytical and methodic or systematic approaches are not suitable (for example when the time to market is too close). A heuristic approach can also be applied when specifications are lacking or when there are high time constraints. Generally, heuristic approaches require experienced testers and do not use test automation tools.

Some organizations prefer approaches where specialist testers are hired with result-oriented objectives instead of means-oriented objectives. This approach saw numerous customers turn towards national or offshore service companies, without taking into account coherent medium- or long-term objectives. Consultants and staff increases can solve specific problems, but introduces long-term risks because the consultant – or external staff – can become a mandatory part of the process if the knowledge and skills are not kept within the organization.

A regression-adverse test approach is important for well-established organizations that do not want any modification in the current services provided by the software. This is important when maintaining software, including third-party software maintenance. An extensive automation of non-regression test suites for regression tests is at the basis of this test approach. Depending on the stability of the GUI software, keeping the test suite up to date will generate important test maintenance effort.

FLO-5.2.4 Differentiate between test planning for a system and scheduling test execution (K2)

Planning and organizing activities ensure the resources and tasks required to reach the objectives have been correctly planned. They are based on hypothesis that can fail to materialize during test execution. It is necessary, during test planning, to determine which tasks are critical and which tasks can be waived if time constraints require it. By prioritizing activities, the highest value-added tasks are carried out first. This is valid during test design tasks, as well as during test implementation and execution tasks.

Organizing activities enables us to define which tasks must be executed before other tasks. It is important to identify these dependences in order to determine the impact of a delay, a cancellation, or a modification of the tasks during the actual execution of test campaigns. During the execution of the test campaign, it will be necessary to adapt the activities to project realities. Some tasks will be postponed, some will be cancelled, and others will be added. Efficient organization will enable the tasks to be sequenced in a coherent order, with the objective of maximum efficiency and effectiveness.

FLO-5.2.5 Write a test execution schedule for a given set of test cases, by considering prioritization and technical and logical dependencies (K3)

When organizing tests and planning, the order in which the tests must be carried out should be defined. A non-homogeneous distribution of tests, with a higher priority for checking common user activities (instead of a systematic search for defects) is important. This aspect called the "happy path" corresponds to the nominal software operation. By default, it should always operate correctly [PAG 09, pp. 69-70] and its validation is a priority. Verifying functionalities and characteristics according to their criticality also needs to be anticipated when sequencing test tasks.

As for military campaigns, the life expectancy of a test plan is limited. The test plan will have to take into account potential delays in software delivery from the development team, test environment installation problems, major defects preventing the resumption of test activities and additional effort to identify defects and inform the development team of their presence. These different issues will impact test organization, and it is necessary to anticipate them where possible. Good test organization must be able to anticipate timing or dependency issues, without impacting the workload (test effort) or the delivery times, while keeping an adequate coverage level. The use of project management tools and linking tasks to each other (i.e. generating actual dependencies with the deliverables) is an efficient way to manage projects.

FLO-5.2.6 List test preparation and execution activities that should be considered during test planning (K1)

Test planning must anticipate and plan an important number of tasks. The following tasks are included among test preparation activities:

– identifying the testing scope, applicable constraints and test objectives;

– definition of the overall test approach, of the test levels, and their entry and exit criteria;

– identifying and prioritizing risks, anticipating tasks to mitigate impacts and to limit the possible occurrence of these risks;

– identifying the activities with which tests will interact, such as development, acquisition, delivery, exploitation, and maintenance activities;

– defining and ordering test basis analysis and design activities, by making sure that adequate traceability is maintained from (and to) the requirements;

– defining and sequencing test implementation activities, selecting test data (including expected results), sequencing test execution and verification activities;

– defining the level of detail, the volume, structure, and templates for test documentation, both in terms of progress reports, periodic status reports, and final deliverables.

We can find the following tasks amongst the test execution activities to anticipate during test planning:

– deciding what will be tested (which quality characteristics), which roles will execute which activities, when and how these activities will be executed, how to evaluate the test results and when to stop the tests (definition of the test exit criteria);

– assigning resources to the different tasks that were defined and taking into account the specialties of each individual, possible issues, holidays, as well as the impact of disease on the limited availability of resources;

– selecting the means required to track and control test preparation and execution, defect removal and risk limitation activities, through the definition of metrics and other appropriate means;

– defining the level of detail for test cases and test procedures, so as to provide enough detail to allow the creation and execution of reusable tests. This greatly depends on the knowledge of the testers in charge of the actual test execution.

FLO-5.2.7 Recall typical factors influencing the test effort (K1)

The test workload is influenced by numerous factors that can be classified in four categories:

– process-dependent factors associated with software development and testing;

– hardware-dependent factors;

– human factors;

– contextual factors.

5.2.1.1. *Process-dependent factors*

The internal structure of the company, as well as the project organization and the position of testing in such organizations have a strong impact on the test effort.

If the organization has a coherent test policy and a good understanding of the value-added provided by tests, the goals of each process will be clearly defined. A coherent definition of the various processes within the organization will facilitate the work of test teams, because it will impact the way testers and test activities are perceived in the organization.

Mature processes according to capability maturity model integration (CMMI) and a coherent organization where each process is defined and perfectly fits within the organization's development scheme lead to a significant decrease in workload, while delivering the same level of quality. We can find amongst the processes facilitating test effort:

– software change management, including the impact analysis of all changes;

– process maturity, specifically if they are continuously monitored and improved (CMMI level 5);

– involvement of the tests from the beginning of the design phases (such as via requirement, specifications, or code reviews), with a continuous comparison of the previous estimates with the actual resource usage and the remaining workload;

– involvement of the whole organization in a continuous test improvement initiative, with measurement and control by metrics policies, as well as analysis of these metrics information during feedback reviews;

– evaluation of the defect detection and correction rates, as a function of their criticality and impact, as well as an evaluation of the test processes efficiency throughout the project.

5.2.1.2. *Hardware-dependent factors*

Many hardware-related issues also influence the test effort. The lack of a dedicated test environment representative of the production – as it is often the case on mainframes, distributed web environments (Cloud), or specific equipment – influences the representatively of the executed tests. This is especially true for performance tests and those requiring a large volume of data and covering specific portability issues.

The lack of tools, of adequate test data, and of appropriate documentation, will have a negative impact on the test effort.

Having too many tools or test environments can also have a negative impact on the test effort. Indeed, these tools, the scripts they use, their environments, and parameter sets will require maintenance. This is an additional effort that we need to take into account when evaluating the test workload.

5.2.1.3. *Human factors*

Here are some of the human factors influencing the test effort:

– testers experience: junior testers or those with less experience in the context will not be able to focus on the most critical aspects of the software being analyzed, nor to select and implement the most appropriate techniques to quickly find the mist significant defects;

– expectations from testers, customers, managers, and other stakeholders: the less precise they are, the more likely it is that they will be questioned during testing; therefore, impacting on the test duration and effort;

– availability of the resources throughout the testing campaign, and their level of technical and business knowledge, will strongly influence the test effort; directly via the level of details that will be necessary to include in the test conditions, cases and procedures, and indirectly, via the support effort from technical or business experts to explain the reasons and impacts of the planned activities;

– the level of support available for the test teams is another factor influencing the test workload: the support aspect here includes both test execution and environment implementation support, but also the functional support from specific users (to explain functional aspects) and the required support for non-functional tasks such as security, performance and stress tests.

– the relationships between test teams and the other stakeholders. If test activities are considered by the designer and development teams as non-value added activities, or as a mandatory milestone that should be reduced as much as possible (commoditized), it is clear that tester requests will not be treated as those of the partners or prescribers.

5.2.1.4. *Context-based factors*

The context in which tests will be executed has also a strong influence on testing workload:

– the complexity of the software or of the system with which the software will interact. This will influence input and output interfaces, as well as the combinatorics of the events and states to simulate during tests;

– the number of stakeholders, because their number will influence the communication and information patterns (contradictory or not) that need to be taken into account throughout the test duration;

– the quality of the software being tested, because if there are more defects in the test process, there will be a greater requirement to write defect reports, to wait for corrections, to execute re-testing and regression testing. This will have an impact in terms of increased workload, but also in terms of the extension of the duration of the test campaign, to achieve a similar level of quality;

– the innovation level of the software: if the software uses new technology or if it represents a technological leap from what currently exists in the market, it will be difficult to base estimates on the experience acquired from other software;

– the geographical distribution of the development and test teams and of other stakeholders also influences the test effort. This is because travel expenses will have to be taken into account, as well as possible delays when asking questions and obtaining responses (e.g. to take into account different time zones). This will reduce the effectiveness and reaction speed of the test teams;

– detailed test documentation, as required in regulated industries (aeronautical, space, medical, etc.) will impact the test workload. It is indeed necessary to verify, validate, and sign most of these documents and to ensure that the version of these referenced documents is correct and corresponds to the software that will be delivered for acceptance testing by official regulatory services;

– fragile test data impacts the workload in terms of creation and maintenance workload, as well as verification of the consistency of the data, leading to an increased workload. This is what happens in some telecom or aerospace environments and for specific areas where the volume of processed data is important (meteorology, geo-localization, etc.);

– logistical aspects, use of specific hardware support (for testing embedded systems), delivery of software components and their integration in software builds (creation of the executable code for the target system in case of multi-systems applications) introduce additional complexity factors that will influence the testing workload;

– the risks and the risk coverage level required in order to reduce these risks, is an important factor when estimating testing workload;

– the quality level of the software and thus the number of failures that testers will discover is an often neglected factor that increases the testing workload. For each defect found, it will be necessary to write a defect report, to have the defect corrected, to ensure the correction is valid (re-testing or confirmation tests) and does not generate regressions in the rest of the software (regression tests), leading to an increased and unplanned workload;

– the expected duration of the test campaign, whether it is for test design, test execution, defect correction in the test elements, and verification of their corrections all influence the test effort;

– the use of test techniques will also influence the testing workload, whether these techniques are based on the structure or the code (white box tests) or based on input data (equivalence partitioning, boundary value analysis, and decision tables), if the number of input (and output) values to check is significant;

– criticality of the software requiring testing; various restrictions of equipment usage of test environments or simulators, as well as the type of system, will also influence the test effort.

FLO-5.2.8 Differentiate between two conceptually different estimation approaches: the metrics-based approach and the expert-based approach (K2)

Niels Bohr, a Danish physicist said that "prediction is very difficult, especially about the future". This is also true about predicting testing workloads. We have seen that many factors influence predictions, but to do so, we have to have a basis for these estimations.

There are two main families of approaches: those based on metrics and mathematical formulas and those based on historical references and experience. A third family of approaches is proposed for the agile world.

5.2.1.5. *Metrics-based estimation*

There are many estimation methods based on metrics. The most frequently mentioned are those based on lines of code, on function points, on formulas such as COCOMOII and those based on test points.

Estimation methods appeared in the frame of software development to evaluate the size and the development effort. They benefited from the works of Dr Barry Boehm on the COCOMO method published in 1981. A more recent version of this method is available COCOMO II ([COC] download possible). This estimation method computes, from a number of characteristics, a workload and a development time, as well as a size in lines of code. From this estimation of the development effort, it is possible to extrapolate a test workload. The parameters used to compute the test workload will have to take into account the different factors we have seen previously.

Estimation methods based on software size in lines of code or on development workload, often do not take into account that the same functionality can be designed with more – or less – lines of code, depending on the programming language used. Some languages are wordier than others and some developers are more concise than others. Numerous published books use lines of code as reference to measure the number of defects and the resulting workload. Frequently, these values merge the defects identified by developers and are corrected without being introduced in a defect management tool, which influences statistics. Other factors influencing testing, which we have previously mentioned, are also applicable.

To bypass the drawbacks from measurements based on lines of code, a software development workload metric has been designed based on the functions to design: function points. This metric is based on an approximation of the functions that need to be designed in the software and on an extrapolation of the development workload from that development workload. Capers Jones [JON 07, pp. 485-515] informs us that the number of defects that we can expect varies from four to seven defects per function point, depending on the type of software.

Estimation methods are mostly used to define the development workload. Erik van Veenendaal [VAN 97, p. 157] and Ton Dekkers proposed a method (TPA®) allowing us to estimate the test workload for a system or acceptance tests with black-box techniques.

As always, hypotheses associated with the selection of an estimation method are often forgotten and later return with a vengeance. The metrics used must correspond to the context, the level of criticality (integrity), and the level of knowledge and skills of the testers.

5.2.1.6. *Experience-based estimation*

Methods based on experience are not based on a series of metrics, but on the experience of experts or those who will execute these tasks. This solution should enable us to bypass the risks of incorrect use of metrics, at the risk of having statistically invalid estimations.

The first experience-based method requires that each individual who will execute the planned tasks estimates the workload and these individual tasks estimations are summed. The drawbacks of this proposed solution is that individuals only have an approximate idea of the workload (based on a number of unconfirmed hypotheses), and that there is frequently a safety factor that is added as a rounding factor (in hours or days).

The second experience-based method requires an experienced tester to estimate the workload. The drawback of this method will depend on the person who will effectively execute the work (are the knowledge and expertise levels similar to that envisaged by the expert tester during the initial estimation?). This drawback can be bypassed by the three-point estimation with the aim of identifying the hypotheses. It requires three estimations: an optimistic one, a pessimistic one, and a third one that must be the most likely.

A third method is based on the similarity between the project to be estimated and previous projects that have been carried out. The hypothesis here is that the context is similar, which is rarely the case. If we test a software that we have already tested, our understanding of the software will be better than before and therefore efficiency should be increased. However, it could be reduced if the test team is different or if the test objectives are modified. If we test a project that is similar to a project we have already executed, we could be tempted to estimate the same workload, but are we in the same context, with the same programming language, the same defect rate, and similar objectives?

There are many different variations of the methods based on experience, each with its own advantages, drawbacks, and underlying hypotheses.

5.2.1.7. *Estimation in the agile world*

In the agile world, there are similar estimation methods, depending on how the teams are organized and on the requirement definition.

This is no longer an experience-based estimation, but an estimation based on "story points", an analogy with other projects or even "planning poker" as proposed by Mike Cohn [COH 06, pp. 35-60]. We remember that agile methods are unable to provide a detailed and exhaustive estimation from the beginning of the project, because requirements and story points are provided one after the other by the customer. Therefore, there will be an iterative re-estimation of the workload and a constant increase of the tasks.

The principle of "story point" estimation consists of estimating each "user story", the complexity of its development and test, whenever the story is received. Workload estimation for a story is influenced by the previous workload estimations in the project. Any change of context from the previous stories (such as increased or decreased complexity, required refactoring, etc.) will impact the estimation.

Scrum proposes estimation methods similar to the second experience-based methods, with a periodical re-estimation of the workloads based on the time spent carrying out the previous tasks and the tasks that remain. This estimation is executed by all members of the team and when a consensus is reached, this value is taken as a reference. To make this estimation quicker or more "agile", estimation can be done by using cards, as seen previously (poker estimations).

Agile estimation methods are similar to traditional estimation methods, but the hypotheses on which they are based are often forgotten by their users.

5.2.2. *Test planning activities*

According to IEEE 829-2008, test organization and planning activities include, depending on the software integrity level, the minimal tasks listed below:

– generation of the master test plan;

– workload estimation review;

– review of the technical support required;

– interface with the organizational and supporting processes;

– identification of test process improvement opportunities.

The organization of test activities and specifically the documentation aspects have evolved between the 1998 and 2008 versions of the IEEE 829 standard. The 2008 version proposes an approach based on tasks while the previous one proposed an approach based on deliverables. For historical reasons, the ISTQB retains the approach based on deliverables and thus the references to the 1998 version.

The master test plan will be based on the models proposed by IEEE 829. It will cover the global test aspects and the way the test activities will be distributed throughout the project phases (development, maintenance, acquisition, sales, etc.). If we follow the IEEE 829-1998 template, the master test plan will have the same structure as normal (level) test plan. The IEEE 829-2008 standard proposes a different model. The test plan is detailed in section 5.2.3.2.

Amongst the test activities to execute during the planning and organizational phases, we also have:

– identification of the test scope, which we will include in section 3 of the test plan;

– risk analysis, which will be conveyed into test tasks (section 10) or in test approach (section 6) or be included in section 15 of the test plan;

– integration and coordination of the test activities with development activities: acquisition, delivery, development, operations, and maintenance;

– organization and scheduling of the analysis and test design activities, creation of test cases and test data, test case execution, and evaluation activities;

– volume, level of detail, structure, and templates for test documentation;

– identification of test control and monitoring activities (test metrics), to prepare and execute tests, eliminate defects, and solve risk-related issues;

– volume, level of detail, and structure of the test procedures to allow reproducible test preparation and test execution.

The test strategy, detailed in the "approach" section of the test plan, can be an adaptation or a combination of those described in section 5.2.1.

5.2.3. *Test documentation*

FLO-5.2.2 Summarize the purpose and content of the test plan, test design specification and test procedure documents according to the "Standard for Software Test Documentation" (IEEE Std 829-1998) (K2)

All the test activities, such as test planning, test data preparation, test design, test execution, verification, and validation, as well as reporting activities are supported by written documentation. There are many document templates for these documentations, whether it is on the Internet or in standards. ISTQB recommends the use of the IEEE 829-1998 standard for software test documentation. This standard has evolved in 2008 to cover systems as well as software.

A description of the IEEE 829 templates is available in Chapter 8.

There are advantages and drawbacks to detailed test documentation:

– precise and detailed tests are less flexible because they will need to be modified if the software undergoing tests is modified; on the other hand, they allow the use of less experienced testers;

– less precise and less directive (or even less documented) tests enable us to cover more test conditions, but they are less reproducible, especially if test execution information (values used, actions executed, etc.) is not detailed and if testers do not have a good knowledge of the user business;

– precise and detailed tests will offer more transparent test criteria, which are not subject to interpretation, but are more difficult and more expensive to maintain;

– less detailed tests are easier to write and design, but the evaluation of their coverage can be difficult.

Let us have a look at the different documents used in the frame of software testing.

5.2.3.1. *Test documentation according to IEEE 829*

In order to be as exhaustive as possible, this book will describe both 1998 and 2008 versions of the IEEE 829 standard. The documentation architecture is as follows, with the 1998 version on the left side and the 2008 version on the right.

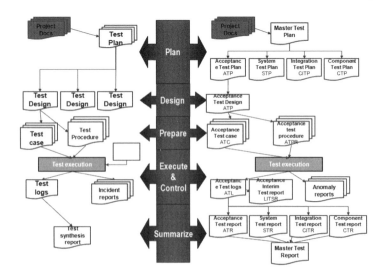

Figure 5.3. *Documentary architecture IEEE 829 v1998 and v2008*

The new version (2008) of the standard proposes documentation focused on test levels. The 1998 version used by the ISTQB enables the use of as many test plans and test design documents as required, and to organize them by test levels or by characteristics, as requested by the specific project needs.

5.2.3.2. *IEEE 829-1998 test plan*

Basing itself on the IEEE 829-1998 standard, ISTQB proposes a test plan with 16 chapters:

1. Test plan identifier, i.e. a unique reference to identify the test plan and its version;

2. An introduction, where the document and its implementation context will be succinctly described;

3. The elements or objects to be tested, the test target (software, hardware, documentation, etc. which will undergo testing);

4. The characteristics to be tested, defining the main test axes;

5. The characteristics that should not be tested. This is important to clearly state the perimeter of the current test campaign;

6. The planned test approach. We will have here a description of the main principles used, planned techniques and methods, and distribution of the test activities depending on the test levels or characteristics;

7. Pass or fail criteria, defining how to evaluate the success or failure of tests. This frequently depends on the number and severity of the remaining defects;

8. Test suspension and resumption criteria, defining the reasons that would justify stopping tests in order to use resources more efficiently (for example, not continuing tests if the smoke tests are not conclusive or if the software does not install correctly);

9. Tests deliverables, including final and intermediary deliverables (test data, statistics, scripts and scenarios, etc.);

10. The test tasks necessary to produce or process the deliverables;

11. Requirements in terms of environment (hardware, but also software and test tools) to execute the tasks identified in point 10;

12. Responsibilities of the different teams, in terms of quality of the deliverables and of the executed tasks;

13. Roles of the different participants and level of knowledge or skills required, both in terms of techniques (tools and methods) and in terms of business;

14. A calendar defining the schedule of the tasks, their duration, and their dependencies;

15. Risks and risk mitigation activities, such as executing the tests – for each testing task – depending on their relative importance (based on their integrity level, on criticality or on the impact of failures);

16. Approval of the test plan by the different stakeholders, whether it be the test team (to validate that the tasks can be done), the development team (to ascertain that they can deliver the software with the expected level of quality at the expected dates), the customers and users who accept – or not – the selected coverage criteria, the upper management who will deliver the necessary means to reach the stated objectives.

5.2.3.3. *IEEE 829-1998 test design document*

Test design documents detail the planned approaches, identify the characteristics to be tested in this domain or for this aspect of the software and list the associated tests. We can envisage as many test design documents as necessary. The following points describe the content of a test design document according to IEEE 829-1998:

1. Identification of the test design document, allowing a unique reference to this document;

2. Aspects to be tested in this design document. This allows the use of multiple views of a single characteristic; views that are described in separate test design documents;

3. Approach refinements, describing the approach – identified in the test plan – in more detail. We can describe here the analysis results demonstrating the interest of the test conditions and of the test case selection. We can also summarize the constraints and environmental requirements identified in this design document or the dependencies of these test cases or test procedures;

4. Identification of the tests and procedures associated with this test design document;

5. Pass or fail criteria for the different aspects and this characteristic, in order to easily determine the quality level expected in this design document.

5.2.3.4. *IEEE 829-1998 test cases*

Test cases are referenced and identified in the test design document and, according to IEEE 829-1998, comprise the following sections:

1. A unique identifier for the test case to enable traceability and a clear identification of the test case;

2. A description of the component to be tested. This component can be the software or any other product, document or hardware – described in the test design document – that will be verified by the test case. We should clearly reference the component and the documentation describing it (requirements or specifications, user guide, operating or installation manual, etc.);

3. Input specification, i.e. all the values or ranges of values used as input or as parameters, all the database references and authorization level, and any relationship between these input data;

4. Characteristics of the expected outputs, including the response time, expected values or ranges of values if there are some tolerances;

5. The environmental needs, clearly identifying the configuration characteristics and specifications of any hardware used in the test case, the versions and parameter levels of the software used and all other hardware needs related to the test;

6. The specific requirements for procedures, such as those necessary to simulate the passing of time between two test cases (for time sensitive transactions), or operator interventions during or after the test case;

7. Dependencies between the test cases, such as the fact that one test case on transfer of funds from account A to account B must ensure that account A is created and sufficiently provisioned.

5.2.3.5. *IEEE 829-1998 test procedures*

Test procedures allow us to combine multiple test cases, to evaluate a set of characteristics or features. They are sometimes also called "test scenarios". Test procedures as proposed by IEEE 829-1998 include the following sections:

1. Test procedure identifier, i.e. a unique identifier to reference this procedure;

2. Purpose of the procedure, including the references of the test cases executed and references to the relevant test documentation;

3. Specific requirements necessary to execute this procedure, which may include prerequisite procedures or test cases, special skills or environment requirements;

4. Procedure steps, describing – where needed – the following steps:

   - special methods for logging test execution results, incidents observed, or specific execution results,

   - setup of initialization actions necessary to execute the procedure,

   - actions to start the procedure,

   - actions necessary during the procedure execution,

- planned means of measurement, for example to measure the response time,

- actions to shut down the procedure, in case of unscheduled events,

- actions to restart the procedure, including restart points,

- actions to properly terminate the procedure,

- actions needed to properly restore the test environment,

- contingency actions to deal with unusual events occurring during the execution.

5.2.3.6. *IEEE 829-1998 test report*

The test report, whether it is a summary test report or a detailed one, describes the test activities carried out, their results, and provides an estimation based on these results. The test report proposed by IEEE 829-1998 includes the following sections:

1. A unique report identifier;

2. A summary describing the evaluation of the tested component, its detailed identification (version, sub-version and build number if applicable), references to the test documentation (test plan, test design document, test case and procedures, defect or anomaly reports and test logs) if they are available;

3. Description of the variations identified between the components that were to be tested and those actually tested, including any differences identified with regards to the test documentation and the reasons for these differences or variations;

4. Comprehensive assessment highlighting the level of coverage of the actions planned in the test plan, with an identification of any aspect or combination of aspects that may have been insufficiently tested;

5. Summary of the test results, with identification of all incidents or defects resolved, summary of these resolutions and the identification of any unresolved anomalies;

6. Global evaluation of each tested component, with identification of any limitations based on the test results and the pass/fail criteria;

7. Summary of the main test activities and notable events, including a synthesis of resource usage;

8. List of the persons that should approve the test report and their signature.

5.2.4. *Entry and exit criteria for test activities*

FLO-5.2.9 Recognize/justify adequate entry and exit criteria for specific test levels and groups of test cases (e.g. for integration testing, acceptance testing, or test cases for usability testing) (K2)

When organizing test activities, it is necessary to define, unequivocally when an activity ends and when another can start. Test activity entry and exit criteria define these criteria for tests. An entry criteria defines that a task can be started, the exit criteria identify that a task can be considered as finished.

5.2.4.1. *Entry criteria for test activities*

The entry criteria define when the activities can start, whether for a test level or for activities within a single test level. Generally these criteria define the availability of:

– adequate documentation (requirements, design, operations manual, etc.) allowing testers to determine the expected behavior of the component to be tested;

– test object (component, software, system) of an appropriate level of quality. This means that the previous phases (test or design phases) were successfully finished (the exit criteria for these previous phases have been successfully reached);

– test environment, test harness, drivers, and stubs necessary to execute the component to be tested, in a format usable by the testers;

– test resources (testers, hardware and software resources, etc.);

– test tools and test scripts;

– test data required for the test to be executed.

The entry criteria become stricter depending on the progress of the test activities. They can also include requirements for evidences of a minimal (pre-defined) level of quality as input (acquired by the execution of tests in a previous phase or by the successful execution of smoke tests in the initial phase of the task).

Samples of entry criteria for a system test level:

– availability of defect-tracking tools and test-execution tracking tools;

– all components are managed with a configuration management tool;

– the test environment – including all the hardware components – is configured. The test team has obtained the required level of access to these systems;

– all planned fixes for this version have been implemented by the development team;

– lower-level tests (component testing and integration testing) have been executed for all functionalities and fixes provided in this version;

– there is no remaining open blocking or critical defect in this version, and they are less than in other open defects for this version;

– the development team has delivered the software to the test team at least 3 days before the start of the system tests;

– the test team have executed 3 days of smoke tests and acceptable results have been provided at this test phase kick-off meeting;

– the management team, during the test phase kick-off meeting (for this level) agrees to continue testing. The elements to cover during this meeting are:

- is the code complete?

- is component testing complete and correct?

- will the remaining identified fixed defects be delivered less than 1 week after the start of the test phase?

5.2 4.2. *Resumption criteria*

The resumption criteria determine if tests can effectively resume, so as not to use unnecessarily resources. It can be considered as a polite way to say the opposite of a "stopping criteria", because stopping a test phase is not appreciated.

These resumption criteria can anticipate environment problems, blocking defects in the software or system being tested, lack of resources, etc.

Examples of resumption criteria for a system test level:

1. Software delivered to the test team is accompanied with a delivery notice (and include adequate references);

2. No modification is implemented on the system, whether it is to the source code, configuration files, or setup instructions, without a defect report. When a change is implemented without an appropriate defect report, the test manager will open an urgent defect report requesting this information and will escalate it to their manager;

3. The number of remaining open defects will remain below 50. Average closure durations (daily and rolling) will remain below 2 weeks (i.e. defects will be corrected in delivery cycles of 2 weeks);

4. A defect review meeting occurs twice a week, until the end of the system testing phase, in order to manage remaining open defects and defect closing durations.

5.2.4.3. *Exit criteria for test activities*

Exit criteria define when test activities can be considered as finished and when the component under test can be delivered to the next tasks.

Activity exit criteria are often based on metrics or on coverage ratio, such as a successful execution of all the previously defined tests cases, coverage of all instructions or all branches, of all functionalities, or of a selected subset of functionalities.

Too strict requirements may become blocking factors during test execution, and it is recommended that mechanisms that prevent testing from being considered as an activity preventing software delivery are included.

Exit criteria are defined per test level, per activity or for the whole software. If the exit criteria are sufficiently detailed, they will help in designing a strategy for unit testing and integration testing. Generally these exit criteria (or stopping criteria) are management decisions.

Amongst possible exit criteria, we can mention:

– 100% statements, branch or decision coverage by the executed tests. This ensures a technical coverage and identifies the areas of the software that have not yet been executed;

– reaching a specific detection ratio for new defects per period of time, but this ratio must be function of the test effort and of the severity of the detected defects;

– the defects detected at this level correspond to the type of defects expected. This confirms the maturity level of the design and test processes preceding the current phase. This also enables us to determine the maturity of the tested product;

– all tests planned for this test level have been successfully executed;

– all tests for "catastrophic" and "critical" (or even "marginal") integrity levels have been designed, implemented and executed successfully on the last version of the software or system.

Some exit criteria should be avoided:

– stopping testing when the planned test termination date is reached. As specified by G. Myers [MYE 97, pp. 122-124], this criterion can be reached without any test being designed or executed. It does not allow measuring any level of quality;

– stopping testing when the planned test effort has been reached. This criterion does not allow measuring the final level of quality of the software or system, and is dependent on the initial level of quality of the software. If the planned workload is too small, the criterion will be reached quickly, without significantly impacting the quality level of the software;

– stopping when all the test cases have been executed without finding new defects. This criterion is simultaneously counterproductive (pushes for the design of test cases that have a small possibility of identifying defects) and depends on the quality of the tests.

If the exit criteria specified in the test planning and organizational phase is ignored, the following phases – including production – provide a system that is not sufficiently mature and will potentially have significant defects. These subsequent phases will be less efficient (increase in the number of defects identified that have to be corrected) and more expensive. If the exit criteria apply to system tests or to acceptance tests, poor-quality, defective software will be delivered to the customers and end users, thereby leading to unhappy users, loss of perceived quality of products, and potential loss of sales for the company.

Potential exit criteria for a system test level as provided by Rex Black [BLA 09, p. 60]:

1. No modification (design, code or characteristics) during the last 3 weeks, except to deal with the defects identified during system tests;

2. No stopping, crash, or inexplicable end of processes on any software servers or systems during the last 3 weeks;

3. No customer systems have become unstable or unusable following an installation failure during system testing;

4. The testing team has run all tests planned on the delivery candidate version of the software;

5. The development team has solved all the "to be fixed" defects, as planned by sales, marketing or customer services;

6. The testing team has checked that all issues identified in the defect management tool have been either closed or postponed to a subsequent version and – where applicable – have been verified by adequate regression and confirmation tests;

7. Test metrics indicate a stable and reliable product, the end of all the planned tests, and adequate coverage of all the critical quality risks identified;

8. The product management team accepts that the product, as defined in the last cycle of system testing, will meet reasonable quality objectives for the customers;

9. The project management team held a meeting for the end of the system testing phase and accepts that system testing can be considered as finished.

Exit criteria must be considered simultaneously on the basis of customer test objectives and selected techniques. For example, from experience-based tests, we can determine whether the distribution of the faults corresponds to industry statistics [BEI 90, pp. 462-466] or shows an improvement in comparison to the previous versions.

5.3. Test progress monitoring and control (FL 5.3)

Considering the number of tasks and their dependencies, it is necessary to ensure adequate progress, in order to anticipate problems and plan necessary adaptations of the test activities. This is called *test control*.

FLO-5.3.1 Recall common metrics used for monitoring test preparation and execution (K1)

The easiest way to measure the progress of test activities is to measure them. Various progress metrics can be used to determine whether tasks are on schedule or if they are falling behind.

We can mention:

– actual progress percentage for the task and comparison of this progress with the planned completion estimated for the task at this point in time;

– coverage rate of the activities carried out with regards to all these types of activities, taking into account integrity levels. This applies to all test conditions, design activities, test implementation, and execution tasks, and can be related to the progress percentage expected at this specific time;

– coverage rate for the requirements, the risks, the specifications or the code, or even of the test cases;

– successful closure of contract or internal milestones and test activity monitoring;

– subjective evaluation by testers of the software quality level;

– comparative evaluation of the risks and the cost of test to limit these risks, in order to prioritize coverage of the highest risks.

FLO-5.3.2 Explain and compare test metrics for test reporting and test control (e.g. found and fixed, and tests passed and failed) related to purpose and use (K2)

Metrics and measurements, just as statistics, can be misleading: the simple visual representation of the tests can be different from their detailed interpretation. Let us take the example of Figure 5.4, showing the progress report of unit tests carried out by a team of external providers for a customer.

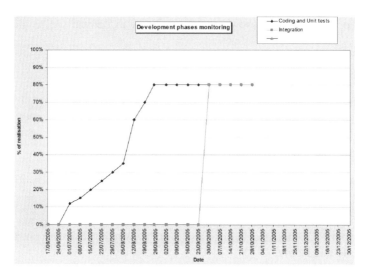

Figure 5.4. *Example of integration*

First, we can conclude that integration seems to have been done according to the "big bang" model. However, this is not entirely true as only 80% of the components have been developed and integrated. What about the remaining 20%? A second reading enables us to identify that no design of new components occurred over a 10 week period. This period is not a holiday period and resources were thus assumed to be available.

A more detailed reading enables us to identify surprising aspects of this graph, such as the progress from the fourth week onwards with an incremental step of 5% and then of 10% from the ninth value. This not statistically realistic and should have raised a red flag for the customer.

We can thus see that such statistics, if they are not more detailed, are not useful to anticipate the end of the component design and testing phase, or the delivery – after integration – of the components for the beginning of system and acceptance tests.

Let us take another example, concerning defect detection and correction, as described in Figure 5.5.

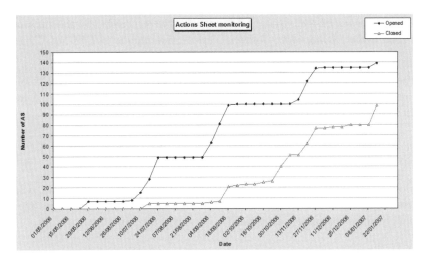

Figure 5.5. *Defect detection and correction ((♦) opened; (△) closed)*

On a first reading it seems to indicate that the lower curve (defect closure) grows more quickly than the upper curve (defect identification) and thus all the identified defects will be fixed.

A trend analysis of these two curves enables us to notice a slight divergence of the two curves and defect detection plateaus. This can indicate a lack of maturity of the software or implementation of different and additional techniques. Here, the main problem is that testing stops after about 3 weeks, because testers reach blocking points, which force testing activities to stop.

A more detailed analysis enables us to identify correction phases, which are limited to 20 or 30 identified defects, instead of processing all the defects identified to date. This can be symptomatic of a tendency for the development team to prioritize easy to fix defects and to defer the processing of more complex defects or more difficult to fix defects to a later stage. This method of processing occurs frequently and leads to a reduction of the defect-fixing rate towards the end of the campaign, by keeping the most complex defect fixes for the end.

Two other elements of information can be taken from Figure 5.5: the vertical space between the two curves shows the number of defects that still need to be fixed at a given point in time while the horizontal space between the two curves gives the average time to fix the defect. We can thus see that the correction time, which was initially equal to about 10 weeks, then becomes more than 3 months at the end of the graph. We can thus assert that the project is not in a good shape.

FLO-5.3.3 Summarize the purpose and content of the test summary report document according to the "Standard for Software Test Documentation" (IEEE Std 829-1998) (K2)

The objective of the test summary report is to summarize the results of the executed test activities and to supply an evaluation based on these results. A model of test summary report is available in section 8.8.1.

5.4. Reporting

Monitoring and control would not be useful without reporting activity (generation of a *test report*), in order to inform the stakeholders and to allow them to knowingly make appropriate decisions for the rest of the project.

However, it is important to know what to say and to whom, because some pieces of information are not relevant to all the stakeholders: customers and the hierarchy are not interested in the same elements as the test or development teams. The information delivered should be defined and depends on the planned audience.

5.4.1. *What to report, to whom, and how?*

Which are the interesting aspects for stakeholders and who are these stakeholders?

Objectives and information of interest for testing teams:

– the workload carried out thus far and what is remaining;

– quality level of services carried out;

– coverage of requirements, of specifications, and of test conditions (depending on the project progress, we will speak about test case design or test case execution);

– the number of identified, fixed, or to-be-retested defects and their impact in terms of regression testing;

– components with more defects than others, in order to adjust testing;

– the number of executed test cases, those successfully carried out, the blocked ones, those at fault, and associated percentages;

– etc.

Development teams are interested in other information provided by the test teams, such as:

– identified defects, their impacts and impacted modules;

– planned test delivery dates;

– quality level of delivered software (number and types of defects) per version.

In the framework of the test action progress monitoring, the testing management is interested in:

– planned software delivery dates by the development team for testing, in order to anticipate required test environment resets and smoke tests;

– functionalities, specifications, or requirement changes compared to the initial requirements, in order to anticipate their impact on tests, whether they are new tests to be designed or existing tests to be modified or removed;

– number of defects detected per period of time (sorted by impact of the failures) and number of duplicated or rejected defects, and by failure level (integrity level or failure criticality) the average correction time;

– effort spent compared to the effort planned and the reasons for any differences, to identify whether are attributable to the test team, the development team, or to other causes;

– average test design, test implementation, and test execution effort, as well as the workload and average cost of the defects;

– etc.

Higher-level hierarchy is interested in:

– the identified quality level;

– use of the planned effort and any difference between the planned and actual effort;

– planned delivery dates;

– improvement of the application maturity;

– evolution of the costs and efforts (planned, carried out or remained to be done);

– evaluation of the effectiveness and maturity of the processes, as well as process improvement actions that need to be considered.

Customers, users, or marketing representatives may be interested in:

– system testing dates, in order to be present if needed;

– provisional date for the beginning of acceptance testing;

– planned delivery date to production or to the market;

– requirements or functionalities postponed to a later delivery date or subject to limitation (e.g., of performances);

– etc.

How can we supply these pieces of information to the various stakeholders? This information is often presented as graphs or statistics, from the metrics supplied during the test project.

5.4.2. *Statistics and graphs*

Graphs with trends and evolutions are useful to show the evolution throughout time. A global view showing an evolution can often clearly show the progress of the project.

Various representation modes can be used to evaluate the project progress. We have for example the quality of each project milestone (see Figure 5.6):

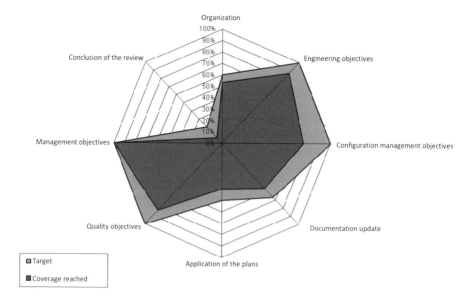

Figure 5.6. *Quality of a milestone*

Evaluating the evolution of the quality of the various milestones (Kick-Off, Specification Review, PDR, CDR, SRR, Test Readiness Review (TRR), Test Review Board (TRB), Acceptance) throughout the project:

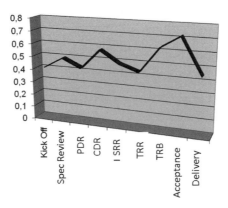

Figure 5.7. *Quality indices of the reviews*

Designing dashboards, which will supply summarized information, such as in Figure 5.8:

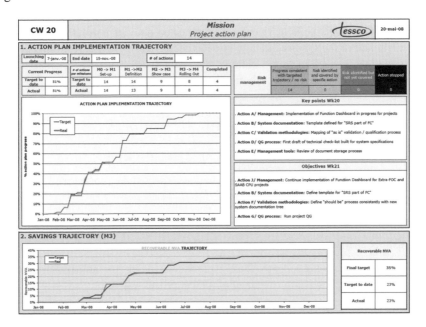

Figure 5.8. *Dashboard*

Or evaluating the delay taken by a project by using time-over-time graphs (Figure 5.9):

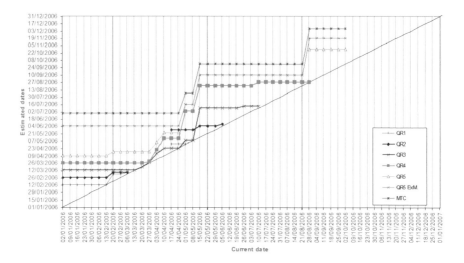

Figure 5.9. *Diagram time after time*

The use of a time-over-time diagram enables us to assess the delays of a project over time. The objective is to visualize the expected date for a milestone (identified on the left side of the graph) and how these expected dates evolve over time. If these curves tend to be parallel to the oblique, the project will never be finished, always producing 1 month delay with each month of progress.

5.5. Transverse processes and activities

Numerous transverse activities are executed at all test levels:

– definition of test data: input data as well as expected data (oracles);

– *configuration management* for all deliverables (inputs or outputs of testing activities);

– change management and *version control*;

– identification of good (or "best") practices, search for anti-patterns or bad practices and continuous improvement of all test processes;

– etc.

5.5.1. *Test data definition*

The search for test data is necessary at all test levels for many functional or non-functional characteristics. This includes several major phases:

– we must identify the necessary input data to exercise all planned data combinations depending on the techniques we use. For each equivalence partition, we must identify the representatives and design test data (in files, database tables or transactions) which will enable us to identify potential failures. These data may need to be combined with one another (such as for decision tables) and include boundary values at the edges of the equivalence partitions;

– we must identify the expected data (test oracles) for all input values, either dynamically during test execution or in a static manner before the test execution, in order to compare the obtained data and to determine the success or failure of each test;

– we must also design large volumes of data to ensure that functional and performances tests apply to volumetric bases, representative of production.

It is possible to copy production data in order to get test data; however, this is not recommended. Production data are confidential and always protected. Test data are not subjected to the same restrictions or even to the same safety measures. If test data are used, it is thus recommended to ensure that they are "anonymized". Moreover, the use of test data with a name can be subjected to regulatory constraints, such as a declaration to the CNIL (*Comission Nationale Informatique et Libertés*; French National Commission of Computer Science and Freedoms).

5.5.2. *Configuration management (FL 5.4)*

Development and design teams use configuration management systems to store and manage software components and to ensure product integrity throughout their cycle of life.

FLO-5.4.1 Summarize how configuration management supports testing (K2)

Configuration management tools enable us to structure the test team's files and directories and how test components are modified. This is necessary due to the significant number of modifications occurring throughout the testing project. An inadequate configuration management process will lead to data loss and significant difficulties to identify the cause of some failures, such as those due to different environments (with different software components).

It is often possible to adapt the configuration management processes used by the development team, as well as the configuration management tools.

Configuration management must also be ensured for all hardware components necessary for testing, as well as for software tools and operating systems.

5.5.3. *Change management*

Project requirements and specifications do not remain set in stone throughout the project. The market evolves and so do customers, their markets, and their requirements. This implies evolutions in terms of requirements and specifications. It is extremely easy to change software and it will lead to a request for modifications, without always taking into account the impact of these changes on the development and test processes or on deadlines or on costs.

The industry estimates at about 2% change per month for evolutions in requirements. It is important to ensure a consistent implementation of these changes, with the evaluation of their impacts on specifications, architecture, code, tests, and documentation.

The integration of change management processes and of the evolutions must be taken into account by the test project management. It is generally made up of a change control board, which, on the basis of the identified impacts, decides on the implementation of the selected evolutions. This committee can also be involved in the selection of the corrections to implement in the different software versions (version control).

5.6. Risks management (FL 5.5)

Risk management is a continuous and iterative process starting with the definition of the concept and finishing with the end of life of the software or system. Risk management in tests is applied on two levels: risks associated with the software product (defects and failures) and risks associated with the test project (overrunning of the deadlines or costs).

FLO-5.5.1 Describe a risk as a possible problem that would threaten the achievement of one or more stakeholders' project objectives (K2)

A risk is described as a probability (lower than 100%) that an event occurs and leads to negative consequences. These negative consequences can be minor or major and jeopardize reaching the objectives, in terms of development (project risks) or of use of the application software (product risk). An event with an occurrence probability of 100% and negative consequences is called a problem, whereas an event with an occurrence probability lower than 100% and a positive consequence is called an opportunity.

It is important to identify and anticipate risks so as to implement in due course the limitation measures applicable to the identified risks. There are several possible answers to the identification of a risk:

– acceptance of this risk and of the consequences of its occurrence. This is often the best solution if no action can be carried out to counter or limit this risk or if the occurrence likelihood or the impact is low;

– reducing the occurrence probability of this risk by implementing risk mitigation actions. The risk occurrence probability still needs to be measured to ensure that mitigation measures are efficient;

– reducing the impact of this risk by taking safeguard and contingency measures. It is important to continuously measure the risk occurrence probability to know whether the safeguard or contingency plans must remain active or may be reduced;

– transfer the risk to another team or organization, for example, via EULA (End User License Agreement) for legal risks coming from the use of software or via insurances. This risk transfer can be a solution if the impacts for the company, the project, or for the product are limited.

These four possible answers are not mutually exclusive, but can be implemented simultaneously, especially the mitigation and contingency aspects.

5.6.1. *Principles of risk management*

The risk management principle is as follows: each risk must be identified, analyzed, prioritized (according to impact and probability of occurrence), and monitored throughout its period of existence.

Risks can evolve independently from the actions carried out by the actors of the project. They evolve according to events outside the project, whether it is in terms of probable impact or in terms of the increase – or decrease – of the occurrence probability.

FLO-5.5.2 Remember that the level of risk is determined by its likelihood (of occurrence) and its impact (damages resulting from it) (K1)

Risk are often evaluated according to their probability of occurrence (depending on the occurrence of the defect and of the frequency of use of the function) and to their impact. The formula of risk evaluation will thus be:

$$\text{Risk} = [(\text{impacts}) \times (\text{likelihood})] \qquad [5.1]$$

We will determine ranges of impact, of occurrence and of frequency as proposed in Table 5.1.

Condition	Description	Likelihood (%)	Level
Critical	The risk will almost certainly materialize	≥90	1 – Very high
High	The risk will not materialize under optimistic conditions	60-90	2 – High
Average	The risk may or may not materialize in normal circumstances; there is no evidence for one eventuality over the other	30-60	3 – Average
Low	The risk will only materialize in pessimistic conditions	0-30	4 – Low

Table 5.1. *Risk likelihood*

By evaluating the risks according to equation [5.1], we obtain a range of values (RPN: risk priority number) going from 1 to 16. We can represent these ranges of values in the form of a matrix, as illustrated in Figure 5.10.

Figure 5.10. *Table of risks: occurrence × impact*

This matrix enables us to order risks according to their criticality (their RPN). Several risk combinations are identical (for example, 2, 3, 4, 6, and 12) and, therefore, such a matrix will not enable us to determine whether it is more important to deal with the risks with a high occurrence probability but a low impact, or with those with a low occurrence probability and a critical impact, or else with those with a high occurrence and impact probability (for example, the value 4 appearing in three places). Although this assessment mode is quite common, it leaves much to be desired, especially if the impacts on the project, the product, or its use are multiple (or are not evaluated).

There are several types of impact that we may wish to evaluate:

– impact on the development, implementation or test planning;

– impact on the product cost;

– impact on the performances of the product.

This enables us to identify and classify the impact severities as follows:

Product cost	Performances	Planning	Severity
Extra cost of more than 25%; significant budget overrun	Inability to produce a deliverable software or system fulfilling the acceptance criteria	Delay of more than 25% and inability to meet the commitments to higher-level project(s)	1 – Critical
10-25% extra cost, much beyond the budget	Inability to reach key criteria and no workaround identified	Delay of 10-25% or inability to meet major milestones	2 – High
5-10% extra cost, limited overrun of the budget	Inability to reach criteria, but workaround and corrections are possible	Delay of 5-10% or delays without any change to the global planning	3 – Average
Less than 5% extra cost, non-negligible overrun of the budget	Inability to reach criteria but possible negotiation with customers	Less than 5% delay, or the delay can be suppressed	4 – Low

Table 5.2. *Impact severity of the risks*

If we wish to sort out risks according to the severities (Table 5.2) and the defined level (Table 5.1), we will be able to obtain the following evaluation:

Global severity of the risk	Very high	High	Average	Low
An aspect of "Critical" severity or else two or more aspects of "High" severity	1	2	4	8
An aspect of "High" severity or else two or more aspects of "Average" severity	3	5	6	10
An aspect of "Average" severity	7	9	11	14
All aspects are of "Low" severity	12	13	15	16

Table 5.3. *Risks by severity and likelihood*

The numbering of the various risk levels (risk priority number) and their coherent organization in the matrix enable us to group risks together and to deal with them according to their classification, their frequency, and their impact.

The classification (or the risk category, called CAT) associated with the levels 1 and 2 (CAT I), 3 to 6 (CAT II), 7 to 12 (CAT III), and 13 to 16 (CAT IV) can help to determine the responsibility level of the person in charge of these risks. Critical risks (CAT I) are often managed at the level of a general direction (upper management), whereas lower risks can be managed at lower hierarchical levels.

For each identified risk, we must assign reduction actions for this risk, called mitigation actions, in order to reduce the risk occurrence or to limit impacts.

As previously mentioned, risks and their impact evolve throughout the project. It is recommended that periodical risk evaluations are carried out to identify new risks; risks with increasing severity, those that are disappearing, and/or those with a decreasing impact (for example after the implementation of mitigation actions). The evolution of the risks of the project over time enables us to see if the project is or is not on a slippery slope. A representation of this evolution on a specific period of time is proposed on Figure 5.11.

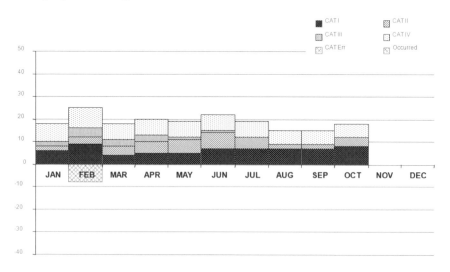

Figure 5.11. *Evolution of the risks throughout time*

We can see in Figure 5.11 that category I risks grow as the project progresses, from March onwards. Such a situation is not recommended and we should tend towards a decrease of the highest risks (categories I and II).

5.6.2. *Project risks and product risks*

FLO-5.5.3 Distinguish between project and product risks (K2)

Risks can be applied to the product (system or software) or to the project.

A project-related risk is a risk whose main impact will be on the project, on its cost or its duration, on the effort required, or the use of the resources associated with the project. An influenza epidemic or social unrests within the company will have an impact on the execution of the project and must be considered as a project risk.

A risk related to the product will have an impact on the software, on its quality level, on its limitations, or on its availability. Missing functionalities or functionalities subjected to important limitations in a software can be considered as risk of non-acceptance of the software or of the system by the customer and must, therefore, be managed as such.

Often, project risks will impact on product risks and vice versa. Indeed, anything that impacts the ability of the project participants to carry out tasks (whether it is for lack of time or of knowledge or for any other reason) will lead to an increase of the number of remaining defects in the product. Similarly, a product for which the number of defects identified during testing is significant, will impact project duration, because of the obligation to write defect reports, to fix these defects, and then to re-test and regression test the software.

FLO-5.5.4 Recognize typical product and project risks (K1)

It is not always easy to determine the impact on the project or product, because often these impacts are merging. An easy way to differentiate project risks from product risks is to determine the initial or major impact and the derived impacts.

A few examples of risks are listed below:

– risks related to logistics, such as those resulting from a late receipt of the software to be tested, from a lack of quality of the delivered product, impacting on the project duration and the product quality. This can be mitigated by the implementation of preventive measures and by an adjustment of the planning;

– a test environment that does not correspond to the production environment, resulting in unidentified defects delivered to customers. The risk here can be transferred towards the management or customers or can be mitigated by a call for outside service providers able to carry out tests in more realistic environments;

– software or components that are incorrectly installed in the environment and impact error reproducibility. This can be mitigated via the implementation of a configuration management process and of a component traceability management process;

– modifications of the product with impacts all over in the software, forcing us to re-test everything, to modify test conditions, test data, and oracles. A change management process enables us to identify and mitigate such risks. It is also possible to transfer and raise these risks towards senior management;

– poorly trained staff or too few staff, leading to an increase of project duration or to the lack of tests on important business or technical aspects. This type of risk can be mitigated by using business experts from amongst the users or by hiring outside technical experts (fixed rate services for example);

– failure of suppliers or subcontractors. These risks can be mitigated by closely monitoring the activities of outside subcontractors and suppliers; contingency plans can be developed and implemented in case of an established risk;

– changing, ambiguous, or contradictory requirements and priorities, generating technical problems. This can be dealt with via change management associated with reviews and with project management taking into account priorities;

– etc.

5.6.3. *Introduction to risk management*

Risk management is a wide and complex field, the detailed study of which is beyond the scope of this book. A number of aspects, however, need to be taken into account and will be tackled in the next sections.

5.6.3.1. *Frequency measurements*

Risks are measured as a function of their occurrence frequency and their impact. Measuring the possible occurrence frequency is not easy. This is rather a "finger in the air" estimate, carried out by taking into account risks that have already occurred (in previous projects) or not.

Such a way to estimate frequencies does not take into account the reasons explaining the increase or decrease of risks. The evolution of development and test projects has an impact on the possible occurrence of a risk or not. It is thus important that the test manager identifies the factors influencing risk occurrence and knows about (tracks) their evolution.

5.6.3.2. *Identifying risks*

We can identify risks with various techniques, which can be more or less formal.

Risk identification includes the following techniques:

– the informal technical meeting, where risks are identified in groups, without any defined guideline (brainstorming). Risks are then evaluated in terms of impact and of probability of occurrence, and measures are taken based on these evaluations;

– failure mode and effect analysis (FMEA), with the possibility to process the criticality impact of these effects (FMECA). This more formal method identifies potential failures, organizes them according to their severity, and defines prevention measures in order to avoid their occurrence or to limit their impact;

– fault tree analysis is another formal method, where the origins of failures of a level are studied on the basis of a combination of lower level defects, in order to produce a tree of failures, which is leading to an unwished result. This method comes from the system safety and reliability field but is also applicable to the software field;

– hazard analysis is a technique used in the aerospace industry, where the system context is taken into account to evaluate failures and the impact of the defects;

– hyperspace of danger is a risk analysis method at the business level enabling us to organize risks according to five major axes. For more information on this method, the reader can refer to [KER 91] and to the article "L'HyperEspace du Danger et son application aux risques logiciels" [HOM 03a, pp. 4-10].

5.6.3.3. *Risk prioritization and scheduling*

Risk identification will give us a fairly extensive list, which we will need to classify and prioritize, to deal with the identified risks.

Risk prioritization must measure the frequency and impact for each risk and whatever increases (or decreases) this frequency or this impact. The simple identification of a risk proves its importance for a person. We risk finding ourselves with a large number of high-level risks. Risk prioritization must be carried out once the frequency and the impact have been determined.

Considering the number of risks, it will not be possible to discuss all identified risks. We will have to implement risk mitigation actions according to the defined priority. This will lead us to neglect some risks.

Implemented mitigation or contingency activities, such as the evolution of the project context over time, justify a periodical re-evaluation of the risks as well as reporting of risk monitoring (top 10 risks) and historic (evolution of the number and level of risks throughout the project) information.

5.6.3.4. *Risk-based testing*

It is possible to design tests using as a basis all identified risks. This risk-based testing method should be applied all along the project after the definition of task durations. For each task, the principle is to carry out the task according to the prioritizations of the identified risks.

Dealing with the tasks is undertaken in the same way we used to prioritizing requirements or ensuring their coverage by test conditions and test cases. Here, instead of focusing traceability on requirements, we will use the identified risks as the basis. This method also considers input requirements as a type of risk that needs to be covered.

5.6.3.5. *Prioritization throughout the project*

While risks, their likelihood of occurrence, and their impact vary throughout the project, it is necessary to periodically re-evaluate and reprioritize risks.

FLO-5.5.5 Describe by using examples how risk analysis and risk management may be used for test planning (K2)

For example, we could identify the risk of disaster leading to the complete loss of the test environment as a significant risk for our test project. Several mitigation and contingency actions can be considered:

– preventing overvoltage, fire, or flood risks by taking the appropriate measures;

– preventing risks of data loss by storing all the data used by the test team on secure backup media (RAID 4 or 5 disks), which will be placed in protected premises;

– making periodical backups (i.e. daily) and ensuring they work by carrying out reinstallations (data recovery) in a clean test environment;

– negotiating the possibility to access a cold site in case of disaster, etc.

Some risk limitation actions are quite repetitive and others are one-off actions. Not making sure that backups are usable is a significant risk, which should be periodically re-evaluated. The negotiation of an access contract to a cold site is a one-off action.

5.6.3.6. *Main risks*

As previously defined, there are project risks and product risks. Some risks are often neglected, as:

– legal risks due to negligence or malpractice,

– use of offshore subcontractors (see the article "L'externalisation des développpments informatiques analysé via l'Hyperspace du danger" [HOM 03b, pp. 8-12],

– etc.

5.7. Defect management (FL5.6)

Besides the supply of information on the level of quality of software and systems, one of the main objectives of the tests is to identify defects so that they are processed – corrected or evaluated – before the software or the system is delivered to customers. This implies identifying and processing defects, as well as checking their correction.

Anomaly discovery is carried out via the static and dynamic techniques studied previously. For software already in use, users can discover failures and ask for their correction. These defects detected in production are defects that were not detected by test processes in previous versions of the software. It will be necessary to improve these processes in order to identify such defects. A link between user support tools (customer support) and defect management tools is thus important.

Defect management is associated with the IEEE 1044-1993 standard (describing anomaly classification) and to the IEEE 829-1998 standard, which suggests a template for anomaly description.

5.7.1. *Introduction to defect management*

The main objective of testing activities is to identify defects in software applications and to participate in the delivery of high-quality software. Therefore, discovered defects must be fixed.

We can apply a management process to defects that is similar to risk management and we may consider not fixing some defects, if their impact is negligible or if there are other (higher) priorities. It may be more important to put a product on the shelf in order to position ourselves on the market – even if the product is not perfect – and even if it means offering up free corrective patches available for downloading.

The level of urgency associated with defect correction, in order to continue testing the software, implies the need to describe defects in a sufficiently detailed way, so that analysis by the developer is quick and clear.

5.7.1.1. *Defect life cycle*

Anomalies generally have a life cycle made of three main phases[1]:

– the recognition or identification phase, during which we identify the difference between the obtained result and the expected one; we assert the reality of the defect and we assess causes and impacts;

– the action phase, during which we determine the actions to be carried out in order to process the defect;

– the disposal phase, during which we define the phases related to defect closure.

5.7.1.2. *Defect classification*

Defects can be classified according to several criteria: the impact on users (often called criticality), the necessary effort to correct the defect, the component where this defect is initially present, etc.

Defect classification enables us to order them according to various criteria and to take measures in order to avoid repeated reporting of already discovered defects.

Once the classification has been carried out, it is possible to determine:

– defect prevention activities that can be implemented, so as to prevent the occurrence of other defects of this type in the software or in future software developments;

– processes effectiveness and test process permeability rates related to defects, in order to determine the most permeable phases (those detecting the fewest number of defects) and to improve them.

5.7.2. *Defect identification*

One of the important aspects of the tests is to ensure that the results obtained during the execution of the application correspond to the expected results. In case of a difference between those two results, we have to determine whether it is an anomalous defect or not.

There are several methods to identify expected results:

– comparison to requirements and specifications provided for the software design. Requirements and specifications should be testable and comprise sufficient information to determine the level of quality of the actual results. This method does

---

1 According to IEEE 1044-1993.

not always enable accurate testing, because the options chosen by developers in case of ambiguities or imprecisions can differ from those chosen by the tester. There will then be the creation of defects, which will be considered as "works as designed" and as "a feature, not a bug" without any added value or information;

– comparison with a previous version of the program or even other competitor software, etc.

We must remember that many defects during tests are to be found in the tests themselves. Tests may have been badly designed or implemented or may not use the right data or context (environment, priorities, users, etc.). The first action of defect identification should thus consist of determining the reality of the error. The defect can be discovered by a tester, a developer, a customer, or by any other user of the software. This is why it is important to have feedback from product support teams towards test teams.

Once the defect has been detected, it is necessary to report it and to reduce the number of execution steps necessary for its manifestation. This helps us to determine the possible probability frequency. After the determination of the defect probability frequency, determination of the impact will be important to determine the urgency applicable to fix the defect. Easy workaround methods will reduce the perceived impact.

Detailed documentation of the defect enables us to note all the information obtained during this identification phase and helps developers to correct the defect and to carry out any subsequent statistical analysis based on defect data (i.e. search for defect clustering in components, identification of the most frequent root causes, identification of the most efficient processes and methods, etc.).

5.7.2.1. *Defect taxonomies*

There are several lists (taxonomies) of defects. You can define your own list or use one of those already available in the industry:

– the root cause is frequently a human error. In order to avoid their future reappearance, we can consider training actions, or check-lists in order to identify them;

– the phase of the development cycle where the defect has been introduced (see [BEI 90, pp. 460-476]);

– listing the characteristics impacted by the defect (see characteristics and sub-characteristics ISO 9126);

– lists of typical defect (see appendix A of [KAN 99, pp. 363-436]).

5.7.2.2. Defect description

The content of the defect reports can follow the model proposed by the IEEE 829-1998 standard.

FLO-5.6.1 Recognize the content of an incident report according to the "Standard for Software Test Documentation" (IEEE Std 829-1998) (K1)

This model has been proposed by the IEEE 829-1998 standard and includes the following sections:

1. Identifier for the defect, enabling us to recognize and identify it uniquely.

2. Summary of the anomaly, often a short sentence. It is quite important to use this field as if it were the title of a press article, so as to potentially influence readers.

3. Description of the defect or incident. We will describe here the following points in separate fields (to enable selections and ordering):

- values introduced as input, including pre-conditions,

- values expected as output, including post-conditions,

- values obtained as output (actual results),

- description of the defect,

- date and time of the identification,

- step of the test procedure or of the test case,

- description of the hardware and software environment (including data and settings),

- actions carried out to isolate and reproduce the anomaly,

- name of the testers,

- name of the witnesses of the anomaly and of the test.

Other pieces of information can be added, such as the test cases previously executed if they influence the anomaly.

4. Impact of the defect, where we will describe the impact for the users and the various stakeholders. This impact will help us determining the urgency or not of the correction. The impact can be on test documentation (test plans, test design document, test cases, etc.) or on other supports (installation manual, maintenance or operation manual, user manual, specifications or requirements, etc.).

Adding specific information to anomaly reports in order to lead to a more efficient management can be useful. It will be necessary to apply similar criteria to those applicable for the redaction of specifications: avoid noise (useless information), avoid ambiguities, and be precise and concise, etc.

Fields enabling statistical analysis of the anomalies and the definitions of axes for future improvement can be required depending on the improvement techniques of the implemented processes:

– the activity being carried out when the defect was identified: for example, if we were rereading a specification during system testing, the activity will be "rereading";

– the environment and conditions that enabled us to identify the defect and more particularly what revealed the defect;

– analysis of the impact for tests and for customers;

– component(s) actually fixed (this can be the requirements or the specifications, in addition to the code);

– type of defect and how (and when) it should have been identified;

– type of fix implemented;

– type of defect source (missing or duplicated code, subcontracted code, library component, etc.);

– age of the defective component (is it new or legacy code?), in order to determine the possible number of latent defects in the code.

The first three fields described above are filled in by testers during defect identification and the last five are filled in by developers during (or after) correction of the defect.

5.7.2.3. *Triage*

It may be necessary to implement a "bug triage" phase, to select which defects must be immediately fixed and which defects can be fixed at a later stage (or even not corrected at all). This means deciding the priority level to allocate to each defect, according to various criteria, such as:

– remaining time before delivery to the market;

– cost and duration of the correction;

– priority and severity of the defect (determined as a function of impact for the user and/or the organization);

– criticality of the module where the defect is located, etc.

Triage can also determine that a detected defect does not need to be corrected, either because it is a required operating mode ("it's a feature not a bug"), or because its impact is not important enough to justify correction.

5.7.2.4. *Attributes of defect reports*

The objective of the defect report is to allow defect fixing. Therefore, it is necessary to share with others (managers, developers, customers) the evaluation of the impact that identified defect can have on the software. This involves reporting the defect in the most succinct and understandable way possible, to allow an understanding by all stakeholders. Determining the impact in an understandable way for developers (data loss, functionality loss, software instability, etc.) and for customers and the hierarchy (impacts in financial terms or in usability terms, non-compliance to requirements, etc.) enables a quick recognition of the anomaly.

FLO-5.6.2 *Write an incident report covering the observation of a failure during testing (K3)*

Rex Black [BLA 09, pp. 152-154] proposed 10 aspects to take into account when writing of a defect report:

1. Structure: tests deliberately carried out while taking notes enable us to find more easily the first indices of a defect;

2. Reproduction: the reproducibility of an anomaly is a necessary attribute to ensure its correction;

3. Isolation: once the defect is reproduced, it is important to isolate the phases leading to its occurrence. Where possible limit the number of steps necessary to reproduce the defect. A defect including seven stages or more is generally difficult to read and its correction will thus be delayed;

4. Generalizing: once the defect is isolated, we need to determine whether it can be generalized. This includes the detection of other defects of a similar structure in other modules of the software;

5. Comparing: determining whether the defect has occurred for the first time in this version of the application or whether it was already present (but undetected) in previous versions;

6. Summarizing: the title of the defect (or its summary) is critical and must show how it can affect customers;

7. Condensing: reducing the size of the defect report so as not to bore readers and reducing the number of acronyms so that it remains readable;

8. Ambiguity: avoiding any ambiguity is important, in order not to be vague or subject to misinterpretation;

9. Neutrality: the anomaly report must be neutral and not be perceived as an attack against developers;

10. Review: once the defect has been written, it should be reread by another tester. This enables us to clarify suggestions and to take them into account.

Other aspects also need to be taken into account:

1. Accuracy:

- name windows by their accurate name (the name displayed in the title bar) to rule out ambiguities,

- ensure that you are using the exact text of the message if an error message appears,

- in case of a GPF (general protection fault), ensure that you include the name of the module and the address of the instruction causing the error;

2. Conciseness: avoid being repetitive, except if it is a characteristic of the defect;

3. Precision: ensure that the stages to reproduce the defect are numbered (without gaps or duplications).

Once the defect is referenced, you do not know who will read it: besides the project manager, it could reach senior management or customer desks or even the Intranet of the company. The defect report is of your making, be proud of it.

5.7.3. *Actions applied to defects*

Various actions can be considered to process a defect:

– an immediate fix;

– a possible fix that can take the form of changes to the code or to the tests, or of an update of project documentation, or of specific operator training or of an action towards a third-party (supplier);

– a postponement of the fix to a subsequent version or a request for deviation/waiver;

– a rejection without fix, because the defect is incorrectly identified, or because a deviation or waiver has already been requested, or because a fix cannot be identified or justified (for economic reasons for example), or refers to a duplicated or obsolete defect that has already been corrected in a version that will be delivered.

5.7.4. *Defect disposition*

The disposition of the defects comprises all the actions to carry out after the action phase. It can be:

– closure after the implementation of a fix;

– closure without fixing because:

  - the identified defect is not deemed a problem,

  - the defect is not located within the radius of the project and will thus have to be escalated,

  - the defect is a problem on the supplier or subcontractor level (we will have to identify the reference),

  - the defect is duplicated;

– postponed to a later version, referenced in the defect;

– merged with another problem (we will supply the reference);

– transferred to another project for action.

After any correction, it is necessary to ensure that:

– the defect has been correctly fixed and the failure has been removed. This is called re-testing;

– the fix did not introduce or reveal new defects. This is called regression testing.

5.8. Synopsis of this chapter

Let us summarize what was learned in this chapter.

Section 5.1 described the organization of tests and has enabled us to identify organization modes, the roles and human aspects related to test management. The following words must be known: tester, test leader, test manager.

Section 5.2 described test planning and workload estimation and also suggested how to arrange tests depending on the priorities and to anticipate project hazards, to organize and evaluate the workloads of test activities. The following terms must be known: test approach, test strategy.

Section 5.3 described how to control test activities and the risk of using metrics. The following terms must be known: defect density, failure rate, test control, test coverage, test monitoring, test report.

Section 5.4 described the information feedback provided to stakeholders and the use of measurements for localized or periodical statistics.

Section 5.5 identified the definition of test data, configuration management, change management as transverse processes and their impacts on tests. The terms to remember are: configuration management, version control.

Section 5.6 explained the principles of risk management and the concepts or project risks and product risks, with the introduction of the concept of risk management. The reader needs to remember the following terms: risks related to the product, risks related to the project, risks, risk-based testing.

Section 5.7 enabled us to understand defect management, its integration in test activities and has proposed a model of defect report. The terms to note are: incident recording, defect management, defect report.

5.9. Sample exam questions

Section 5.1. Test organization (K2)

FLO-5.1.1   Recognize the importance of independent testing (K1)

FLO-5.1.2   Explain the benefits and drawbacks of independent testing within an organization (K2)

FLO-5.1.3   Recognize the different team members to be considered for the creation of a test team (K1)

FLO-5.1.4   Recall the typical tasks of test leaders and testers (K1)

Ref	Questions
75.	FLO-5.1.1 (K1)
	Why should we call upon independent testers?
	A. They are cheaper than company testers.
	B. They are more efficient than company testers.
	C. They do not need to have any technical or business knowledge.
	D. They can reduce the responsibility level of developers.

76.	FLO-5.1.2 (K2)
	You wish to put together a test team, with yourself in the role of test manager. You need to demonstrate the advantages of using independent testers, in order to convince your hierarchy. What are the advantages you could list?
	A. Independent testers are not biased and can identify different types of errors.
	B. It is possible to transfer risks on these subcontractors.
	C. Costs will be more predictable because testing will be paid at fixed rate.
	D. Quality problems can have an impact on the public.
77.	FLO-5.1.3 (K1)
	You have just been named project manager for a future project. What type of person will be best qualified to work at component testing level?
	A. A business analyst.
	B. An independent tester.
	C. A developer.
	D. A user.
78.	FLO-5.1.4
	Name an example of a task typically carried out by a test project manager?
	A. Designing test specifications.
	B. Coordinating the test strategy with the development project manager.
	C. Writing the test plan and the test design document.
	D. Reviewing and commenting the test plan.
79.	Terms (K1)
	What is a test manager?
	A. A test management tool, to facilitate test monitoring and execution.
	B. A tool facilitating the control and providing support to the project manager.
	C. A qualified professional testing a management software component
	D. An individual directing, organizing, controlling, administrating, and planning software test activities.

Section 5.2. Test planning and estimation (K3)

FLO-5.2.1   Recognize the different levels and objectives of test planning (K1)

FLO-5.2.2   Summarize the purpose and content of the test plan, test design specification and test procedure documents according to the "Standard for Software Test Documentation" (IEEE Std 829-1998) (K2)

FLO-5.2.3   Differentiate between conceptually different test approaches, such as   analytical,   model-based,   methodical,   process/standard   compliant, dynamic/heuristic, consultative, and regression-averse approaches (K2)

FLO-5.2.4   Differentiate between test planning for a system and scheduling test execution (K2)

FLO-5.2.5   Write a test execution schedule for a given set of test cases, while considering prioritization and technical and logical dependencies (K3)

FLO-5.2.6   List test preparation and execution activities that must be considered during test planning (K1)

FLO-5.2.7   Recall typical factors influencing the test effort (K1)

FLO-5.2.8   Differentiate between two conceptually different estimation approaches: the metrics-based approach and the expert-based approach (K2)

FLO-5.2.9   Recognize/justify adequate entry and exit criteria for specific test levels and groups of test cases (e.g. for integration testing, acceptance testing or test cases for usability testing) (K2)

Ref	Questions
80.	FLO-5.2.1 (K1) What is the master test plan useful for? A. To cover components, system and acceptance level tests. B. To cover all test levels. C. To cover all the tests executed during the project. D. To cover maintenance and technical tests.
81.	FLO-5.2.2.(K2) As test project manager, you wish to specify the entry and exit criteria of test tasks, as well as the specificities of the test environment. In which document will you define that? A. The master test plan. B. The test plan. C. The test design document. D. The test case.

Ref	Questions
82.	FLO-5.2.3 (K2) Quite early on in the project, at the moment of the first draft (rough draft) of the specifications, your manager asks you to take part in a brainstorming session in order to identify the project risks. What is probably the primary approach of this project? A. A dynamic and responsive approach. B. An analytical and systematic approach. C. An approach based on outsourcing and consulting. D. An approach focused on impact analysis and maintenance.
83.	FLO-5.2.4 (K2) Let us consider the following activities: I. Defining the project risks. II. Introducing a configuration management tool. III. Installing a defect management tool. IV. Filling in a defect or incident report. V. Scheduling test tasks. VI. Selecting metrics for test control and monitoring. Which assertion is correct? A. All these activities are test planning activities. B. Only I, III, and V are test planning activities. C. Only II, IV, and VI are test planning activities. D. Only I, V, and VI are test planning activities.

Ref	Questions
84.	FLO-5.2.5.(K3) Let us consider the following test case list, the priority (from the lowest to the highest priority) and the dependencies. | N° of the test case	Name of the test case	Priority	Dependency | |---|---|---|---| | T.001 | Visualizing the elements | 3 | None | | T.002 | Putting the elements into the basket | 3 | T.001 | | T.003 | Paying for purchases | 1 | T.002 | | T.004 | Keeping the basket without paying | 4 | T.002 | | T.005 | Going back to the shop, fetching a kept basket, paying | 4 | T.004 | Amongst the following execution sequences, which one is considering at the same time priorities and dependencies? A. T.001, T.002, T.001, T.002, T.003, T.004, T.005. B. T.002, T.001, T.004, T.005, T.002, T.001, T.003. C. T.001, T.002, T.003, T.001, T.002, T.004, T.005. D. T.001, T.002, T.004, T.005, T.001, T.002, T.003.
85.	FLO-5.2.6.(K1) Which activities are defined during test planning and evaluated during the test execution? A. Test tasks. B. Needs for test environments. C. Test entry criteria. D. Training level of the testers.

86.	FLO-5.2.7
	
	Let us consider the following factors:
	    I. The number of business use cases, which is defined in the specifications.
	    II. The result of test execution.
	    III. The time zones between the test team member.
	    IV. The quality of the product software produced by the designers.
	Which assertion is true?
	A. All these factors influence the test effort for all projects.
	B. The factors I, II, and III influence the test effort for all projects.
	C. The factors I, II, and IV influence the test effort for some projects.
	D. The factors II, III, and IV influence the test effort for all projects.

Ref	Questions
87.	FLO-5.2.8 (K2) Which assertion is true? A. Task estimation by those who will execute them will always be more specific than estimation by metrics. B. Task estimation by those who will execute them can be used in addition to metrics estimation. C. Task estimation by those who will execute them will always be less specific that a metrics estimation. D. An estimation of the effort by metrics should always precede an estimation of the effort by those who will execute the tasks.
88.	FLO-5.2.9. (K2) Let us suppose that you find the following extract in the test plan as an entry criterion of acceptance testing: "The system will contain all the required characteristics, all the defects requiring fixes will be fixed by the development team and checked by the test team as being fixed and all regression tests will be successfully passed before delivery of the product for the acceptance phase." What could be the reason for such an entry criterion? A. Acceptance testing will be carried out by business experts, whose time is precious and who should not be subjected to failures or test an incomplete system. B. The quality of system testing could be too low if this criterion was not included. C. Developers and the hierarchy could require the delivery of the product if this criterion was not included. D. The objective of acceptance testing is to find as many defects and failures as possible.
89.	Terms (K1) What is the test plan? A. A document specifying why tests are carried out within the organization. B. A document listing the test cases to be carried out, sometimes in a hierarchical way. C. A document specifying the action sequences of test execution and the measures to be taken in order to note down results. D. A document specifying amongst other things the test approach and the entry and exit test conditions.

Section 5.3. Test progress monitoring and control (K2)

FLO-5.3.1   Recall common metrics used for monitoring test preparation and execution (K1)

FLO-5.3.2   Explain and compare test metrics for test reporting and test control (e.g. defects found and fixed, and tests passed and failed) related to the purpose and use (K2)

FLO-5.3.3   Summarize the purpose and content of the test summary report document according to the "Standard for Software Test Documentation" (IEEE Std 829-1998) (K2)

Ref	Questions
90.	FLO-5.3.1.(K1) Which metric is frequently used to measure the progress of test execution? A. The number of executed test cases. B. The number of covered conditions. C. The number of covered lines of code. D. The number of identified and solved defects.
91.	FLO-5.3.2.(K2) During the test execution, the test manager describes the following situation to the project team: "90% of the test cases have been executed. 20% of these test cases have identified 127 defects. 112 of the latter have been fixed and confirmed as fixed. The management has decided not to fix the 15 remaining defects before delivery." What is the most reasonable interpretation of this test report? A. The 15 remaining defects should be re-tested before delivery. B. The 10% of the remaining test cases should be tested before delivery. C. The management considers that the system is ready for delivery without any additional tests necessary. D. Developers should concentrate their efforts on the correction of the remaining defects before delivery.

Ref	Questions
92.	FLO-5.3.3. (K2) In a test summary report, the test manager writes the following: "The card-management sub-system does not deal correctly with AMEX cards, which are considered as a priority aspect of this version". In which section will we find this assertion? A. Evaluation. B. Summary of the activities. C. Variation. D. Description of the incidents.
93.	Terms (K1) What is test control? A. An activity of test management that ensures the good test execution as planned in the test plan. B. A test management activity that enables us to control test results and to ensure that validations have been correctly obtained. C. A test management activity that defines the metrics that will enable us to ensure the good execution of the actions and their control. D. A test management activity measuring the progress of the tests and defining corrective actions when the metrics indicate a deviation in relation to the plans.

Section 5.4. Configuration management (K2)

FLO-5.4.1   Summarize how configuration management supports testing (K2)

Ref	Questions
94.	FLO-5.4.1 (K2) During a previous test phase, a defect has been identified, solved and confirmed as solved by re-testing, but has been discovered again in a subsequent test phase. Amongst the following aspects, which one should probably be improved the most? A. Traceability. B. Confirmation tests (re-test). C. Non-regression tests. D. Configuration management.

Ref	Questions
95.	Terms (K1) What is configuration management useful for? A. To evaluate, coordinate, trace, and implement modifications of elements of a project after their identification. B. To ensure that the identified defects have been fixed. C. To ensure that the information of the modifications of the software components are correctly saved. D. To evaluate, trace and implement modifications of test cases in case of requirement modification.

Section 5.5. Test and risks (K2)

FLO-5.5.1   Describe a risk as a possible problem that would threaten the achievement of one or more stakeholders' project objectives (K2)

FLO-5.5.2   Remember that the risk level is determined by its likelihood (of occurrence) and impact (damages resulting from it) (K1)

FLO-5.5.3   Distinguish between project and product risks (K2)

FLO-5.5.4   Recognize typical product and project risks (K1)

FLO-5.5.5   Describe, by using examples, how risk analysis and risk management can be used for test planning (K2)

Ref	Questions
96.	FLO-5.5.1.(K2) What aspect is NOT important in risk evaluation? A. The occurrence likelihood of the risk in production. B. The impact on users during use. C. The duration, cost, and effort of the defect correction. D. Impact on the load and deadlines of the project.

Ref	Questions
97.	FLO-5.5.2.(K1) Let us consider the following aspects concerning the project risks: I. Occurrence likelihood of the risks. II. Number of days before delivery. III. Impact of the risk in terms of costs and delays. IV. Number of persons involved in the resolution. V. Frequency of the risk analysis. For an identified individual project risk, what are the factors directly impacting the identified risk level? A. I and III. B. I, II, and III. C. I, III, and V. D. All the five aspects.
98.	FLO-5.5.3.(K2) Let us consider the following risks and mitigation actions: I. The actions to be implemented in case of absence of a team member. II. The actions to carry out in order to limit too long transaction times. III. The means to prevent data corruption. IV. The non-execution of a key use case by lack of time. V. The actions that will not be carried out after a late delivery of the code. VI. The actions to implement following late delivery of the code. During the writing of the test plan, following the IEEE 829-1998 model, what should you include in the section "risks and mitigation actions"? A. II, III, and V. B. I, II, and VI. C. IV, V, and VI. D. I, V, and VI.

Ref	Questions
99.	FLO-5.5.4.(K1) Take the list of risks below: I. Bankruptcy of a supplier or a partner. II. Response time longer than what is required. III. Ambiguous or contradictory requirements. IV. Staff without the appropriate technical knowledge. V. Problem with the quality of the test data. VI. Quality of the code design. What is the correct assertion? A. I, II and III are project risks, IV, V and VI are product risks. B. I, III and IV are project risks, II, V and VI are product risks. C. I, IV and VI project risks, II, III and V are product risks. D. I, III, IV and VI are project risks, II and V are product risks.
100.	FLO-5.5.5.(K2) You are working as a test project manager on an in-house development project. During the planning phase, you gather representatives of the stakeholders, in order to identify and prioritize the software risks. During test planning and test design phases, for what will you use the result of this meeting? A. To determine the test levels to implement for each risk. B. To determine the intensity of the test to be considered for each risk. C. To prepare test execution and its traceability towards risks. D. To write a test report focusing on these risks.
101.	Terms (K1) A risk is: A. An event that may occur with negative consequences. B. An event that may occur with positive consequences. C. An event that will occur with negative consequences. D. An event that can occur whatever the consequences.

Section 5.6. Risk management (K3)

FLO-5.6.1   Recognize the content of an incident report according to the "Standard for Software Test Documentation" (IEEE Std 829-1998) (K1)

FLO-5.6.2   Write an incident report covering the observation of a failure during testing (K3)

Ref	Questions
102.	FLO-5.6.1.(K1) Consider the following elements: I. Input data II. Expected results III. Obtained results IV. Description of the incident In the section "Description of the anomaly or incident" of the defect report according to the IEEE 829 standard (version 1998 and 2008), which of the following should be present? A. All of them B. I, II and III C. I, III and IV D. II, III and IV
103.	FLO-5.6.2 (K3) Let us consider the extract of the defect report below: "Despite repeated tests with several types of cards, the system does not recognize as valid the numbers of the Visa and MasterCard." Which objective or information is fulfilled by this extract? A. Description of the incident or the anomaly. B. Evaluation of the importance of the impact for users. C. Information on the executed confirmation actions. D. Relevant data in order to facilitate the correction.
104.	Terms (K1) What is incident or anomaly management useful for? A. To identify, follow, and fix incidents or anomalies. B. To identify, evaluate, and process incidents or anomalies. C. To decide on the actions to be applied to incidents or anomalies. D. To ensure that anomalies are correctly fixed.

Chapter 6

Tools Support for Testing (FL 6.0)

In the previous chapters, we studied several testing techniques and mentioned possible tools to aid testing. Several tools are available to aid the execution of tests procedures in a simple, automated way, whatever the technical environment or context of the software might be.

These tools are used in two main cases:

– to automate the execution of tedious, repetitive, or meticulous tasks, such as the comparison of files of several thousands of lines, so that testers can concentrate on tasks of higher importance;

– to execute or monitor tasks that cannot be easily carried out by humans, such as performance testing or the analysis of response times (usually measured in hundredths of seconds).

We identify here the types of tools frequently used to support test execution, even if they are not directly tools specifically devoted to testing. In the framework of the International Software Testing Qualifications Board (ISTQB) foundation level for certified testers, no specific tool knowledge is required.

6.1. Types of test tools (FL 6.1)

Tools can be used to support most test activities, whether they are management, design, execution, test monitoring or control, or test reporting activities. Generally, for each type of tool there are commercial and open-source tools.

In general, the use of automated tools increases test reliability, enables us to carry out execution tasks without any human presence in the room, and improves the efficiency of repetitive tasks, such as regression tests.

6.1.1. *Test tool classification*

FLO-6.1.1 Classify different types of test tools according to their purpose and to the activities of the fundamental test process and the software life cycle (K2)

FLO-6.1.3 Explain the term test tool and the purpose of tool support for testing (K2)

Test tools can be classified in different ways. We will classify them here according to the tasks they support:

– tools supporting test management;

– requirement management tools;

– reviewing and static analysis tools;

– modeling tools;

– test design tools;

– tools for test design and test basis analysis;

– tools for test execution;

– support tools for test environments;

– data comparison tools;

– coverage measurement tools;

– security tools;

– performance testing, load and dynamical analysis tools;

– other tools.

6.1.2. *Tools supporting test management*

Tools supporting test management provide:

– support for project management, generally from task planning up to monitoring of the activity progress;

– test traceability, from their design up to their execution, including monitoring of test execution results, whether the tests are automated or manually executed;

– incident and defect management support, from identification up to closure or disposition;

– version and configuration management of the components to be tested, but also of all the components, drivers, stubs, documents used during testing activities;

– support for risk analysis, including identification, evaluation, and risk monitoring;

– reporting tools, whether they supply directly information from test data or indirectly via data extraction. Amongst other things, reporting tools include spreadsheets, text processors, presentation design tools, and graphical tools.

6.1.3. *Tools supporting requirement management*

Tools supporting requirement management enable us:

– to store requirements and specifications;

– to check consistency and avoid ambiguities in requirements;

– to prioritize requirements and specifications;

– to ensure traceability of each test – and of its execution – with regards to each customer requirements, in order to provide evidence of its coverage.

6.1.4. *Tools supporting static tests*

This category includes:

– support tools for the reviewing process, which:

   - monitor (i.e. workflow and task monitoring tools) and deal with reviewing processes,

   - enable us to store and convey review comments,

   - identify the defects and planned correction actions, which interface with the defect management tools,

   - manage references to check-lists and applicable rules,

   - ensure the traceability between source documents and the code;

– static analysis tools, which:

    - enable defect identification before the dynamic test execution,

    - ensure compliance to coding standards,

    - compute metrics from the code or the architecture,

    - analyze structures and their dependencies.

This category also includes tools, which are mainly used by developers, such as compilers, link analyzers, or cross-reference generators for the use of variables and function calls.

6.1.5. *Modeling tools*

Modeling tools are mainly used by developers and include business behavior modeling tools and those allowing the validation of the created models.

These tools can also be related to test design tools.

6.1.6. *Tools supporting test design and test data creation*

The generation of the expected data, of drivers and stubs, of simulators and specific test environments is included in this category. This category of tools enables us to generate tests or test data from:

– requirements;

– a graphical user interface;

– design models;

– the code.

Test data are necessary as test inputs, but are also required to compare actual test outputs with expected ones (oracles). Test data management tools will enable us to:

– manipulate or create files, data bases, individual data, or messages, used during test execution;

– create large volumes of useful data for testing, e.g. by defining data combinations for all the equivalence partitioning;

– validate test data according to specific management rules, in order to ensure consistent operations and degraded operation of the system under test;

– analyze statistical frequencies regarding conditions and risks;

– anonymize actual production data to ensure confidentiality of customer data for example.

6.1.7. *Tools supporting test execution*

Test execution tools help us to execute tests by submitting input data to the software under test via:

– graphical user interfaces (screens, keyboard, input fields, etc.);

– API (application programming interfaces) without going through the graphical interface;

– command lines, where the data are used as parameters.

Generally, these tools include comparators, which help to identify successfully passed test cases from failed ones. Execution monitoring information is supplied in the form of test execution reports.

Test execution tools and the interfaces they use are often handled by specific languages, called scripting languages. These tools record user actions and then replay them. They are called record/playback tools and record the user actions in a script that can be modified via these scripting languages.

When properly used, record/playback tools can produce automated test scripts and processes, which enable us to re-execute tests with various input data and to repeat the same tests in the framework of regression tests for example.

When used improperly, with an imbrication of actions and test data, record/playback tools can be very fragile and may not be reusable (leading to shelving of the tool).

6.1.8. *Tools supporting test environment management*

These tools enable us to replace missing equipment or software or those who can potentially create problems. They include:

– simulators simulating equipment behavior, by reproducing the operation of the equipment (including output data) on the basis of a sub-set of determined output.

– emulators emulating external behavior of equipment or software, without reproducing their internal behavior. It is thus possible to emulate terminals via PC software (terminal emulator VT220, 3270, or 5250) and to emulate mobile phones or network equipment, by reproducing the same behaviors as the original equipment. For network simulators, a latency and limitations of the corresponding bandwidth will be generated similarly to the one generated by the actual network environment;

– environments in order to test languages, operating systems or hardware, by replacing missing components by the creation of other components, such as drivers, stubs, system parts or equipment, which are not available for testing.

There are also tools enabling us to intercept the requests sent to the operating system and to modify these requests. It is also possible to simulate specific conditions of use, such as when the internal memory or the central processing unit (CPU) is limited, when the capacity of the storage system is reached or when the network is defective. With these tools, we can generate exceptions that would otherwise be difficult to simulate.

6.1.9. *Tools supporting test data comparison*

These tools enable us to check the content of files, data bases, or test execution results with respect to expected data, during or after test execution.

The comparisons can include automatic oracles, a dynamic comparison (during the test execution), or a comparison by batches. They can be equipped with a certain level of intelligence, for example to process dynamic data such as dates and hours.

6.1.10. *Tools supporting test coverage measurement*

These tools are mainly used by developers and specialized technical testers and enable them to:

– identify memory leaks and incorrect memory management (allocation and deallocation) by the software;

– evaluate the system behavior in simulated loading conditions;

– generate loading conditions for the application, the database, the network, or servers, by following more or less realistically defined load increase scenarios;

– measure, analyze, verify, and report information on system resources and enable us to anticipate potential problems.

6.1.11. *Other test supporting tools*

There are many other tools supporting software and system tests:

– website analysis tools, able to identify missing pages;

– spellers and syntax checkers;

– tools to test network safety or vulnerability;

– specific tools for embedded systems, such as those measuring the voltage evolution on each bus wires;

– etc.

Testers also use a significant number of office automation tools (spreadsheets, graphical tools, word processors, project management tools, etc.) and data and database management tools.

6.2. Assumptions and limitations of test tools (FL 6.2)

The use of test tools does not guarantee the improvement of the software quality: just because we have a Ferrari, does not mean that we are as good as Fangio or Senna.

First, it is necessary to use tools where they can bring added value. They should also not be used for tasks to which they are not suited. This could lead to the purchase and use of several tools, each for a specific usage.

It is also important to keep in mind the hypotheses, assumptions, and limitations associated with the use of tools. Indeed, the use of tools generates a layer of additional complexity in tests, an additional traceability level, and test scripts that we need to maintain and to change consistently in step with the evolutions of the software or system under test. This leads to an increase of the test maintenance activities (and costs), without any proportional increase of the ability to identify additional defects.

Thirdly, we have to remember the seven general principles that are always applicable, including for automated tests.

6.2.1. *Advantages and risks of the tools*

FLO-6.2.1 Summarize the potential benefits and risks of test automation and tool support for testing (K2)

Acquiring a tool does not guarantee the success of your testing activities. We have seen in previous chapters that tests are not limited to the simple use of tools, however sophisticated they might be. The use of human intelligence, of various test techniques, and of the acquired experience is essential to organize, plan, and implement test activities. Tools can help the execution of a certain number of these activities, but their use adds a certain number of risks to the project.

The main advantages to using tools are:

– a reduction of repetitive manual actions, such as regression tests, by the automation of these tests, which enable testers to concentrate on testing other software functionalities;

– an increase of reliability and repeatability of regression testing, and of comparison of large volumes;

– an ability to stimulate an increase of users or transactions (for load, stress and performance testing) or to stimulate complex or unusual environments;

– easy acquisition of metrics and measurements, including when data are not easily visible (for example, bandwidth on a network, transaction response time, etc.);

– an ability to evaluate how objectives have been reached (coverage, compliance measurements, etc.) and to compare the actual objectives reached with the planned ones;

– simplification of reporting activities, amongst other things for the comparison of historic data and identification of trends, and for comparison between planned and actual achievements.

The use of tools to support testing does not only have advantages; there are also a certain number of risks. The main risks related to the use of these tools are:

– underestimating the effort required to achieve the expected benefits with the tool. This includes all aspects of training, coaching, and external support;

– failing to take into account possible *probe effects*. Probe effects are the impact that tools can have on the measured object, such as the use of the bandwidth by a record/replay tool impacting the available bandwidth for the application;

– unrealistic expectations regarding tools. This is increased due to the high cost of such tools and the wish to limit tool acquisition expenses;

– underestimation of the effort required to maintain the scripts, data and parameters related to tools and the workload needed to adapt these pieces of information to the evolutions of the software or system tested;

– over-confidence in tools, often related to gullibility towards the performances expressed by the tools' vendors or some experts;

– lack of version management and of configuration management of the tools, the scripts, data, and parameters related to the versions of the software or system to be tested;

– intrinsic limitations of the tools when they are ported to a new platform or to your environment;

– possibility of bankruptcy of the tool vendor or supplier or of a change in the development policy of the tool supplier, or of its buyout by a competitor and of the end of support of the chosen tool;

– lack of a quality technical support from the supplier or the community (for open source software) for tools and their adaptation to your various environments;

– lack of interoperability of this tool with other tools or systems that you have implemented, whether it is for requirement, configuration, or incident management, for interfaces with test, measurement, or reporting management tools, for the difficult acquisition of metrics, etc.

– inability to reach the desired effectiveness, reliability, and quality objectives with the tool;

– regarding open-source software, the licenses required are often restrictive and force you to release to the whole community, any specific development you may have carried out to this software.

We can thus note that there are a number of risks related to the introduction or use of tools supporting tests. It is important to prevent the occurrence of such risks for our projects when we acquire such tools.

6.2.2. Specific considerations for some tools

FLO-6.2.2 Recall special considerations for test execution tools, static analysis, and test management tools (K1)

All tools are associated with assumptions, hypotheses, and limitations. The CFTL- (*Comité Français des Tests Logiciels*) ISTQB syllabus suggests focusing on three types of tools:

– test execution tools;

– static analysis tools;

– test management tools.

The aspects we will evaluate for these three types of tools are typical and can be applied to other types of tools.

6.2.2.1. *Test execution tools*

Test execution tools are those enabling us to dynamically execute test cases. Just as manual dynamical tests, they require a known initial state, actions applied on test data, and then a comparison of the obtained and expected results. The main advantage of this type of tool is to be able to execute sequences of test cases, test scenarios, or processes without the physical presence of a tester. Execution can thus be carried out at night, in the absence of testers. Testers would thus be able to analyze test results the following morning.

It is necessary to ensure a sequencing of test cases without any hitch and with check points. All testers' intelligence must thus be transmitted in execution scripts, to ensure that:

– the initial state is the expected one (and what should happen if it is not the case);

– all the required human actions have been recorded and are correctly planned and initiated in response to known stimuli;

– the comparison between actual result and the test oracle provides identical results (and what actions to implement if it is not the case);

– the resulting state of a test case is the start-up state for the next test case;

– success or failure information are correctly logged, to identify failing test cases, the components involved, and as much information as possible to define the failure and identify the defect.

Nowadays, there are three main families of test automation tools:

1. The pure record and replay, where the script is reused as such or else copied or reused by modifying the recorded values. There will thus be as many test scripts as data sets to be tested. Any modification of the user interface – even of only one transaction screen – will lead to a modification or re-recording of all the scripts where this screen is used. This solution is easy to implement, but requires a huge maintenance effort on each test level;

2. Data-driven testing, where the test script is separated from the data it is using. The script is modified to replace the data introduced by calls for variables. The data associated with these variables are stored in files or databases (comprising test input data but also the expected results). The modified script is then encapsulated in a piece of code that will:

- read the input data in the file,

- execute the script with input data, which are introduced in variables,

- compare the obtained data with the expected ones,

- note the success or failure of the test for this set of data,

- recondition the test environment in the expected state to restart,

- start again the cycle with the next piece of data of the input file, until there is no more data to process in the file.

Using this method, we can execute the same test activity for every combination of equivalence partition or of boundary values and thus process large volumes of data (this can be useful to create a valid test data set). When all these pieces of data associated with a test case have been processed, we can then move on to the next test case and to its associated input data file. We thus have an abstraction level, where data are extracted, which enables us to limit the changes (or the script re-recording and its modification in order to process data) to the script alone whenever the user interface changes;

3. Keyword-driven tests, add an additional abstraction level: tests are business actions whose rendering regarding user interface can use one or several screens. Business actions can be summarized by keywords (also called action words) and are applicable to data set (the input values of the business transaction). We have seen previously (data-driven tests) that data sets can be grouped together in files. Keywords can be associated with the necessary test scripts (one script per keyword) and user interfaces to implement the chosen business actions. Using a keyword with a data sequence will lead to the script execution with the specified data. Keywords can be grouped together in a language that is easily understandable by the user representatives. Test scenarios can thus be designed without the "business" testers knowing how to use the execution tool. In case of a modification of the user interface, it is only necessary to modify the script associated with the keyword and it will do the trick. The piece of software processing the action words is in charge of:

- reading the scenario keyword, the input and expected data,

- loading the necessary script and executing it with input data,

- comparing the obtained data with the expected data,

- if the result is correct, go on to the applicable line of the scenario and start the process at the beginning with the reading of the next keyword, etc.

- if the result is not correct, the anomaly is written down and it is possible to specify the execution of another keyword, enabling for example the reconditioning of the environment or the re-run of the process at an identified check point.

This method enables a much quicker design of the test scenario and does not require any technical knowledge for most testers. We can note that, depending on the defined keywords, it is possible to design a high-level language, enabling interactions between various scenarios, or even between various workstations. For more information on this method, the reader can refer to the work of Hans Buwalda from 2002 [BUW 02, pp.155-192]. A small number of technical testers could maintain the tool and supply support to a significant number of functional testers. This technique has proved its efficiency and effectiveness, e.g. testing character-mode applications on large systems (mainframes IBM ES9000 and RISC RS6000) and on high-level graphical interfaces.

6.2.2.2. *Static analysis tools*

Applying static analysis tools on old code frequently reveals a significant number of defects because of non-compliance to coding standards. Similarly, developers often decide not to display the warning messages provided by the complier, so as to concentrate on the actual compilation errors. However, this can hide many potential problems. It can be important for testers to have access to these lists of compilation warnings, in order to identify potential error zones.

Not complying with some development practices can be completely justified: once, a young programmer studied a software component that did not comply to the rules of structured procedural programming, which forbid, for example, the use of the "GOTO" statement and suggested replacement of the statements by instructions such as "PERFORM UNTIL" or "PERFORM WHILE". After many days of work and tests that helped to ensure that the operation of the new component was similar to the previous one, the new component has been placed into production. The performances of all the applications were strongly affected, with very mediocre response times for the users. The previous component reinstallation was rushed through (with the offending "GOTO" statements) and the system became effective once again. Why?

The component was very frequently used by all the software in the company and was optimized to be very quick in its execution. At compilation time, a GOTO statement is translated by a single instruction, whereas a "PERFORM ..." statement leads to many instructions (about 20). The execution of a single instruction is much quicker than the execution of 20 instructions, especially if we multiply this by the number of times this component has been called during the day. Therefore, caution should be excised before imposing coding rules and it should be ensured that the expected benefits will actually be reached.

6.2.2.3. *Test management tools*

The test manager must integrate data coming from many tools, from each of the testers, from all the elements of the test environment and from all the test levels. It is thus essential that the data are supplied in the best suited format for statistics, graphs, and reports.

Using the tools of an integrated suite coming from a same editor can be a solution to ensure this good integration. However, nothing guarantees that all the necessary tools come from this software tool vendor. It is thus important to ensure that the data coming from each of the tools can be integrated in some kind of tester dashboard, whether it is periodical (even once a day) or continuous.

A continuous dashboard could be permanently displayed on a workstation or a dedicated window of the manager workstation and debrief on the progress of the tests from the inquiries of the tester workstations and test software. These metrics could summarize the state of the various aspects of the test project and supply to the test manager the equivalent of the head-up display for fighter pilots. For more information on this subject, the reader is referred to the work of James Whittaker [WHI 10, pp. 124-132].

6.3. Selecting and introducing tools in an organization (FL 6.3)

With more than 700 test tools commercially available, choosing a tool is a complicated process. Many test tools display promising performances, the latest trendy words, and promise that the tool is easy to use. These promises only engage those believing in them.

We will study three important aspects when choosing test tools:

– main principles related to the introduction of a tool;

– tool selection process;

– tool introduction and generalization process.

6.3.1. *Main principles*

The introduction of a tool into an organization starts with the organization itself and not with the tool. If we plan to introduce a tool, this is usually to improve test efficiency in defect detection, or to reduce the duration of the test campaign or the testing costs. Short-, mid- and long-term views must be considered to evaluate the profitability of the considered choices and, therefore, evaluate the benefits for the organization.

The most efficient way to find defects is to use several complementary techniques. We shall thus need to consider tools for each one of these techniques and methods. This is why we need to carry out an evaluation of the benefits expected by the organization from the introduction of new tools.

It is also important to realize that a tool is not the universal panacea or a miracle solution (snake oil or silver bullet) that will solve all your testing problems with a magic wand. You have to be very wary of editor promises and of the capacity of a single tool to meet all your needs. In fact, it might be necessary to select several tools.

Moreover, you should not underestimate the cost of the investment surrounding the tool, such as training (even self-training), implementation of scripts, and their maintenance over time, etc. The purchase price of a tool is a relatively small part of the total investment that you will make in a tool. If the tool in which you have invested is not suited to your needs, does not give you reliable information, does not enable you to reach the expected benefits, or even forces you to purchase another tool later on, its profitability will be affected; one of the consequences may be the abandonment of the tool (sometimes it can go as far as getting rid of the whole test team).

6.3.2. *Tools selection process*

There are several stages in the selection process:

– first, evaluate the expected benefits from the introduction of a test tool in the organization, which includes an analysis of the test process maturity level of the organization and a profit and loss estimation to the use of this tool;

– secondly, the selection of a tool or set of tools, which answers the previously defined profitability and efficiency objectives;

– thirdly, the actual selection of the tool, which best answers the identified selection criteria.

To succeed in the selection and introduction of a tool, we must first clearly define what we expect from it, ensure that the organization is of a sufficient maturity level and determine – in actual figures – the expected benefits, before considering choosing a tool.

FLO-6.3.1 State the main principles related to the introduction of a tool into an organization (K1)

6.3.2.1. *Objective evaluation*

The evaluation of the planned objectives is built around two main aspects:

– evaluation of the maturity of the organization processes, of its strengths and weaknesses and of the possible improvement to the test processes by the use of tools. The advanced ISTQB level syllabus for test managers suggests several evaluation and improvement methods applicable to the test and development processes. Such an evaluation enables us to list and measure the expected benefits of the improvement of the processes and the types of tools enabling us to reach this objective;

– implementation of an economic analysis of the expected costs and benefits in the short-, mid-, and long-term.

Evaluation of the test process maturity enables us to identify those which will benefit the most from improvements. There are several ways to evaluate the test organization maturity. The best methods are based on an internal frame of reference and the simplest ones to implement are based on an external reference frame.

A measurement of the processes requiring improvement will enable us to identify those where the implementation of a tool will be most profitable.

6.3.2.2. *Pre-selection*

You can draw up a list of tools in different ways, but each one has advantages and drawbacks:

– from research on the Internet via search engines;

– from discussion forums and user groups;

– from advertisement or leaflets handed out during conferences, seminars or congresses such as the *Journée Française des Tests Logiciels* (French Software Testing Day);

– from discussions with colleagues and competitors.

These methods all have advantages and drawbacks. Inquiries on the Internet with search engines can provide really interesting results. You will maybe have to make a search with English keywords: a search on a search engine with the French expression "outil de test" gives 5,400,000 answers; whereas a search with the English translation of this expression, "test tools" gives 154,000,000 answers (the ISTQB glossary compiles software testing definitions in English). Adding keywords helps to refine a search, but at the risk of producing first search results listing companies that have invested a lot in marketing.

There are a few discussion forums on the Internet focusing on software tests. From their own experience, a certain number of people will suggest one tool or another. There are several frequent case scenarios: a person with experience with only one tool recommends a tool, without taking into account your specific context; or a person recommends a tool and you later realize that they work for the editor or the supplier of this tool; or else – and this is quite frequent – some people recommend commercial tools while only having used the open-source tool. Thus, you need to be really cautious. It could be wiser to make contact with user groups of several tools (such as the ECUME club for users of HP tools) or to ask for information from people who are not selling anything, and have experience of various tools.

Leaflets and ads, demonstrations during conferences or congresses are a very interesting source of information. As mentioned previously, it is advised to remain vigilant, because demonstrations are often efficient and quick, but the people making the demonstration are sales people and the use case may not be representative of your own application context. In France, the *Journée Française des Tests Logiciels* is organized by the CFTL (representing France at the ISTQB). This is a major French-speaking event, where you can meet with editors and providers, but also where you can exchange information with other users.

In France and French-speaking countries, the software test scene is not as widely developed as the software development scene. Only a limited number of people are significantly involved. They meet within the CFTL, either as simple members or as members of the Technical Committee of this association, or as a training provider accredited by the CFTL as ISTQB accredited provider. These various people are known for their professionalism and can be useful sources of information about tools and on how they have been implemented in various environments.

From all this information collected from various sources, you should be able to select a short list of tools, which could answer to your needs. Afterwards, you can determine which of these tools will best answer your selection criteria.

6.3.2.3. Tool selection

For each aspect to be covered, you will need to select which characteristics and criteria will be taken into account during the selection process, including cost, expected benefits, need for preliminary training (learning curve), etc.

From the pre-selection of tools associated with the aspect you wish to cover, you will have to choose the most suitable one according to your selection criteria.

FLO-6.3.2 State the goals of a proof-of-concept for tool evaluation and a piloting phase for tool implementation (K1)

The CFTL and ISTQB recommend asking editors and providers for a proof of concept executed in your own environment or with a representative subset of your application. You can thus ensure that the tool in question can supply the expected benefits in your environment. Too frequently, advertisements embellish the truth and do not take into account some aspects of your environment or sometimes they cover them only in return for additional expenses, which are not included in the basic license.

The evaluation of the few tools you have preselected should be done with objective and comparable criteria. In order to be as transparent as possible, create a list of criteria and weighting factors before starting comparing tools; therefore avoiding being overly influenced by a specific criterion or tool.

The phases of proof of concept and evaluation must be carried out for all the preselected tools on the basis of the same environments, characteristics, and criteria. Numerical measurements must be taken in order to have measurable decision elements.

At the end of the proof of concept phase, conclusions can be drawn from a technical review and a suggestion submitted to the hierarchy concerning the purchase of one tool or the other.

6.3.3. *Test tool implementation*

FLO-6.3.3 Recognize that factors other than simply acquiring a tool are required for good tool support (K1)

Acquiring a tool is not an automatic guarantee for success during the generalization and the use of this tool. Other factors come into play: some are procedural, technical, or human. To enable their proper recognition, it is recommended that:

– a pilot project be implemented, which will:

- enable your testers to familiarize themselves with the selected tool,

- identify the need to adapt the technical or business processes within the company,

- measure the actual benefits,

- help determining specific metrics suitable for the selected tool,

- enable you to design specific in-house training sessions to the organization's tasks and processes,

- enable the members of the pilot project team to acquire practical experience,

– conduct lessons learned (return on experience) meetings once the pilot project is finished. During this meeting, all positive and negative aspects associated with the use of the tool, the advantages and drawbacks, the adaptations to be implemented, and the need for additional training will be identified. Moreover, during this meeting decide whether or not to generalize the tool, depending on whether it has reached the initially planned objectives or not.

The generalization of a tool within the company should be carried out incrementally, project by project, with publication of the obtained results and advantages. This will create demand for the tool, instead of a voluntarist or mandatory decision policy, which can sometimes be seen as a unilateral decision of the hierarchy and does not take into account the requirements of the project.

Throughout the tool generalization on projects, it is necessary to:

– continue measuring the benefits and compare the benefits reached to the ones expected;

– identify improvements to be made, if:

- the pilot project was not sufficiently representative of the organization's projects,

- some projects have specific characteristics.

6.3.4. *To build or to buy test tools?*

6.3.4.1. *Open-source and free software*

In the open-source software community, there may be some tools that could be adjusted to your needs, in return for only limited modifications. It is thus tempting to consider selecting such a tool, as it leads to an equivalent reduction of the initial investments. However, several aspects must be considered. Open-source software is often associated with use and development licenses, forcing private specific developments to be put at the disposal of the free software community according to the same license as the original software. Therefore, the developments that you will invest for will have to be made available to your potential competitors. Moreover, corrections to free software cannot immediately be carried out and the documentation or the technical support can also be quite difficult to obtain.

6.3.4.2. *Commercial software*

Commercial software is often very expensive and the initial purchase expenditure does not include yearly maintenance costs. It is very important to study long-term needs and their impact in terms of maintenance and the necessary investment to maintain the automated test cases in operational conditions.

Communication aspects between the different software and the ease of metrics generation should also be evaluated for tools, whether they are commercial or developed within your own organization.

6.3.4.3. *Building your own tools*

Developing specific test tools in-house can be an interesting solution when working in specific fields, where commercial test tools may not be available. This is quite common for organizations at the forefront of their technology for which a commercial development is not considered. This is often the case with proprietary technology or when the number of potential customers is too low for a commercial development to be profitable.

When developing specific tools, it is important that the various probe effects and reporting aspects are correctly identified and managed. If it is not the case, the odds are that the results of the test tools will not meet the objectives. It is also more difficult to validate and verify the proper operation, as these tools must also be tested.

6.4. Synopsis of this chapter

Let us summarize what was learned in this chapter.

Section 6.1 helped us to identify the various types of test tools and how we can classify them. The following terms should be known: configuration management tools, coverage measurement tools, debugging tools, dynamic analysis tools, defect management tools, load test tools, modeling tools, test monitoring, performance testing tools, probe effect, requirement management tools, review tools, security tools, static analysis tools, stress testing tools, test comparator, test data preparation tools, test design tools, test harness, test execution tools, test management tools, structural, and unit test tools.

Section 6.2 taught us that tools have lots advantages, but also a number of risks. We are able to identify some important aspects related to the use of some of these tools. The followings terms should be known: data-driven testing, keyword-driven testing, and scripting language.

Section 6.3 enabled us to identify the main phases related to the introduction of a tool in an organization: tool selection phase, implementation phase on a pilot project, and generalization phase.

6.5. Sample exam questions

Section 6.1. Types of test tools (K2)

FLO-6.1.1   Classify different types of test tools according to their purpose and to the activities of the fundamental test process and the software life cycle (K2)

FLO-6.1.3   Explain the term test tool and the purpose of tool support for testing (K2)

Ref	Questions
105.	FLO-6.1.1 (K2)
	You are working as a test manager on a very large project. You identify the need for a tool supporting test traceability from requirements up to test execution, test execution monitoring, test basis, and results monitoring. What type of tool do you need?
	A. A requirement management tool.
	B. A test management tool.
	C. A coverage tool.
	D. A test reporting tool.

106.	FLO-6.1.3 (K2)
	Which test tool is mainly used by developers?
	A. A test harness.
	B. A coverage and execution monitoring tool.
	C. A spreadsheet program for test data management.
	D. A defect monitoring tool.
107.	Terms (K1)
	What is the probe effect?
	A. The impact of a measurement tool on the measured element.
	B. The impact when a probe is introduced on a processor.
	C. The effect of a probe on the network bandwidth.
	D. A specific impact for probes.

Section 6.2. Assumptions and limitations of test tools (K2)

FLO-6.2.1   Summarize the potential benefits and risks of test automation and tool support for testing (K2)

FLO-6.2.2   Recall special considerations for test execution tools, static analysis, and test management tools (K1)

Ref	Questions
108.	FLO-6.2.1 (K2)
	You are working on a third-party testing project for a banking application with a large number of identified risks. One important aspect is the re-execution of 8264 test cases to be applied on each of the test deliveries (i.e. release candidates). Amongst the following benefits, which one will be the more convincing for the test team?
	A. The fact that it is easy to measure the coverage of the executed or not tests.
	B. Reduction of repetitive activities.
	C. Reduction of the test costs and therefore equivalent reduction of the test effort.
	D. The fact that it is easy to fill in defect reports.

Ref	Questions
109.	FLO-6.2.2 (K1) Let us consider the following techniques: I. Exploratory. II. Data driven. III. Keyword driven. IV. Portability. V. Record/replay. VI. TPI. Which assertion is correct for automation techniques? A. II and III are recognized efficient and profitable techniques for automated test management. B. I, II, III, and V are recognized efficient and profitable techniques for automated test management . C. I, IV, and VI are recognized efficient and profitable techniques known for automated test management. D. None of these techniques are recognized as efficient and profitable for automated tests.
110.	Terms (K1) What is a scripting language? A. A language of test scenario and script representation. B. The abbreviated language used by scribes to write during reviews. C. A software component representing a missing component of the test harness. D. The programming language used for test scripts.

Section 6.3. Selecting and introducing tools in an organization (K1)

FLO-6.3.1   State the main principles of introducing a tool into an organization (K1)

FLO-6.3.2   State the goals of a proof-of-concept for tool evaluation and a piloting phase for tool implementation (K1)

FLO-6.3.3   Recognize that factors other than simply acquiring a tool are required for good tool support (K1)

Ref	Questions
111.	FLO-6.3.1 (K1) Which one of the following is an important principle during tool selection? A. Trusting the seller's ability. B. Automating as many tests as possible and in the fastest possible way in order to be profitable. C. Automating as many tests as possible to increase the coverage. D. Evaluating the seller, on technical and commercial levels.
112.	FLO-6.3.2 (K1) When introducing a test tool in your organization, what should be absolutely taken into account? A. A proof of concept to confirm the adequacy of the tool to the context. B. A commercial negotiation to reduce the price to pay for the tool. C. An impact analysis to identify where the tool will be the most efficient. D. The implementation of metrics to validate the expected benefits by the tool.
113.	FLO-6.3.3 (K1) What is not related to the introduction of tools and yet influences the success of the deployment of a tool? A. An evaluation of the in-house training needs. B. A measurement of the rate of use and of the expected benefits with the tool. C. An evaluation of the support supplied by the seller throughout the project. D. Clear requirements that are correctly traced up to the test cases.

Chapter 7

Mock Exam

This is not a real CFTL (*Comité Français des Tests Logiciels*) or ISTQB (International Software Testing Qualifications Board) exam, but a mock exam provided by the ISTQB, which holds the copyright. Its questions should not appear in real exams. The ISTQB certified tester foundation level exam has 40 questions and should be answered in 60 minutes or less. Each question is worth one point and the pass rate is 65%. You must have a minimum of 26 questions answered correctly to succeed. The questions start on the next page. For more realism, use the suggested response sheet below. Start counting 60 minutes from the moment you turn this page. The answers are in Chapter 9. This ISTQB sample exam is reproduced with kind permission of © ISTQB 2011.

Question	Answer	Question	Answer	Question	Answer	Question	Answer
Q01		Q11		Q21		Q31	
Q02		Q12		Q22		Q32	
Q03		Q13		Q23		Q33	
Q04		Q14		Q24		Q34	
Q05		Q15		Q25		Q35	
Q06		Q16		Q26		Q36	
Q07		Q17		Q27		Q37	
Q08		Q18		Q28		Q38	
Q09		Q19		Q29		Q39	
Q10		Q20		Q30		Q40	

Ref	Questions
Q01	Which of the following statements BEST describes one of the seven key principles of software testing? a) Automated tests are better than manual tests for avoiding the exhaustive testing. b) Exhaustive testing is, with sufficient effort and tool support, feasible for all software. c) It is normally impossible to test all input/output combinations for a software system. d) The purpose of testing is to demonstrate the absence of defects.
Q02	Which of the following statements is the MOST valid goal for a test team? a) Determine whether enough component testing was executed. b) Cause as many failures as possible so that faults can be identified and corrected. c) Prove that all faults are identified. d) Prove that any remaining faults will not cause any failures.
Q03	Which of these tasks would you expect to perform during test analysis and design? a) Setting or defining test objectives. b) Reviewing the test basis. c) Creating test suites from test procedures. d) Analyzing lessons learned for process improvement.
Q04	Below is a list of problems that can be observed during testing or operation. Which is MOST likely a failure? a) The product crashed when the user selected an option in a dialog box. b) One source code file included in the build was the wrong version. c) The computation algorithm used the wrong input variables. d) The developer misinterpreted the requirement for the algorithm.
Q05	Which of the following, if observed in reviews and tests, would lead to problems (or conflict) within teams? a) Testers and reviewers are not curious enough to find defects. b) Testers and reviewers are not qualified enough to find failures and faults. c) Testers and reviewers communicate defects as criticism against persons and not against the software product. d) Testers and reviewers expect that defects in the software product have already been found and fixed by the developers.

Ref	Questions
Q06	Which of the following statements are TRUE? A. Software testing may be required to meet legal or contractual requirements. B. Software testing is mainly needed to improve the quality of the developer's work. C. Rigorous testing and fixing of defects found can help reduce the risk of problems occurring in an operational environment. D. Rigorous testing is sometimes used to prove that all failures have been found. a) B and C are true; A and D are false b) A and D are true; B and C are false c) A and C are true, B and D are false d) C and D are true, A and B are false
Q07	Which of the following statements BEST describes the difference between testing and debugging? a) Testing pinpoints (identifies the source of) the defects. Debugging analyzes the faults and proposes prevention activities. b) Dynamic testing shows failures caused by defects. Debugging finds, analyzes, and removes the causes of failures in the software. c) Testing removes faults. Debugging identifies the causes of failures. d) Dynamic testing prevents causes of failures. Debugging removes the failures.
Q08	Which statement below BEST describes non-functional testing? a) The process of testing an integrated system to verify that it meets specified requirements. b) The process of testing to determine the compliance of a system to coding standards. c) Testing without reference to the internal structure of a system. d) Testing system attributes, such as usability, reliability, or maintainability.
Q09	What is important when working with software development models? a) To adapt the models to the context of project and product characteristics. b) To choose the waterfall model because it is the first and best proven model. c) To start with the V-model and then move to either iterative or incremental models. d) To only change the organization to fit the model and not vice versa.

Ref	Questions
Q10	Which of the following characteristics of good testing apply to any software development life cycle model? a) Acceptance testing is always the final test level to be applied. b) All test levels are planned and completed for each developed feature. c) Testers are involved as soon as the first piece of code can be executed. d) For every development activity there is a corresponding testing activity.
Q11	For which of the following would maintenance testing be used? a) Correction of defects during the development phase. b) Planned enhancements to an existing operational system. c) Complaints about system quality during user acceptance testing. d) Integrating functions during the development of a new system.
Q12	Which of the following statements are TRUE? A. Regression testing and acceptance testing are the same. B. Regression tests show if all defects have been resolved. C. Regression tests are typically well-suited for test automation. D. Regression tests are performed to find out if code changes have introduced or uncovered defects. Regression tests should be performed in integration testing. a) A, C, and D and E are true; B is false. b) A, C, and E are true; B and D are false. c) C and D are true; A, B, and E are false. d) B and E are true; A, C, and D are false.
Q13	Which of the following comparisons of component testing and system testing are TRUE? a) Component testing verifies the functioning of software modules, program objects, and classes that are separately testable, whereas system testing verifies interfaces between components and interactions with different parts of the system. b) Test cases for component testing are usually derived from component specifications, design specifications, or data models, whereas test cases for system testing are usually derived from requirement specifications, functional specifications or use cases. c) Component testing focuses on functional characteristics, whereas system testing focuses on functional and non-functional characteristics. d) Component testing is the responsibility of the technical testers, whereas system testing typically is the responsibility of the users of the system.

Ref	Questions
Q14	Which of the following are the main phases of a formal review? a) Initiation, status, preparation, review meeting, rework, follow-up. b) Planning, preparation, review meeting, rework, closure, follow-up. c) Planning, kick-off, individual preparation, review meeting, rework, follow-up. d) Preparation, review meeting, rework, closure, follow-up, root cause analysis.
Q15	Which TWO of the review types below are the BEST fitted (most adequate) options to choose for reviewing safety critical components in a software project? Select 2 options. a) Informal review. b) Management review. c) Inspection. d) Walk-through. e) Technical review.
Q16	Which of the following statements about static analysis is FALSE? a) Static analysis can be used as a preventive measure with appropriate process in place. b) Static analysis can find defects that are not easily found by dynamic testing. c) Static analysis can result in cost savings by finding defects early. d) Static analysis is a good way to force failures into the software.

Ref	Questions
Q17	One of the test goals for the project is to have 100% decision coverage. The following three tests have been executed for the control flow graph shown below. Test A covers path: A, B, D, E, G Test B covers path: A, B, D, E, F, G Test C covers path: A, C, F, C, F, C, F, G Which of the following statements related to the decision coverage goal is correct? a) Decision D has not been tested completely. b) 100% decision coverage has been achieved. c) Decision E has not been tested completely. d) Decision F has not been tested completely.
Q18	A defect was found during testing. When the network got disconnected while receiving data from a server, the system crashed. The defect was fixed by correcting the code that checked the network availability during data transfer. The existing test cases covered 100% of all statements of the corresponding module. To verify the fix and ensure more extensive coverage, some new tests were designed and added to the test suite. What types of testing are mentioned above? A. Functional testing. B. Structural testing. C. Re-testing. D. Performance testing. a) A, B, and D. b) A and C. c) A, B, and C. d) A, C, and D.

Ref	Questions
Q19	Which of the following statements about the given state table is TRUE?

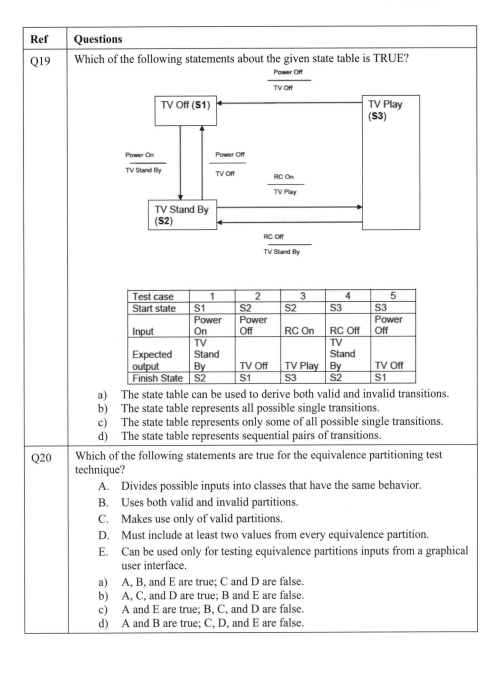

Test case	1	2	3	4	5
Start state	S1	S2	S2	S3	S3
Input	Power On	Power Off	RC On	RC Off	Power Off
Expected output	TV Stand By	TV Off	TV Play	TV Stand By	TV Off
Finish State	S2	S1	S3	S2	S1

a)   The state table can be used to derive both valid and invalid transitions.
b)   The state table represents all possible single transitions.
c)   The state table represents only some of all possible single transitions.
d)   The state table represents sequential pairs of transitions.

Ref	Questions
Q20	Which of the following statements are true for the equivalence partitioning test technique?

A.   Divides possible inputs into classes that have the same behavior.

B.   Uses both valid and invalid partitions.

C.   Makes use only of valid partitions.

D.   Must include at least two values from every equivalence partition.

E.   Can be used only for testing equivalence partitions inputs from a graphical user interface.

a)   A, B, and E are true; C and D are false.
b)   A, C, and D are true; B and E are false.
c)   A and E are true; B, C, and D are false.
d)   A and B are true; C, D, and E are false.

Ref	Questions
Q21	Which TWO of the following solutions below lists techniques that can be categorized as black-box design techniques? Select 2 options from the following: a) Equivalence partitioning, decision tables, state transition, and boundary value. b) Equivalence partitioning, decision tables, use case. c) Equivalence partitioning, decision tables, checklist based, statement coverage, use case. d) Equivalence partitioning, cause-effect graph, checklist based, decision coverage, use case. e) Equivalence partitioning, cause-effect graph, checklist based, decision coverage, and boundary value.
Q22	An employee's bonus is to be calculated. It cannot become negative, but it can be calculated to zero. The bonus is based on the duration of the employment. An employee can be employed for less than or equal to 2 years, more than 2 years but less than 5 years, 5 to 10 years, or longer than 10 years. Depending on this period of employment, an employee will get either no bonus or a bonus of 10%, 25%, or 35%. How many equivalence partitions are needed to test the calculation of the bonus? a) 3 b) 5 c) 2 d) 4
Q23	Which of the following statements about the benefits of deriving test cases from use cases are most likely to be true? A. Deriving test cases from use cases is helpful for system and acceptance testing. B. Deriving test cases from use cases is helpful only for automated testing. C. Deriving test cases from use cases is helpful for component testing. D. Deriving test cases from use cases is helpful for testing the interaction between different components of the system. a) A and D are true; B and C are false. b) A is true; B, C, and D are false. c) A and B are true; C and D are false. d) C is true; A, B, and D are false.
Q24	Which of the below would be the best basis for fault attack testing? a) Experience, defect and failure data, knowledge about software failures. b) Risk analysis performed at the beginning of the project. c) Use cases derived from the business flows by domain experts. d) Expected results from comparison with an existing system.

<table>
<tr><th>Ref</th><th>Questions</th></tr>
<tr><td>Q25</td><td>Which of the following would be the best test approach when there are poor specifications and time pressures?
a) Use case testing.
b) Condition coverage.
c) Exploratory testing.
d) Path testing.</td></tr>
<tr><td>Q26</td><td>Which one of the following techniques is structure-based?
a) Decision testing.
b) Boundary value analysis.
c) Equivalence partitioning.
d) State transition testing.</td></tr>
<tr><td>Q27</td><td>You have started specification-based testing of a program. It calculates the greatest common divisor (GCD) of two integers (A and B) greater than zero.
calcGCD (A, B);
The following test cases (TC) have been specified.
<table>
<tr><th>TC</th><th>A</th><th>B</th></tr>
<tr><td>1</td><td>1</td><td>1</td></tr>
<tr><td>2</td><td>INT_MAX</td><td>INT_MAX</td></tr>
<tr><td>3</td><td>1</td><td>0</td></tr>
<tr><td>4</td><td>0</td><td>1</td></tr>
<tr><td>5</td><td>INT_MAX+1</td><td>1</td></tr>
<tr><td>6</td><td>1</td><td>INT_MAX+1</td></tr>
</table>
INT_MAX: largest integer
Which test technique has been applied in order to determine test cases 1 through 6?
a) Boundary value analysis.
b) State transition testing.
c) Equivalence partitioning.
d) Decision table testing.</td></tr>
</table>

Ref	Questions
Q28	Consider the following state transition diagram and test case table.

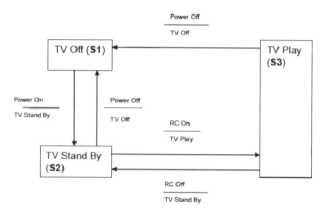

Test Case	1	2	3	4	5	6	7
Start state	S1	S1	S2	S2	S3	S3	S3
Input	Press Power On	Press Power On	Press RC On	Press RC On	Press RC Off	Press Power Off	Press RC Off
Expected Output	TV Stand By	TV Stand By	TV Play	TV Play	TV Stand By	TV OFF	TV Stand By
Next state	S2	S2	S3	S3	S2	S1	S2
Input	Press Power Off	Press RC On	Press Power Off	Press RC Off	Press RC On	Press Power On	Press Power Off
Expected Output	TV Off	TV Play	TV Off	TV Stand By	TV Play	TV Stand By	TV Off
Finish state	S1	S3	S1	S2	S3	S2	S1

Which of the following statements are TRUE?

    A.   The test case table exercises the shortest number of transitions.
    B.   The test case gives only the valid state transitions.
    C.   The test case gives only the invalid state transitions.
    D.   The test case exercises the longest number of transitions.

    a)   Only A is true; B, C, and D are false.
    b)   Only B is true; A, C, and D are false.
    c)   A and D are true; B, C are false.
    d)   Only C is true; A, B, and D are false.

Ref	Questions
Q29	Which of the following best describes the task partition between test manager and tester? a) The test manager plans testing activities and chooses the standards to be followed, while the tester chooses the tools and controls to be used. b) The test manager plans, organizes, and controls the testing activities, while the tester specifies, automates, and executes tests. c) The test manager plans, monitors, and controls the testing activities, while the tester designs tests. d) The test manager plans and organizes the testing and specifies the test cases, while the tester prioritizes and executes the tests.
Q30	Which of the following can be categorized as product risks? a) Low-quality requirements, design, code, and tests. b) Political problems and delays in especially complex areas in the product. c) Error-prone areas, potential harm to the user, poor product characteristics. d) Problems in defining the right requirements, potential failure areas in the software or system.
Q31	Which of the following are typical test exit criteria? a) Thoroughness measures, reliability measures, test cost, schedule, state of defect correction, and residual risks. b) Thoroughness measures, reliability measures, degree of tester independence, and product completeness. c) Thoroughness measures, reliability measures, test cost, time to market and product completeness, availability of testable code. d) Time to market, residual defects, tester qualification, degree of tester independence, thoroughness measures, and test cost.

Ref	Questions
Q32	As a test manager you have the following requirements to be tested: Requirements to test: R1 – Process anomalies – high complexity. R2 – Remote services – medium complexity. R3 – Synchronization – medium complexity. R4 – Confirmation – medium complexity. R5 – Process closures – low complexity. R6 – Issues – low complexity. R7 – Financial data – low complexity. R8 – Diagram data – low complexity. R9 – Changes on user profile – medium complexity. Requirements logical dependencies (A → B means that B is dependent on A): How would you structure the test execution schedule according to the requirement dependencies? a) R4 > R5 > R1 > R2 > R3 > R7 > R8 > R6 > R9 b) R1 > R2 > R3 > R4 > R5 > R7 > R8 > R6 > R9 c) R1 > R2 > R4 > R5 > R3 > R7 > R8 > R6 > R9 d) R1 > R2 > R3 > R7 > R8 > R4 > R5 > R6 > R9
Q33	What is the benefit of independent testing? a) More work gets done because testers do not disturb the developers all the time. b) Independent testers tend to be unbiased and find different defects than the developers. c) Independent testers do not need extra education and training. d) Independent testers reduce the bottleneck in the incident management process.

Ref	Questions
Q34	Which of the following would be categorized as project risks? a) Skill and staff shortages. b) Poor software characteristics. c) Failure-prone software delivered. d) Possible reliability defect (bug).
Q35	As a test manager you are asked for a test summary report. Concerning test activities and according to IEEE 829 standard, what should you consider in your report? a) The number of test cases using black-box techniques. b) A summary of the major testing activities, events and its status in respect of meeting goals. c) Overall evaluation of each development work item. d) Training taken by members of the test team to support the test effort.
Q36	You are a tester in a safety-critical software development project. During execution of a test, you find out that one of your expected results was not achieved. You write an incident report about it. What do you consider to be the most important information to include according to the IEEE Std 829? a) Impact, incident description, date and time, your name. b) Unique ID for the report, special requirements needed. c) Transmitted items, your name, and your feelings about the defect source. d) Incident description, environment, expected results.
Q37	From the list below, select the recommended principles for introducing a chosen test tool in an organization? 1. Roll the tool out to the entire organization at the same time. 2. Start with a pilot project. 3. Adapt and improve processes to fit the use of the tool. 4. Provide training and coaching for new users. 5. Let each team decide their own standard ways of using the tool. 6. Monitor that costs do not exceed initial acquisition cost. 7. Gather lessons learned from all teams. a) 1, 2, 3, 5 b) 1, 4, 6, 7 c) 2, 3, 4, 7 d) 3, 4, 5, 6

Ref	Questions
Q38	Which one of the following best describes a characteristic of a keyword-driven test execution tool? a) A table with test input data, action words, and expected results, controls execution of the system under test. b) Actions of testers recorded in a script that is rerun several times. c) Actions of testers recorded in a script that is run with several sets of test input data. d) The ability to log test results and compare them against the expected results, stored in a text file.
Q39	Which of the following is NOT a goal of a pilot project for tool evaluation? a) To evaluate how the tool fits with existing processes and practices. b) To determine use, management, storage, and maintenance of the tool and test assets. c) To assess whether the benefits will be achieved at reasonable cost. d) To reduce the defect rate in the pilot project.
Q40	Below is a list of test efficiency improvement goals a software development and test organization would like to achieve. Which of these goals would best be supported by a test management tool? a) To build traceability between requirements, tests, and bugs. b) To optimize the ability of tests to identify failures. c) To resolve defects faster. d) To automate selection of test cases for execution.

Chapter 8

Templates and Models

This annex lists all documentation templates proposed in the frame of the test activities.

Use of these templates without previous thought as to advantages and risks of customization can have an adverse effect on your test project. It is thus highly recommended to evaluate what level of detail is necessary in these documents.

8.1. Master test plan

The master test plan is considered by IEEE 829-1998 to have the same structure as the test plan (see section 8.2). IEEE 829-2008[1] is different and represented hereafter:

1. Introduction

    1.1. Document identifier

    1.2. Scope

    1.3. References

    1.4. System overview and key features

    1.5. Test overview

        1.5.1. Organization

---

1 IEEE829:2008 and IEEE829:1998 and its content are copyright of IEEE. These are used here only as extracts for example purposes.

3.1. Glossary

3.2. Document change procedures and history

8.2. Test plan

8.2.1. *Test plan as per IEEE 829-1998[2]*

1. Test plan identifier

2. Introduction

3. Test items

4. Features to be tested

5. Features not to be tested

6. Approach

7. Item pass/fail criteria

8. Suspension criteria and resumption requirements

9. Test deliverables

10. Testing tasks

11. Environmental needs

12. Responsibilities

13. Staffing and training needs

14. Schedule

15. Risks and contingencies

16. Approvals

8.2.2. *Test plan as per IEEE 829-2008[3]*

1. Introduction

  1.1. Document identifier

  1.2. Scope

---

2 Copyright IEEE.
3 Copyright IEEE under the term "Level test plan".

1.3. References

1.4. Level in the overall sequence

1.5. Test classes and overall test conditions

2. Details for this level of test plan

2.1. Test items and their identifiers

2.2. Test traceability matrix

2.3. Features to be tested

2.4. Features not to be tested

2.5. Approach

2.6. Item pass/fail criteria

2.7. Suspension criteria and resumption requirements

2.8. Test deliverables

3. Test management

3.1. Planned activities and tasks; test progression

3.2. Environment/infrastructure

3.3. Responsibilities and authority

3.4. Interfaces among the parties involved

3.5. Resources and their allocation

3.6. Training

3.7. Schedules, estimates, and costs

3.8. Risk(s) and contingency(s)

4. General

4.1. Quality assurance procedures

4.2. Metrics

4.3. Test coverage

4.4. Glossary

4.5. Document change procedures and history

8.3. Test design document

8.3.1. *Test design specifications as per IEEE 829-1998[4]*

1. Test design specification identifier

2. Features to be tested

3. Approach refinements

4. Test identification

5. Feature pass/fail criteria

8.3.2. *Test design document as per IEEE 829-2008[5]*

1. Introduction

    1.1. Document identifier

    1.2. Scope

    1.3. References

2. Details of the level test design

    2.1. Features to be tested

    2.2. Approach refinements

    2.3. Test identification

    2.4. Feature pass/fail criteria

    2.5 Test deliverables

3. General

    3.1. Glossary

    3.2. Document change procedures and history

---

4 Copyright IEEE under the name "Test design specification".
5 Copyright IEEE under the name "Level test design".

8.4. Test case

8.4.1. *Test case document as per IEEE 829-1998[6]*

1. Test case specification identifier

2. Test items

3. Input specifications

4. Output specifications

5. Environmental needs

6. Special procedural requirements

7. Intercase dependencies

8.4.2. *Test case document as per IEEE 829-2008[7]*

1. Introduction (once per document)

   1.1. Document identifier

   1.2. Scope

   1.3. References

   1.4. Context

   1.5. Notation for description

2. Details (once per test case)

   2.1. Test case identifier

   2.2. Objective

   2.3. Inputs

   2.4. Outcome(s)

   2.5. Environmental needs

   2.6. Special procedural requirements

   2.7. Intercase dependencies

3. Global (once per document)

---

6 Copyright IEEE under the name "Test case specification".
7 Copyright IEEE under the name "Level test case".

3.1. Glossary

3.2. Document change procedures and history

8.5. Test procedure

8.5.1. *Test procedure document as per IEEE 829-1998[8]*

1. Test procedure specification identifier

2. Purpose

3. Special requirements

4. Procedure steps

8.5.2. *Test procedure document as per IEEE 829-2008[9]*

1. Introduction

   1.1. Document identifier

   1.2. Scope

   1.3. References

   1.4. Relationship to other procedures

2. Details

   2.1. Inputs, outputs, and special requirements

   2.2. Ordered description of the steps to be taken to execute the test cases

3. General

   3.1. Glossary

   3.2. Document change procedures and history

---

8 Copyright IEEE under the name "Test procedure specification".
9 Copyright IEEE under the name "Level test procedure".

8.6. Test log

8.6.1. *Test log as per IEEE 829-1998[10]*

1. Test log identifier

2. Description

3. Activity and event entries

8.6.2. *Test log as per IEEE 829-2008[11]*

1. Introduction

   1.1. Document identifier

   1.2. Scope

   1.3. References

2. Details

   2.1. Description

   2.2. Activity and event entries

3. General

   3.1. Glossary

8.7. Defect report

8.7.1. *Defect report as per IEEE 829-1998[12]*

1. Test incident report identifier

2. Summary

3. Incident description

   3.1. Inputs

   3.2. Expected results

   3.3. Actual results

---

10 Copyright IEEE under the name "Test log".
11 Copyright IEEE under the name "Level test log".
12 Copyright IEEE under the term "incident report".

3.4. Anomalies

3.5. Date and time

3.6. Procedure step

3.7. Environment

3.8. Attempts to repeat

3.9. Testers

3.10. Observers

4. Impact

8.7.2. *Defect report as per IEEE 829-2008*[13]

1. Introduction

1.1. Document identifier

1.2. Scope

1.3. References

2. Details

2.1. Summary

2.2. Date anomaly discovered

2.3. Context

2.4. Description of anomaly

2.5. Impact

2.5.1. Inputs

2.5.2. Expected results

2.5.3. Actual results

2.5.4. Unexpected outcomes

2.5.5. Procedure step

2.5.6. Environment

2.5.7. Attempts to repeat

---

13 Copyright IEEE under the term "anomaly report".

2.5.8. Testers

2.5.9. Observers

2.6. Originator's assessment of urgency

2.7. Description of the corrective action

2.8. Status of the anomaly

2.9. Conclusions and recommendations

3. General

3.1 Document change procedures and history

8.8. Test report

8.8.1. *Test report as per IEEE 829-1998[14]*

1. Test summary report identifier

2. Summary

3. Variances

4. Comprehensive assessment

5. Summary of results

6. Evaluation

7. Summary of activities

8. Approvals

8.8.2. *Interim test report as per IEEE 829-2008[15]*

1. Introduction

1.1. Document identifier

1.2. Scope

1.3. References

2. Details

---

14 This test report is copyright IEEE, under the name "Test summary report".
15 This test interim report is copyright IEEE.

2.1. Test status summary

2.2. Changes from plans

2.3. Test status metrics

3. General

3.1. Document change procedures and history

8.8.3. *Level test report as per IEEE 829-2008*[16]

1. Introduction

1.1. Document identifier

1.2. Scope

1.3. References

2. Details

2.1. Overview of test results

2.2. Detailed test results

2.3. Rationale for decisions

2.4. Conclusions and recommendations

3. General

3.1. Glossary

3.2. Document change procedures and history

8.8.4. *Master test report as per IEEE 829-2008*[17]

1. Introduction

1.1. Document identifier

1.2. Scope

1.3. References

2. Details of the master test report

---

16 Copyright IEEE under the name "Level test report".
17 Copyright IEEE under the name "Master test report".

2.1. Overview of all aggregate test results

2.2. Rationale for decisions

2.3. Conclusions and recommendations

3. General

3.1. Glossary

3.2. Document change procedures and history

Chapter 9

Answers to the Questions

You will find hereafter the answers to the questions located at the end of the different chapters.

9.1. Answers to the end of chapter questions

1.	A	13.	B	25.	B
2.	D	14.	C	26.	C
3.	B	15.	A	27.	C
4.	C	16.	B	28.	A
5.	D	17.	C	29.	B
6.	A	18.	B	30.	A
7.	D	19.	D	31.	A
8.	D	20.	D	32.	C
9.	C	21.	A	33.	D
10.	B	22.	C	34.	D
11.	B	23.	A	35.	B
12.	D	24.	C	36.	A

37.	B	65.	C	93.	D
38.	D	66.	D	94.	D
39.	D	67.	B	95.	A
40.	C	68.	D	96.	C
41.	C	69.	B	97.	A
42.	A	70.	C	98.	D
43.	C	71.	D	99.	D
44.	C	72.	D	100.	B
45.	C	73.	B	101.	A
46.	D	74.	D	102.	B
47.	B	75.	B	103.	B
48.	C	76.	A	104.	B
49.	A	77.	C	105.	B
50.	A	78.	B	106.	A
51.	A	79.	D	107.	A
52.	D	80.	C	108.	B
53.	C	81.	B	109.	A
54.	A	82.	B	110.	D
55.	B	83.	D	111.	D
56.	A	84.	C	112.	A
57.	C	85.	C	113.	B
58.	D	86.	C		
59.	A	87.	B		
60.	C	88.	A		
61.	D	89.	D		
62.	D	90.	D		
63.	B	91.	B		
64.	A	92.	A		

9.2. Correct answers to the sample paper questions

Question	Reponse	Syllabus reference	Question	Reponse	Syllabus reference
Q01	C	1.3.1	Q21	A and B	4.3.1
Q02	B	1.2.1	Q22	D	4.3.1
Q03	B	1.4.1	Q23	A	4.3.5
Q04	A	1.1.5	Q24	A	4.5.1
Q05	C	1.5.1	Q25	C	4.2.1
Q06	C	1.2.2	Q26	A	4.4.2
Q07	B	1.2.3	Q27	A	4.3.1
Q08	D	2.3.2	Q28	B	4.3.4
Q09	A	2.1.2	Q29	B	5.1.4
Q10	D	2.1.3	Q30	C	5.5.3
Q11	B	2.4.2	Q31	A	5.2.9
Q12	C	2.3.5	Q32	C	5.2.5
Q13	B	2.2.1	Q33	B	5.1.1
Q14	C	3.2.1	Q34	A	5.5.4
Q15	C and E	3.2.3	Q35	B	5.3.3
Q16	D	3.3	Q36	A	5.6.2
Q17	A	4.4.2	Q37	C	6.3.1
Q18	C	4.4.2	Q38	A	6.2.2
Q19	B	4.3.1	Q39	D	6.3
Q20	D	4.3.1	Q40	A	6.1.3

Bibliography

Books and publications

The following publications were referenced in this book.

[BEI 84] BEIZER B., *Software System Testing and Quality Assurance*, Van Nostrand Reinhold, 1984.

[BEI 90] BEIZER B., *Software Testing Techniques*, Van Nostrand Reinhold, 1990.

[BEI 95] BEIZER B., *Black-Box Testing Techniques for Functional Testing of Software and Systems*, John Wiley & Sons, 1995.

[BIN 00] BINDER R., *Testing Object-Oriented Systems, Models, Patterns and Tools*, Addison-Wesley, 2000.

[BLA 09] BLACK R., *Managing the Testing Process, Practical Tools and Techniques for Managing Hardware and Software Testing*, Wiley, 2009.

[BOE 86] BOEHM B., "A spiral model of software development and enhancement", *ACM SIGSOFT Software Engineering Notes*, August 1986

[BOE 88] BOEHM B., "A spiral model of software development and enhancement", *IEEE Computer*, vol. 21, no. 5, May 1988, pp. 61-72.

[BUW 02] BUWALDA H., *Integrated Test Design and Automation*, Addison-Wesley, 2002.

[COH 06] COHN M., *Agile Estimating and Planning*, Pearson Education, 2006.

[COP 03] COPELAND L., *A Practitioner's Guide to Software Test Design*, Artech House, 2003.

[GIL 93] GILB T., GRAHAM D., *Software Inspections*, Pearson Education, 1993.

[GIL 05] GILB T., *Competitive Engineering, A Handbook for Systems Engineering, Requirements Engineering, and Software Engineering using Planguage*, Elsevier, 2005.

[HUT 03] HUTCHESON M., *Software Testing Fundamentals, Methods and Metrics*, Wiley, 2003.

[JON 07] JONES C., *Estimating Software Costs, Bringing Realism to Estimating*, 2nd edition, McGraw-Hill, 2007.

[JOR 08] JORGENSEN P., *Software Testing, a Craftman's Approach*, 3rd edition, Auerbach Publications, 2008.

[JOR 09] JORGENSEN P., *Modeling Software Behavior, a Craftman's Approach*, CRC Press - Taylor and Francis Group, 2009.

[KAN 03] KAN S., *Metrics and Models in Software Quality Engineering*, 2nd edition, Addison-Wesley, 2003.

[KAN 99] KANER C., FALK J., NGUYEN H., *Testing Computer Software*, 2nd edition, John Wiley & Sons, 1999.

[KER 91] KERVERN G.-Y., RUBISE P., *L'archipel du Danger, introduction aux cyndiniques*, Economica, 1991.

[LEV 93] LEVESON, N.G. TURNER, C.S., "An investigation of the Therac-25 accidents", *IEEE Computer*, vol. 26, no. 7, pp. 18-41, July 1993.

[MYE 79] MYERS G., *The Art of Software Testing*, John Wiley & Sons, 1979.

[PAG 09] PAGE A., JOHNSTON K., ROLLISON B.J., *How We Test at Microsoft*, Microsoft Press, 2009.

[UTT 07] UTTING M., LEGEARD B., *Practical Model-Based Testing*, Morgan Kaufmann, 2007.

[VAN 97] VAN VEENENDAAL E., MCMULLAN J. (eds), *Achieving Software Product Quality*, Uitgeverij Tutein Nolthenius, 1997.

[WHI 03] WHITTAKER J., *How to Break Software, a Practical Guide to Testing*, Addison-Wesley, 2003.

[WHI 04] WHITTAKER J., THOMPSON H., *How to Break Software Security, Effective Techniques for Security Testing*, Addison-Wesley, 2004.

[WHI 10] WHITTAKER J., *Exploratory Software Testing, Tips, Tricks, Tours and Techniques to Guide Test Design*, Addison-Wesley, 2010.

Standards and norms

[ESA 08] ECSS-M-ST-10-01C Space management, organization and conduct of reviews, European Space Agency 2008 for the members of ECSS.

[EUR 00] Considérations sur le Logiciel en vue de la Certification des Systèmes et Equipements de bord, 2nd edition, DO178B/ED12B, EUROCAE 2000.

[IEE 08a] IEEE Std 829™-2008, IEEE Standard for Software and System Test Documentation, IEEE 2008.

[IEE 08b] IEEE 1028-2008, IEEE Standard for Software Reviews and Audits, IEEE 2008.

[ISO 01] Standard International ISO/CEI 9126-1:2001 Génie du logiciel – Qualité des produits – Partie 1: Modèle de qualité, 1st edition, ISO 2001.

[ISO 05] Standard International ISO 9000, Systèmes de management de la qualité – Principes essentiels et vocabulaire, 3rd edition, ISO 2005.

Other references

[AGI] Manifesto for agile software development, http://agilemanifesto.org/

[BAC 03] BACH, J., "Exploratory testing explained", http://www.satisfice.com/articles/et-article.pdf

[COC] Center for Systems and Software Engineering, http://sunset.usc.edu/csse/research /COCOMOII/cocomo_main.html

[ELE] http://www.boulogne-billancourt.lesverts.fr/spip.php?article298

[EVA] eValid, Automated web Testing Suite, http://www.soft.com/evalid

[HOL] Security Innovation, http://www.securityinnovation.com/holodeck/index.shtml

[HOM 03a] La Lettre des Cindyniques, no. 39, July 2003, available from: http://www.imdr.eu/v2/extranet/lettre039.pdf

[HOM 03b] La Lettre des Cindyniques, no. 40, November 2003, available from: http://www.imdr.eu/v2/extranet/lettre040.pdf

[KER 04] The Washington Post, "Ohio voting machines contained programming error that dropped votes", http://voices.washingtonpost.com/44/2008/08/21/ohio_voting_machines _contained.html

[LEM 10] Le Monde, "Un bug bloque 30 millions de cartes bancaires en Allemagne", http://www.lemonde.fr/europe/article/2010/01/05/un-bug-bloque-plus-de-20-millions-de-cartes-bancaires-en-allemagne_1287784_3214.html

[LEP 10] Le Point, "Fausse explosion d'un TGV – cette incroyable erreur de la SNCF sur son site", http://www.lepoint.fr/archives/article.php/434105

[LET 10] Le Télégramme, "SNCF. Un pirate a accédé aux données confidentielles des clients", http://www.letelegramme.com/ig/generales/france-monde/france/sncf-un-pirate-a-accede-aux-donnees-confidentielles-des-clients-17-03-2010-829457.php

[LOG] IBM, http://www-01.ibm.com/software/awdtools/logiEtendue/

[TPA] VAN VEENENDAAL E.P.W.M., DEKKERS T., "Testpointanalysis", http://www.ifpa.nl/ Images/ESCOM1999%20Test%20Point%20Analysis%20-%20A%20method%20for%20 test%20estimation_tcm158-35882.pdf

Index